PRIMITIVE
MAN
AS
PHILOSOPHER

PRIMITIVE
MAN
AS
PHILOSOPHER

Paul Radin, Ph.D.
professor of anthropology brandeis university

with a foreword by john dewey
second revised edition

dover publications, i

6-20392-1

: 57-13107

America

nc. new york

International Standard Book Number: 0-48

Library of Congress Catalog Card Number

Manufactured in the United States of
Dover Publications, Inc.
180 Varick Street
New York, N.Y. 10014

PREFACE

In this present edition of *Primitive Man as Philosopher*
I have introduced no changes whatsoever in the older text.
I have, however, added certain additional material: an in-
troductory chapter on methods of approach in the study of
aboriginal philosophies and an essay on new religious-philosophical formulations attempted by an American Indian.
This latter essay was published in Volume XVIII of the
Eranos-Jahrbuch, pp. 249-290. (Rhein-Verlag, Zuerich
1950). It is being reprinted here, with certain changes,
with the kind permission of the Bollingen Foundation of
New York City.

PAUL RADIN

Lugano, 1956

PREFACE

When a modern historian desires to study the civilization of any people, he regards it as a necessary preliminary that he divest himself, so far as possible, of all prejudice and bias. He realizes that differences between cultures exist, but he does not feel that it is necessarily a sign of inferiority that a people differs in customs from his own. There seems, however, to be a limit to what an historian treats as legitimate difference, a limit not always easy to determine. On the whole it may be said that he very naturally passes the same judgments that the majority of his fellow countrymen do. Hence, if some of the differences between admittedly civilized peoples often call forth unfavorable judgments or even provoke outbursts of horror, how much more must we expect this to be the case where the differences are of so fundamental a nature as those separating us from people whom we have been accustomed to call uncivilized.

The term "uncivilized" is a very vague one, and it is spread over a vast medley of peoples, some of whom have comparatively simple customs and others extremely complex ones. Indeed, there can be said to be but two characteristics possessed in common by all these peoples, the absence of a written language and the fact of original possession of the soil when the various civilized European and Asiatic nations came into contact with them. But among all aboriginal races appeared a number of customs which undoubtedly seemed exceedingly strange to their European and Asiatic conquerors. Some of these customs they had never heard of; others they recognized as similar to observances and beliefs existing among the more backward members of their own communities.

Yet the judgments civilized peoples have passed on the aborigines, we may be sure, were not initially based on any calm evaluation of facts. If the aborigines were regarded as innately inferior, this was due in part to the tremendous gulf in custom and belief separating them from the conquerors, in part to the apparent simplicity of their ways, and in no small degree to the fact that they were unable to offer any effective resistance.

Romance soon threw its distorting screen over the whole primitive picture. Within one hundred years of the discovery of America it had already become an ineradicably established tradition that all the aborigines encountered by Europeans were simple, untutored savages from whom little more could be expected than from uncontrolled children, individuals who were at all times the slaves of their passions, of which the dominant one was hatred. Much of this tradition, in various forms, disguised and otherwise, has persisted to the present day.

The evolutionary theory, during its heyday in the 1870's and '80's, still further complicated and misrepresented the situation, and from the great classic that created modern ethnology—Tylor's *Primitive Culture,* published in 1870—future ethnologists were to imbibe the cardinal and fundamentally misleading doctrine that primitive peoples represent an early stage in the history of the evolution of culture. What was, perhaps, even more dangerous was the strange and uncritical manner in which all primitive peoples were lumped together in ethnological discussion—simple Fuegians with the highly advanced Aztecs and Mayans, Bushmen with the peoples of the Nigerian coast, Australians with Polynesians, and so on.

For a number of years scholars were apparently content with the picture drawn by Tylor and his successors. The rebellion against it came in large measure from the American ethnologists, chiefly under the influence of Prof. Franz Boas. Through methods of work foreshadowed by some of Boas' immediate predecessors but more penetratingly and systematically developed by him, a large body of authentic information has been gathered on the American Indians. Add to this the great monographs produced by European ethnologists for other parts of the world, and we have, for the first time in the history of the science, a moderately favorable opportunity for examining anew the nature of primitive man's mentality.

That it is important to the ethnologist, the historian, the sociologist, and the psychologist to understand the true nature of the mentality of primitive man is, of course, self-evident. But practical questions of far more general import are also involved. In Asia, Africa, the islands of the Pacific, Mexico, and South America there exist to-day millions of so-called primitive peoples whose relation to their white and Mongolian conquerors is of vital importance both to the conquerors and to the conquered, or semi-conquered, aborigines. Up to the present all attempts that have been made to understand them, or to come to any reasonable adjustment with them, have met with signal failure, and this failure is in most instances due to the scientifically accredited theories of the innate inferiority of primitive man in mentality and capacity for civilization quite as much as to prejudice and bias. Some governments, notably those of Great Britain and France, have already begun to recognize this fact. But how can we expect public officials to take an unbiased view of primitive mentality when the dominant tradition among ethnologists, among those who ostensibly devote their lives to the subject, is still largely based on an unjustified, or at least undemonstrated, assumption?

The most pressing need in ethnology, then, is to examine anew the older assumptions which, wittingly or unwittingly, ethnologists themselves have harbored for two generations and which threaten to become fixed traditions among psychologists, sociologists, and historians. Among the more important of these assumptions is the notion that there is a dead level of intelligence among primitive peoples, that the individual is completely swamped by and submerged in the group, that thinkers and philosophers as such do not exist— in short, that there is nothing even remotely comparable to an intellectual class among them.

These conceptions of primitive mentality the writer regards as wholly unjustified, and it is with the object of contraverting them that the following pages have been written. Since the contrary view still holds the field among most scholars, including not a few ethnologists, I have been at considerable pains to collect my material in as irreproachable a manner as possible.

The first requisite of all proof is, of course, that data be accurate and subject to control. To meet this requirement I have, in almost all cases, used only data that have been obtained at first hand and have been published in the original with a translation that could be vouched for. This, perhaps, may appear unduly pedantic, and it may possibly entail the omission of valuable material; but it cannot be too strongly emphasized that if the ethnologist wishes to obtain credence among the more skeptically inclined public, he must be willing to adopt a method of presentation that commends itself to them as meeting every critical test.

A good deal of the data presented in the following chapters were obtained by the author himself. Perhaps I should ask indulgence for using my own published and unpublished material so extensively. This is not due to any over-evaluation of either its accuracy or its importance, but simply to the fact that I happened to be interested specifically in a question which other ethnologists had touched only in passing. In the interests of greater accuracy, and in order to substantiate statements that unsupported might seem incredible to the reader accustomed to obtaining his descriptions of primitive culture from secondary works, native sources have been voluminously quoted. If certain tribes have been stressed more than others, it is simply because we happen to have for them better specific data of the kind desired. Yet it is my firm conviction that the conclusions arrived at on the basis of the study of a necessarily limited number of tribes will hold for practically every tribe.

Perhaps it is not necessary to emphasize the dangers besetting the path of anyone venturing to describe and characterize the ideas and mental workings of others, particularly those of races so different ostensibly from ourselves as are primitive peoples. Added to the ordinary risk of misunderstanding, ethnologists often find it necessary to give what are simply their own impressions and interpretations. But to this there can hardly be objection provided the ethnologist is fully aware of all pitfalls, for, surely, the impressions and interpretations of a person who has spent many years among primitive peoples must possess a value in a high degree. Yet the layman, on the other hand, is right in demanding that the investigator prove that he is not confusing facts with impressions. I must confess myself to have had frequent recourse to impressions and interpretations, which I have then sought to illustrate by appropriate examples. But I realize quite clearly how easy it is to obtain appropriate examples, and mine, I hope, have been chosen judiciously.

The following chapters are in no sense a description of all the aspects of what properly belongs to a complete account of the exceptional man in primitive communities. Art and material culture have been completely excluded. To have discussed them would have unduly enlarged the size and the scope of the book. Besides, these subjects have already been well treated in a fair number of works.

It is fitting that here I should express my gratitude to a number of teachers and friends. To two teachers in particular, Prof. James Harvey Robinson and Prof. Franz Boas, I owe a great deal of my whole conception and approach. To the former I owe the initial inspiration for the studies underlying this work. It was the influence of his lectures on the history of the intellectual class in Western Europe, delivered more than twenty years ago, that subsequently fired me with the idea of studying the rôle and the attitude of the intellectual class among primitive peoples. To Professor Boas I owe an equal debt. Not only have I obtained numerous suggestions from his works and his lectures, but a great part of my method of approach toward ethnological data is due to his influence. To the late Dr. W. H. R. Rivers, like all those who came in contact with that remarkable man, I owe more than I can adequately express. I wish gratefully to mention three other friends, Prof. Edward Sapir of the University of Chicago, Mr. P. L. Faye of Berkeley, California, and Mr. W. E. Armstrong of Cambridge University, England, all of whom in many ways, often unknown to them, have been instrumental in stimulating my thought and giving me new outlooks. In conclusion, I wish to express my sincere thanks to Prof. John Dewey for his kindness in reading the proof and consenting to write the foreword.

PAUL RADIN

CONTENTS

PART I
MAN AND SOCIETY

PART II
THE HIGHER ASPECTS OF PRIMITIVE THOUGHT

FOREWORD

Dr. Radin's work opens up an almost new field. It may not go contrary to the beliefs which are implicitly current among workers in the anthropological field. But even an outsider, like the present writer, can see that it surely introduces a new emphasis, fixing attention upon phases of the culture of primitive man which are usually passed over lightly, if they are not overtly denied. There are at least many premises and many conclusions which have gained popular currency which are incompatible with the material and interpretations which he presents. From the standpoint of the specialist in this intellectual territory, Dr. Radin's work is pioneering in quality; it introduces new perspectives in its assertion of the existence of a definite intellectual class, proportionate in numbers and influence to the "intellectuals" in any civilized group, and one which is possessed of ideas upon most of the themes which have formed the staples of philosophical discussion. It is easy to imagine his contribution becoming the center, almost a storm-center, of animated debate and heated controversy among the special students of primitive life.

In that discussion a laymen like myself has no place. But no one concerned with the intellectual history of mankind, especially with the background of what has now become more or less conventionally set apart as philosophy, can fail to be intensely interested in the material which he has advanced. There are not lacking recent writers on the origins of philosophy who have dealt with its emergence from primitive speculations, especially from the material connected with religious beliefs and rites, and who have insisted upon the influence of the latter upon the formation of early philosophic notions. But in the light of Dr. Radin's material their views need reconsideration. For if he is even approximately right, philosophic origins are not to be sought for in the cruder and conventionalized forms which religious beliefs assumed among the populace at large, but rather in the interpretations of the small intellectual class, whose ideas may have been crude because of limitations of subject matter at their command, but which at least were bold, independent, and free within these limitations.

It may be worth while, even at the expense of a hasty traversing of ground which Dr. Radin has covered in detail, to point out some of the matters of the background of philosophic origins with respect to which the material of Dr. Radin demands either authoritative refutation or else a pretty thoroughgoing revision of notions which have become current. Among these points is the secondary and auxiliary place of supernatural and magical practices and beliefs in connection with practical achievement. If we trust the material, primitive man was in fact more "tough-minded," more realistic in facing facts, than is currently believed. The student of morals and social philosophy must give serious attention to the weighty mass of evidence which is adduced to show that early man instead of being enslaved to the group to the point of absorption in it was in fact highly individualistic, within certain limits more so than modern civilized man. The extent to which early ethical judgments in the way of social condemnation were limited to special occasions instead of being generalized into judgments of character at large raises the question whether their moral

standpoint was not in so far sounder than that which civilized "progress" has developed. The prevalent idea that the
customs of the group provide automatic moral standards and
rules receives a severe shock when we find that along with
great freedom of "self-expression" there is equal emphasis
upon responsibility for personal control of actions so as not
to harm others. The conception that primitive man attributes an independence to the existence of the group comparable to that of the "external world" seems not only to
do justice to the facts which the upholders of the incorpora-
tion theory rely upon, without falling into their excesses, but
to be also a valuable contribution to any sociological theory.
And these are only a few of the points with respect to which
the material of the first part of Dr. Radin's work demands
serious attention together with reconstruction of current beliefs as to the background and origin of later moral and social
speculations.

For the abstract phases of philosophy the second part,
entitled "The Higher Aspects of Primitive Thought," is
equally significant. The titles of the chapters are themselves
sufficient to indicate the precious nature of the material to
those interested in the development of metaphysical speculation. Dr. Radin would doubtless be the first to deny that he
is breaking entirely new ground in his presentation of the
actual facts regarding aboriginal man's notion of what constitutes reality and human personality. But I do not know
where one would turn for such a complete and convincing
picture of the dynamic and qualitative way in which the
world presented itself to the primitive speculator on existence. Under the influence of modern philosophic theories,
it has been assumed that the object and world were first regarded as collections of sense-data, while the obvious inconsistencies with this notion have been accounted for as

animistic and supernatural injections. Dr. Radin explodes this traditional notion. He makes it clear that objects and nature were conceived dynamically; that change, transition, were primary, and transformation into stability something to be accounted for. His account makes clear that effects, emotional and practical, were the material of the thought of real objects, and that thinkers, in their doctrine of an inner "form," stated in rational terms a notion which was expressed mythically by the mass, a notion which has marked affiliations with a persistent strain in the classic philosophic tradition.

To continue, however, would be merely to summarize what the book itself vividly presents. I only hope that the cases selected by way of illustration may serve to indicate to those interested in the development of philosophic ideas and to the larger number interested in the growth of the intellectual phase of human culture, the rich and provocative material which Dr. Radin has freshly provided.

John Dewey

METHODS OF APPROACH

There can be little doubt that every human group, no matter how small, has, from time immemorial, contained individuals who were constrained by their individual temperaments and interests to occupy themselves with the basic problems of what we customarily term philosophy. It is equally evident that at no time could the number of such individuals have been very large. What is not so clear, however, to the overwhelming majority of scholars and laymen, even if we grant the existence of individuals with philosophic interests and the capacity for philosophic thinking, is that the languages at their disposal were adequate either in structure or in vocabulary for the formation of abstract and generalized ideas and philosophical concepts. And even if the language can be shown to be adequate, many scholars would contend that the stage of cultural development reached by aboriginal peoples, to say the least, did not encourage such formulations except to a minimal degree. Since a large part of the following pages will be devoted to indicating that the so-called complexity of a civilization has only indirectly much bearing on the existence of philosophers and of philosophic formulations, there is no need for dwelling here upon the second of the objections raised above and I shall accordingly turn directly to the question of the nature and structure of aboriginal languages. My remarks on this subject will have to be of a summary character.

It may seem strange to many readers, but it would be easy to demonstrate that the languages of aboriginal peoples are frequently more complex structurally than are our own, that the vocabularies are just as large, sometimes even larger, that words with abstract or generalized connotations are as frequent, indeed, in some native idioms more frequent than in our own, and that the abstract connotation of a word quite commonly is expressed formally by affixes. I would like to stress the third point particularly because there are a certain number of comparative philologists and philosophers of language, such as E. Cassirer and L. Lévy-Bruhl, who seem to believe that aboriginal peoples do not think abstractly and cannot form generalized concepts because most of their abstract words can be shown to be built up of stems that, etymologically, possess concrete meanings.

Assuredly it is not necessary to point out the large number of words with abstract significance in our own language that are compounded of stems with the most concrete of meanings. To contend, for instance, that the etymology of the Winnebago Indian word for *sacrifice* which means *to-cut-off-a-finger-joint* or the word for *to bite* which signifies *to-bring-together-two-*

horizontal-surfaces-by-the-action-of-the-mouth tells us anything about the capacity of the Winnebago for abstract thinking or generalized thought would be as ridiculous as if we were to draw inferences concerning the lack of ability of Europeans for abstract thinking from the etymology of words like *religion, understand, hypothesis.* Nor should it be necessary to recall to any philologically-trained individual the obvious fact that the possession of affixes with abstract connotation, as well as their number, is due to secondary historical causes and has nothing to do with a people's mentality nor, basically, with a people's interests. In some languages, aboriginal and civilized, such affixes abound, in some they do not; in some the special vocabulary for philosophical formulations is at hand, in others it is not. Kant, we know, had to coin the term *das-Ding-an-sich* (the-thing-in-itself). He would have been saved that necessity had he written in Achomawi, an Indian language of northern California, spoken by a tribe with the simplest of civilizations. In that idiom every noun, pronoun and verb appears in two forms, an absolute-abstract form and a relative-concrete one. This distinction is as fundamental for an understanding of Achomawi as is that of sex-gender for Indo-European.

In short, the language basically required for the expression of philosophical ideas is present in aboriginal civilizations. That in itself, however, means little as we have just seen. It did not necessarily lead to the development of substantial philosophical formulations or integrated philosophical systems. That depends upon other circumstances, particularly upon the presence of a certain type of social-economic structure. Much, of course, admittedly depends upon what we mean by philosophical formulations. If we mean integrated philosophical systems of the type which began in Western Europe with Plato and Aristotle the answer must emphatically be no. But we find no such systems in India or China where very substantial philosophical formulations obviously flourished. On the other hand, in ancient Egypt and Babylonia there is no evidence, apart from religious speculations, that general philosophical formulations were attempted except on a minor scale. Complexity of civilization has, apparently, comparatively little to do with the existence of such formulations. Indeed a complex civilization may very well stifle the urge to philosophize where it does not actually prohibit it.

That theorists like Lévy-Bruhl and Cassirer should question the adequacy of aboriginal languages to express philosophical ideas can perhaps be explained as due to insufficient information. That a linguist of the distinction of Diedrich Westermann[1] should do so is incomprehensible. Perhaps, however, it is no stranger than the claim once made for the superiority of Latin and Greek over all other languages.

By itself, however, it means very little to say a given language is adequate for philosophical formulations. It is not the structure of a language that produces them but the intellectual superstructure accompanying certain social-political conditions. Much, of course, will depend upon what we understand by philosophical formulations. Is, for example, such a proverb as the following West African one a philosophical formulation?

> He went far away;
> He went long ago;
> He went before anyone came.
> Which of them is the eldest?[2]

Manifestly it is. Yet one such philosophical formulation is not enough. What, however, if you find a whole series of philosophical statements in the form of proverbs such as Danquah gives on pages 188-197 of his afore-mentioned book? Will that suffice? I think most of my readers would say no and for a simple reason. They really mean by philosophy a very special thing, namely the integrated philosophical systems which began in Western Europe with Plato and Aristotle. Naturally this cannot be found among primitive peoples. Nor can it be found in India or China. Yet clearly these two countries produced substantial philosophies, although many historians of philosophy admit this rather grudgingly. The development of formal integrated philosophical systems is however only one form which the evolution of philosophy has taken. All the problems with which it is concerned can be adequately formulated without ever being integrated into a system. This should never be forgotten.

It has been contended that only certain types of civilization—I am speaking here of the complex civilizations of Western Europe and Asia—produce formulated philosophies and reasons have been found for explaining this fact. Thus recently Professor Frankfort[3] has insisted that the ancient Egyptians and Babylonians, in fact the Ancient Near East in general, had no true philosophy because for them the phenomenal world was primarily what Frankfort calls a "Thou" while for modern man, that is, with the period beginning, let us say, with the pre-Socratics, it is an "It."[4] There is no need for me to stop here to refute this contention. This will be done abundantly, I hope, in the following pages. Frankfort is here simply following Lévy-Bruhl and Cassirer who based their conclusions on a complete misunderstanding of the data presented by many ethnologists. That the ethnologists often misled them by presenting the data vaguely and confusedly is true enough. But that is no excuse. At bottom all these theorists as well as many of the ethnologists whose data they have used, whether they admit it to themselves or not, predicate a special kind of mentality for all but the Greeks and their cultural descendants.

Except in the case of Lévy-Bruhl and his followers it is not always clear what is the nature of the mentality they predict. In an exceedingly suggestive article on primitive mentality G. Lienhardt[5] has at-

tempted to steer clear of many of the implications of
Lévy-Bruhl, although he agrees with him, on the
whole, in his main contention, namely that we are
dealing here with a special type of mentality. He insists that the distinction between primitive man's
formulations and our own depends upon the fact that
we "think about thought" and primitive peoples do
not. "It is not true, of course," so Lienhardt contends,
"that primitive peoples are less practical and logical
than ourselves in the ordinary course of their daily
lives. All value empirical knowledge and exercise skill,
foresight and common sense, and to this extent we
understand their reasoning without effort. We should
not therefore suppose that all thought *attempts to
become like our own, as our own appears when we
reflect upon it as 'thought'—either concerned, that is,
with the logical demonstrations of truth and error or
meditative and imaginative. If we suppose this, we
introduce into primitive thought distinctions which we
have arrived at by elaborate systematic reflection upon
our own. We do not see it as it is.*"[6]

I believe Lienhardt is quite wrong in the distinction
he here draws between our mentality and that of
primitive man—for that is what his contention
amounts to—and that he has been led to this error
because he thinks the elaborate systematic reflection
upon thought that is necessary could not have been
made where there was no method for preserving the
thoughts, reflections, demonstrations of truth and

error, etc., of a long line of thinkers, that is, writing. The best way, however, to demonstrate that Lienhardt and the large number of individuals who agree with him are in error is to show by examples the extent to which primitive peoples indulge in the same type of philosophic speculation as we do.

This I have attempted to do in the following pages. To the examples given in various parts of this book there must now be added the very remarkable philosophical speculations which M. Griaule obtained from the Dogon of the French Sudan.[7]

On the face of things, then, there is nothing in primitive civilizations that prevents philosophical formulations from being attempted. Individuals with a philosophical temperament are present, the languages are adequate, the structure of their societies places no obstacles in the way. But before we try to discover whether philosophical problems were actually attacked and to determine of what type they were, it is necessary to go into some detail concerning the facts upon which we have to rely and the method by which they were obtained.

Since writing was unknown among aboriginal peoples, all information had to be obtained orally. This meant that individuals had to be induced by outsiders —administrators, missionaries, travellers, ethnologists —to give it to them. For reasons we cannot go into here but which are well known, this information was rarely given willingly. A very special kind of relationship had to be established between the investigator and the investigated and this was very difficult of achievement. Ideally the investigator's role should have been confined to seeking his philosopher, explaining to him what he wished and, having persuaded him to talk, to record what he said. That, however, would have required not only a native philosopher who was willing to give the information but an investigator who was a philosopher and who had neither prejudices nor preconceived notions as to the mentality of the people he was studying. Such investigators are extremely rare. As a result the philosophies in question have, generally, been described either by the investigator himself or elicited, question by question.

The first of these two methods is by far the most commonly employed. It is clearly extremely dangerous even in the hands of those whose knowledge is extensive and deep. Professor Mair is quite right, then, when she insists that "the anthropologist is (not) justified in crediting the peoples whom he is studying with explanations of their beliefs which they do not themselves offer."[8] When, therefore, a distinguished missionary and student like Father Tempels[9] devotes a special volume to Bantu philosophy in which he not only gives no direct formulations from the Bantu themselves but insists, among other reasons, that they could not make them because of the inadequate nature of their vocabulary, his presentation is of value only insofar as it tells us what ideas he thinks are implicit in Bantu philosophy. Even though, as he insists, he submitted his formulation to the people themselves and they agreed that he had correctly stated what they meant, we are not helped much. If, as he says, "it is only we Europeans who can tell them in a precise way what constitutes the nature of their conception of being," if this is really so, then the Bantu, very definitely, are incapable of philosophizing.

This does not mean that attempts such as those of Father Tempels and others are not valuable and legitimate. Indeed it is essential that they be made. I shall indulge in them repeatedly myself. But it must not be forgotten that they are made by outsiders and can be subjective to a dangerous degree. They must not under any circumstances be regarded as primary sources. Not infrequently such formulations may be essentially valid—there is ample evidence for believing that those of Father Tempels are. But they can be demonstrated only by actual texts from philosophically-minded aboriginal philosophers. That is why it is unfortunate, to say the least, that so distinguished a student as S. F. Nadel in his recent book *Nupe Religion*[10] still employs his own formulations instead of attempting to obtain adequate descriptions from native philosophers. That they exist among the Nupe is clear enough. Formulations by outsiders are simply not enough if we wish to remove all doubts as to the capacity of aboriginal peoples to make philosophical generalizations. Moreover such formulations

can be quite erroneous, particularly with complicated religions such as those of native West Africa. How erroneous they can be in enabling us to discover what is implicit in the philosophy of African civilizations, for example, an Akan thinker like J. B. Danquah— granted that one has to be very careful in accepting all he says—has shown very clearly in his book *The Akan Doctrine of God*.[11]

A more authentic method of obtaining information, although also fraught with considerable danger, is direct questioning. Here the value of the record, in large measure, depends upon the relationship between the investigator and his informant. If that is satisfactory and the investigator is competent, knows the language, has an adequate knowledge of the tribe and realizes fully what he is doing, this can become something analogous to a true philosophical dialogue. The difficulty then arises, of course, as to whether we can interpret the answers received as giving evidence of the existence of true philosophical formulations and systematizations. Whether this can or cannot be done can, however, be best brought out by an example. To indicate how valuable and revealing such a method can be, I shall therefore quote in detail one such long dialogue between a highly competent observer, although not a trained one, and an American Indian priest belonging to the Oglala-Dakota tribe.[12]

I heard you exclaim when a meteorite fell and heard you address the people immediately afterwards. Then I saw you burning sweet-grass. Will you tell me why you did this?

You are a white man's medicineman and you want to know the mysteries of the Lakota. Why do you want to know these things?

The old Indians who know these things will soon be dead and gone and as the younger Indians do not know them they will be lost. I wish to write them so they will be preserved and your people can read them in years to come. Will you tell them to me?

My father was a shaman and he taught me the mysteries of the shamans and I will tell them to you. What is it you want to know?

When the meteor fell you cried in a loud voice, "*Wohpa. Wohpe-e-e-e.*" Why did you do this?

Because that is *wakan.*

What is *wohpa?*

It is what you saw. It is one of the stars falling.

What causes the stars to fall?

Taku Skanskan.

Why does *Taku Skanskan* cause the stars to fall?

Because he causes everything that falls to fall and he causes everything to move that moves.

When you move what is it that causes you to move?

Skan.

If an arrow is shot from a bow what causes it to move through the air?

Skan.

What causes a stone to fall to the ground when I drop it?

Skan.

If I lift a stone from the ground what causes the movement?

Skan. He gives you power to lift the stone and it is he that causes all movement of any kind.

Has the bow anything to do with the movement of an arrow shot from it?

Taku Skanskan gives the spirit to the bow and he causes it to send the arrow from it.

What causes smoke to go upward?

Taku Skanskan.

What causes water to flow in a river?

Skan.

What causes the clouds to move over the world?

Skan.

Are *Taku Skan* and *Skan* one and the same?

Yes. When the people speak to him, they say *Taku Skanskan.* When a shaman speaks of him, he says *Skan.* *Skan* belongs to the *wakan* speech used by the shamans.

Is *Skan, Wakan Tanka?*

Yes.

Is he *Wakan Tanka Kin?*

No. That is *Wi,* the Sun.

Are *Wi* and *Skan* one and the same?

No. *Wi* is *Wakan Tanka Kin* and Skan is *Nagi Tanka,* the Great Spirit.

Are they both *Wakan Tanka?*

Yes.

Are there any other *wakan* that are *Wakan Tanka?*

Yes. *Inyan,* the Rock and *Maka,* the Earth.

Are there any others?

Yes. *Wi Han,* the Moon; *Tate,* the Wind; *Wakinyan,* the Winged; and *Wohpe,* the Beautiful Woman.

Are there any others that are *Wakan Tanka?*

No.

Then there are eight *Wakan Tanka,* are there?

No, there is but one.

You have named eight and say there is but one. How can this be?

That is right. I have named eight. There are four, *Wi, Skan, Inyan,* and *Maka.* These are the *Wakan Tanka.*

You named four others, the Moon, the Wind, the Winged, and the Beautiful Woman and said they were *Wakan Tanka,* did you not?

Yes. But these four are the same as the *Wakan Tanka.* The Sun and the Moon are the same, the *Skan* and the Wind are the same, the Rock and the Winged are the same, and the Earth and the Beautiful Woman are the same. These eight are only one. The shamans know how this is, but the people do not know. It is *wakan* (a mystery).

Did the *Wakan Tanka* always exist?

Yes. The Rock is the oldest. He is grandfather of all things.

Which is the next oldest?

The Earth. She is grandmother of all things.

Which is next oldest?

Skan. He gives life and motion to all things.

Which is the next oldest after *Skan?*

The Sun. But he is above all things and above all *Wakan Tanka.*

Lakota have told me that the Sun and *Taku Skanskan* are one and the same. Is that true?

No. Many of the people believe that it is so, but the shamans know that it is not so. The Sun is in the sky only half the time and *Skan* is there all the time.

Lakota have told me the *Skan* is the sky. Is that so?

Yes. *Skan* is a Spirit and all that mankind can see of him is the blue of the sky. But he is everywhere.

Do you pray to *Wakan Tanka?*

Yes, very often.

To which of the eight you have named do you pray?

When I pray I smoke the pipe and burn sweetgrass and *Wohpe* carries my prayer to the *Wakan Tanka.* If the prayer is about things of great importance, it is carried to the Sun; if about my health or my strength it goes to *Skan;* if about my implements, to *Inyan;* if about food or clothing and such things, to the Earth.

Are such prayers ever carried to the Moon, or the Wind, or the Winged, or to *Wohpe?*

They may be carried to the Moon and to the Wind; but this is the same as if to the Sun or *Skan.* Lakota do not pray to the Winged. They defy him. They do not pray to *Wohpe,* for she carries all prayers. The Lakota may pray to any *Wakan,* but if to a *Wakan* that is below *Wakan Tanka,* such must be named in the prayer and it will be carried to the one named.

You say *wohpa* is a falling star. Is *Wohpe* in any way related to a falling star?

She first came like a falling star.

Where did she come from?

From the stars.

What are the stars?

Waniya.

What are *waniya?*

They are ghosts. *Skan* takes from the stars a ghost and gives it to each babe at the time of its birth and when the babe dies the ghost returns to the stars.

Is *Wohpe* a ghost?

She is *Wakan Tanka*. A ghost is *Wakan,* but it is not *Wakan Tanka*.

Has a Lakota ever seen *Wohpe?*

Yes. When she gave the pipe to the Lakota she was in their camp for many days.

How did she appear at that time?

Like a very beautiful young woman. For this reason the people speak of her as the Beautiful Woman. The people do not speak of her as *Wohpe*. Only the shamans call her that.

Lakota have told me that her *ton* is in the pipe and in the smoke of the sweetgrass. Is that true?

It was a shaman who told you that. When the people say *ton* they mean something that comes from a living thing, such as the birth of anything or the discharge from a wound or a sore or the growth from a seed. Only shamans speak of the *ton* of the *Wakan*. Such *ton* is *wakan* and the shamans only know about it. The people are afraid to talk of such *ton* because it is *wakan*. The people smoke the pipe and burn sweetgrass because *Wohpe* will do no harm to anyone.

You say the Rock is the grandfather of all things and the Earth the grandmother of all things. Are the Rock and the Earth as a man and wife?

Some shamans think they are, and some think they are not.

Who were the father and mother of all things?

The *Wakan* have no father or mother. Anything that has a birth will have a death. The *Wakan* were not born and they will not die.

Is anything about a Lakota wakan?

Yes. The spirit, the ghost, and the *sicun*.

Do these die?

No. They are *wakan*.

What becomes of them when the body dies?

The spirit goes to the spirit world, the ghost goes to where *Skan* got it, and the *sicun* returns to the *Wakan* it belongs to.

What is the *sicun?*

It is the *ton* of a *Wakan*. *Skan* gives it at the time of the birth.

What are its functions?

It remains with the body during life, to guard it from danger and help it in a *wakan* manner.

How does the spirit get to the spirit world?

It goes on the spirit trail.

Where is the spirit trail?

It can be seen in the sky at night. It is a white trail across the sky.

Is it made of stars?

No. It is like the clouds, so that nothing but *Wakan* can travel on it. No man knows where it begins or where it ends. The Wind alone knows where it begins. It moves about. Sometimes it is in one direction and sometimes in another.

How does the ghost go to the place where *Skan* got it?

The ghost is like smoke and it goes upward until it arrives at the stars.

What becomes of the body when it dies?

It rots and becomes nothing.

Admittedly no Oglala priests ever indulged in such dialogues. That they conversed on these subjects frequently and deeply we know. It is also quite possible that something in the nature of such dialogues occurred when priests were instructing others. What concerns us here is, of course, not the question of form but whether the answers to Walker's questions indicate that a true and systematic formulation of these ideas existed. Walker, like Father Tempels, insists that no one priest could have given them in a comprehensive or sequential manner. Yet it is perfectly clear that the answers he received constitute just such a formulation. He apparently was thinking of formal philosophical systems after the model of Aristotle and modern European philosophers. Moreover I do not doubt for a moment that the Oglala transmitted their ideas as a unified whole, as a unified system. Such formal teachings are quite common among many Siouan-speaking and Central Algonquian-speaking tribes. All that Walker apparently did was to bring what he considered a desired harmony between the various formulations of the priests. This was quite an error on his part because it obscured the fact that there was considerable difference of opinion, which our quotation clearly indicates, on many of the matters involved.

At best, however, the question and answer method is not an ideal one. It is far better for the investigator to stay in the background and let the native philosopher expound his ideas with as few interruptions as possible. This is the great merit of the account M. Griaule has given us in his remarkable little book cited above. The fact that his African philosopher did so through the stimulation of Griaule and under new conditions, while it must have had some influence, does not constitute a great distortion, particularly not with regard to the question with which we are concerned, the existence of philosophical formulations among primitive peoples and the capacity of certain individuals for constructing philosophical systems.

Only with the introduction of writing was the intervention of an outsider reduced to a minimum. Much of the information was, of course, even then still given at the request of the investigator, but a considerable amount was free from even this minimal type of pressure. The best of this material is to be found in the great collections of native texts. These collections contain not only traditional imaginative narratives— myths, novelettes, historical occurrences, proverbs, riddles, poetry—but likewise both traditional and new philosophical speculations on every conceivable subject from the nature of God and of man to the meaning of the circle or why stones at the top of a mountain tend to be round. Some of these speculations, as I have just said, are new and relate to modern problems as might have been expected considering the crises through which native civilizations have been passing during the last fifty years. Others consist of revaluations of old traditional conceptions. Unquestionably the amount of philosophical speculation of the latter type is much greater today than when the native civilizations were functioning normally. But philosophic speculation generally flourishes most luxuriantly in times of crisis and change. This held, let me recall, for the great periods of Greek or Chinese philosophy as well. Nor must it be supposed that times of crisis and change had not occurred long before contact with the complex Western European or Asiatic civilizations. Native Africa and the Americas, for example, have had a number of such crises which are clearly reflected in the traditional narratives of philosophical import found there. Most of these, except those of ethical import, relate to religion because, as in many of the complex European and Oriental civilizations, speculations on religion were the only ones deemed worthy of transmission. However, considering the large variety of subjects on which individuals speculated in the past, there is no reason for believing there was any more restriction as to subject-matter then than is found today.

Thus it can be contended that there exist ample materials, of various degrees of authenticity and validity, for enabling us to determine whether aboriginal civilizations possessed articulate and systematic philosophies and what their nature was. At times we shall see that it is even possible, with some degree of accuracy, to trace their development.

METHODS OF APPROACH

[1] Cf. *Die Kpelle*, Goettingen, 1921, pp. 139ff.

[2] J. B. Danquah, *The Akan Doctrine of God*, London 1944, p. 27.

[3] *Before Philosophy*, Penguin Books, 1954. Originally published under the title of *The Intellectual Adventure of Ancient Man*, Chicago 1946.

[4] Frankfort, pp. 12 ff.

[5] "Modes of Thought in Primitive Society," *Blackfriars*, Oxford, June 1953, pp. 269-278.

[6] P. 277. The italics are mine.

[7] Cf. his *Dieu d'Eau Entretiens avec Ogotemmeli*, Paris 1948, and M. Griaule and G. Dieterlen, "The Dogon," in *African Worlds*, edited by Daryll Forde, London 1954.

[8] I. L. Mair, *An African People in the Twentieth Century*, London 1934, p. 236.

[9] Placide Tempels, *La Philosophie Bantoue*. Translated from the Dutch. Paris 1949, p. 24.

[10] London 1954.

[11] London 1944.

[12] J. R. Walker, *Oglala Sun Dance, Anthropological Papers of the American Museum of Natural History*, Vol. XVI, 1917, pp. 154-156.

PRIMITIVE
MAN
AS
PHILOSOPHER

Primitive Man as Philosopher

CHAPTER I

INTRODUCTION

THE study of primitive peoples is a comparatively recent discipline. It can be said to have been first definitely and adequately formulated by Edward B. Tylor. To-day, after more than two generations of development, compared with such older disciplines as history it is still barely out of its swaddling clothes. There are comparatively few places where its principles are taught and as a result it is still, to an appreciable extent, the happy hunting ground of well-meaning amateurs. It would be a gross injustice to minimize the services these amateurs have rendered. But amateurs are enthusiasts and, as a class, likely to be both sentimental and uncritical; and while the academic intolerance of them is often unfair and ridiculous, it is nevertheless true that no science can be said to have attained its full majority until the number of amateurs engaged in it, as compared with those specially qualified, is reasonably negligible.

Judged by this criterion, ethnology to-day is still in its adolescent stage. Yet adolescence has its charms, and among these charms is optimism and faith. Optimism is, in fact, the keynote of present-day ethnology. How else can we explain the nonchalance with which an ethnologist embarks on the task of describing, single-handed, the language, mythology, religion, material culture, art, music, and social organization of a people whose language he very rarely can speak and whose mode of thought and life is far more remote from his own than is that of an Illinois farmer from the mode of life and thought of a Hindu?

The keepers of the older disciplines, where specialization often reaches its apotheosis of aridity and futility, sit back in half-contemptuous bewilderment at the boyish pranks of the adventurer-ethnologist who sets out to conquer a new world. Perhaps in the end the laugh will be on the critics. For the present, however, it must be admitted that their bewilderment and incredulity are amply justified. Every statement, for example, that an historian makes is expected to be controlled by a large body of corroborative material. Surely, it is contended, the ethnologist does not expect us to take his uncorroborated word for everything. Unfortunately he does, and there are practical reasons why, dangerous as this situation avowedly is, it must be accepted and made the best of.

With very few exceptions, the descriptions of primitive peoples cannot be controlled in the manner that is customary in subjects like history. The observer not only collects the facts, but to him belongs the power to fix, often for all time, what precisely those facts shall be. It is clearly dangerous to entrust such power to any man, yet for practical reasons attendant upon the collection of ethnological data, it is somewhat difficult to avoid this fundamentally undesirable and unreasonable condition. Since, however, his work is so conditioned, the observer's emotional and intellectual approach, his expressed and his unexpressed assumptions, the many intangible trifles that influence even the most careful and critical, all these naturally assume a greater significance for the ethnologist than for the historian.

It cannot be said that the majority of ethnologists are fully aware of the ways in which certain tacit or conscious attitudes make themselves felt, and how definitely such attitudes are likely to color their records. There is only one way of avoiding this danger, and that is the old way, the one in vogue in history for centuries—to obtain the facts in the original and to attempt no manipulations and no rearrangements of them whatsoever. Whatever interpretations are necessary must be completely separated from the original data. This rather obvious procedure is only now becoming at all common in ethnology. Some of the most famous monographs written by Europeans and Americans, for instance, sin most egregiously against this elementary rule.

But if the historian to-day differs markedly from the ethnologist in the degree of trust he is willing to place in the uncontrolled reports of a single man, no matter how qualified he may be, he differs equally in another even more important regard, namely, the selection of the aspect of culture most to be emphasized. In all recent treatments history has come to be the history of the intellectual class, and at all times it has been the history of the exceptional man. In ethnology, on the contrary, partly owing to its genesis, partly to paucity of material, the emphasis has been quite otherwise, and it is the group beliefs as such that are described. Ethnologists have not always been conscious of this fact, yet even when they are well aware of marked individual differences among primitive men, these are dismissed with the summary comment that they do not represent the general consensus of opinion.

On the whole, it can justifiably be claimed that the prevalent descriptions of primitive peoples represent the beliefs and customs of the non-intellectual class among them, or at best a hopeless mixture of the viewpoint of the intellectual and the non-intellectual class which no lay reader can possibly disentangle. This defect would be in no way mitigated even if it should eventually be shown that ninety-nine per cent of all primitive peoples belong to the non-intellectual class. There would still be one per cent of the aboriginal population to be accounted for, and for this one per cent our present descriptions would be just as distorted and inadequate as if we were to accept Frazer's *The Golden Bough* as a true picture of the beliefs and customs of the intellectual class of Western Europe.

Throughout this book I am making one assumption, namely, that among primitive peoples there exists the same distribution of temperament and ability as among us. This I hold to be true in spite of all the manifest differences in the configuration and orientation of their cultures. In justice to myself I should add that the predication of an identical distribution of ability and temperament for civilized and primitive peoples is not the result of any general theory that I happen to hold; it represents a conviction that has been slowly forced upon me from my observations and contact with a number of aboriginal tribes.

To repeat, then, my object here is to describe primitive cultures in terms of their intellectual class, from the viewpoint of their thinkers. Thinkers, however, are not, and can not be, isolated from life among primitive peoples in the same way as this has repeatedly been done among us, nor do they probably exercise the same degree of influence on their fellows. To attempt, therefore, to envisage primitive culture from their standpoint is equivalent to looking at it through a very restricted lens. I am fully aware of this. The result will give only a partial picture, one which will necessarily hold true for only a very small number of individuals in each group, and it must not be mistaken for anything else. That would be as great an error as the one committed by those who assume that there is no intellectual class in primitive culture.

The following book is grouped into two parts, the first dealing with the relation of man to society and to his fellow men, and the second with what I have called the higher aspects of primitive thought. In this way, it is hoped, it will be possible to indicate to what extent each thinker shared and participated in the ideas of the average man of his group and in what way he transcended them.

Throughout it has been my endeavor to allow the natives to talk for themselves, interpreting their thoughts only in those cases where explanation seemed necessary and of value. Perhaps I shall be criticized for quoting too much and for giving the book more the appearance of an anthology of the thoughts of primitive people than a discussion of them. But, in a sense, what I have really tried to do is to be a commentator. I need not say that this rôle has at times been changed into that of an interpreter.

Had it been possible, I should have much preferred to gather all the sources available to-day into a separate volume and to restrict the present one simply to discussion. But the time for such a procedure has not yet arrived, although it is clearly not far off. It is perhaps better at the present stage, considering the ignorance, incredulity, and prejudice still prevalent even among otherwise well-informed laymen on the whole subject of primitive culture, to carry our proof along with us and to substantiate every unusual statement as soon as it is made.

Let me repeat, before we begin our study, that in the present condition of our knowledge any attempt to describe the intellectual view of life of primitive peoples is destined to be tentative, provocative of further investigation and interpretation rather than permanent and final. I can only say with an unknown Hawaiian poet:

The day of revealing shall see what it sees:
A seeing of facts, a sifting of rumors.

PART ONE

MAN AND SOCIETY

CHAPTER II

THE PRIMITIVE VIEW OF LIFE

PARADOXICAL as it may seem, it is nevertheless a fact that few people are, on the whole, so unfitted by temperament to study the simpler aspects of the life of primitive people, and by implication their emotional and intellectual manifestations, as the average cultured scholar and university-trained ethnologist. It is really a marvel that they have done so well. Both lead a definitely sheltered life and look upon the world from a highly specialized point of vantage. Being largely dependent upon books for stimulation, they are apt, like the generality of historians, to set too high a value upon the rôle of thought in culture. This holds particularly true of the English ethnologists, and ethnological theorists from Tylor to Frazer, Andrew Lang always being excepted. Yet when they sense this danger and consciously guard themselves against the possible overevaluation of the intellectual side, they frequently fall into the opposite error— that of reducing most of the spiritual values of primitive civilizations to those of mere delight in sensations, to simple, unintegrated responses to an uncontrollable environment. It is this latter tendency that we find not infrequently exhibited in works on aboriginal culture written by the professional ethnologist.

It is conceivably demanding too much of a man to whom the pleasures of life are largely bound up with the life of contemplation and to whom analysis and introspection are the self-understood prerequisites for a proper understanding of the world, that he appreciate corporate and individual expressions which are largely non-intellectual—where life seems, predominatingly, a discharge of physical vitality, a simple and naïve release of emotions or an enjoyment of sensations for their own sake. Such undiluted pleasure in spending long periods of time in doing apparently nothing is difficult for a man of intellectual interests to understand. It is just as difficult for a man of action to comprehend. Ethnologists are definitely the one or the other. Yet, in large measure, it is just such an absorption in a life of sensations that is the outward characteristic of primitive peoples.

The reaction of the nonprofessional ethnologist and the layman when he discovers this to be one of the characteristic traits of primitive culture is generally one of puzzled irritation, and is coupled with the suspicion that primitive peoples are possibly, after all, possessed of an inherently lower mentality. Even William James, as a passage in one of his letters clearly shows, could not, for all his affectionate view of life and of man, completely rid himself of this feeling.

This must be expected. Indeed, we indulge in such judgments and inferences all the time. Does not the popular northern mind look with contemptuous be-

wilderment upon the charming ability of so many
Mediterranean nations to enjoy their *dolce far niente?*
Have we not frequently been told that however pic-
turesque, spontaneous, and gifted in the arts the
Latins may be, they are useless for the sterner realities of life and inferior in the higher realms of logical
and integrated thinking?   And would it not be correct
to say that this latter inference has been drawn from
their unadulterated appreciation of sensations?

   To a considerable extent the cultured ethnologist,
often unwittingly, makes an analogous judgment in
his efforts to evaluate primitive cultures.   He does not,
it is true, make so devastating a generalization, but
he does show a marked inclination to regard all culture
as made up of two types of activity—the intellectual
and the practical, setting a higher value upon the
former than upon the latter.   The ordinary man, the
man of the street, the farm boy who is so predominatingly a man of action, is quite right when he smiles
indulgently at the naïveté and lack of real understanding of the world shown by the scholar.   Yet, in
the end, it is the scholar who laughs last, for, owing to
the man of action's unwillingness and inability to
write, histories are generally written by the former.
And the scholar quite naturally makes history a selection of facts which interest and seem of most importance to him and these are largely intellectual although
the practical side is by no means neglected.   What is
neglected is the sensational aspect.   Indeed, this side
of life is not merely neglected: it is definitely distorted

and underrated, faring just as badly whether it is a professional scholar or a gentleman-traveler who is making the evaluation.

We spoke above of the opposition of the northerner and the southerner. To most northerners—and the overwhelming majority of ethnologists are northerners —the enjoyment of sensations as such is still the sign of inferior thinking powers. Now the ethnologist is not merely a northerner: he is a specially selected northerner, an academically trained man, or a traveler —individuals in whom the sensational side is likely to be markedly suppressed. To this specially selected type of investigator an unkind fate has entrusted the task of recording, for all time, the story of civilizations that are, to an overwhelming degree, stressed on the sensational side. What complicates the situation still further and weights the scales still more heavily against a correct understanding of primitive peoples, is that this sensational view of life is accompanied by apparent contradictions of elementary logical thinking and of palpable fact. All the elements in the case thus conspire to reënforce the ethnologist—there are of course noteworthy exceptions—in his belief that the mentality of primitive people is essentially inferior to our own.

That the scholar and ethnologist should be bewildered by the cultures of primitive peoples need elicit no wonder. Through unfortunate circumstances connected with the collection of data, and by too rigid a definition of what constitutes practical activity, many of the native customs fall into a nonpractical plane. On the other hand, through an obvious lack of desire for analysts, primitive mentality clearly does not run along what we have been accustomed to regard as the prescribed channels. Primitive peoples will, for instance, indulge in magical rites for the attainment of purely practical ends—the killing of deer, for instance —under circumstances in which they could by no conceivable means fail to do so. Yet they will seek the most tenuous of religious sanctions for a hazardous undertaking such as a warpath. They may tell you, if directly interrogated, that a poisoned arrow discharged for a short distance into a deer trail will cause the death of a deer that is to be hunted on the following day. What inference can we very well expect a person to draw from such a statement but that a magical nonrational rite has achieved a practical and all-important result? Must we not insist, then, that the mentality of people who accept such a belief is different in degree and possibly in kind from our own? There seems indeed to be no escape.

The first error that we here commit is that of expecting the answer to a direct question put to a native to be either complete or revealing. It is similarly an error even to expect that such a question touches the core of the real problem involved. Let us take the last example given. We are not to imagine that after discharging the arrow into the deer trail our native returns to his family and informs them that he has potentially killed a deer, nor are we to imagine that he tells them he has performed the preliminary part of his work. What he has done is one indissoluble whole —he discharges the arrow in the proper way, waits for the morrow, and then follows the trail until he has killed the deer. Any question whereby it is assumed, consciously or unconsciously, that one part of this series of activities is more important than the other or that a causal relation exists between them, is misleading and entails a misleading answer. So much for our initial error. But we have likewise no justification for assuming that some general principle underlies the native's activities in this particular instance. He did not select any trail at any time of the year, but a particular trail at a particular time of the year. We must assume that he knows from unlimited practical experiences that he is selecting the proper conditions for his task. I once asked a Winnebago Indian whether the rite of shooting an arrow into a trail of which he had no knowledge would be effective and received a prompt and amused denial. Similarly it was discovered that although in certain tribes a vision from a deity was regarded as adequate sanction for embarking on a war party, in actual practice certain very practical conditions had to be fulfilled before an individual was permitted to depart.

Therefore, when ethnologists contend that a direct question should never be put, we mean that its immediate answer does not reflect any necessarily true or complete analysis of the situation. It remains an answer of restricted meaning connected with an indi-

vidual fact momentarily detached from its proper setting.   But even though we give it full meaning, we
must be careful to find out whose view it represents.
Now the two answers given above were given by individuals whom I have reason to believe were medicine-
men or priests—men whose position in the tribe corre-
sponds roughly to that occupied by our scholars and
thinkers.   In answering my question we may suppose
that these individuals tried to explain something.   But
many natives, had they been interrogated, would have
made no' reply at all, or if they had answered, their
answer would have been merely mechanical and would
have carried practically no significance.

What, then, does the rite of discharging an arrow
mean to such people?   Intellectually, indeed even
symbolically, it may mean nothing.   To the ordinary
man it is primarily and essentially one of a series of
actions that is to culminate in the more or less
immediate future, in certain practical results.   All his
energies, all his thoughts, are fixed upon this one and
avowed object.   The medicine-man, the thinker, he
who, in other words, enjoys analysis and possesses an
intellectual envisaging of life, may indeed tell the
practical man that his concentration upon the purpose
in view will enable him to gain his end more definitely
and more effectively; and this statement may in fact
be mechanically repeated by the ordinary practical-
minded man.   But it has no real significance for him.
Action is to him the all-important fact and this it is
that absorbs all his attentions and energies.   As far

as explanations are concerned, any will do. An individual who gives you detail upon detail about the proper method of approaching a deer during the breeding season will inveigh in the next breath against the stupidity of the American game laws that prevent you from killing deer whenever you desire. As though deer propagated their kind after the fashion of other animals and did not, in reality, emerge out of wells! We cannot too strongly insist that there is no logical contradiction involved here nor are we dealing with what the French scholar Lévy-Bruhl has called "prelogical mentality." The matter seems simple enough. Something that the medicine-man and thinker has formulated in intellectual or symbolical terms is being repeated mechanically by a practical-minded man. The thinker's formula stands on its own and the actual fact stands on its own. Neither can possibly contradict the other for they lie in different planes.

Now it is exactly by this envisaging of life in terms of a series of activities of a practical nature that our over-intellectualized modern scholar and ethnologist is apt to misunderstand. Perhaps this is why so many ethnological monographs so often develop into semi-arid tracts containing unconsciously distorted presentations of primitive culture, and why, at times, some individual totally unqualified from the viewpoint of specific training but with a well-developed sensational side to his nature, can give an inherently more correct picture.

CHAPTER III

THE COERCION OF THE WORLD

I T is one of the salient traits of so-called primitive man, we have just seen, that he allows a full and appreciative expression to his sensations. He is pre-eminently a man of practical common sense just as is the average peasant. Now this does not merely mean manual dexterity or an exclusive interest in the purely material side of life. It has much deeper implications. This tough-mindedness leads to a recognition of all types of realities, realities which primitive man sees in all their directness and ruggedness, stripped of all that false and sentimental haze so universal among civilized peoples. We cannot dwell upon this point now but will return to it later. Here we desire merely to point out that primitive man is endowed with an overpowering sense of reality and possesses a manner of facing this reality, which to a western European implies an almost complete lack of sensitiveness. And this is true of even the more avowedly intellectual among them, such as the medicine-men and the leaders of the ceremonies. It is true that the facts of everyday life, in every primitive community, are clothed in a magical and ritualistic dress, yet it is not unfair to say that it is not the average native who is beguiled into an erroneous interpretation of this dress but the ethnologist.

To illustrate what I mean I shall give an example that came under my own observation. An American Indian, pursued by the enemy, took refuge in a cave where he could easily defend himself against direct attack but where escape was apparently completely cut off. This particular individual was not religious. He had during his lifetime had so little interest in getting into the proper *rapport* with the deities of his tribe that he knew the conventional methods of addressing them but little else. In his dilemma, with death staring him in the face, he mechanically offers tobacco to the spirits. That much he knew. But he did not know what to say nor whom to address. So he prayed—if we are inclined to call this a prayer—"To you, O spirits, whoever you are, wherever you are, here is tobacco. May I be saved!" Through an almost miraculous piece of good luck the enemy fled and he was saved. "By the will of God," a devout Christian would have ejaculated; in Indian phraseology, "The spirits have heard me." Here, if anywhere, we might have expected an almost mystical feeling of heavenly intervention and a well-nigh complete obliteration of the mere workaday world. Yet nothing of the kind occurred to this very hard-minded individual. He sought to explain nothing. I can picture him saying to himself in his humorous way—for he was the professional humorist in the tribe—"Let the medicine-men explain; they like such things. All I know is that I was pursued by the enemy; I took refuge in a cave; my attackers withdrew and here I am." The ritualistic paraphernalia were all there but they did not obscure his vision of the nature of a true fact.

This man was of course an unusual specimen of the tough-minded species. So much will have to be granted unhesitatingly. Yet this intense realism, this refusal to be deluded by the traditional phraseology employed, is a salient feature of most primitive communities. That there are many individuals who take the phraseology more seriously we know. The medicine-man, the thinker, the poet, these insist upon a less matter-of-fact explanation and clearly enjoy the wrappings. Did they not in fact devise these explanations and are they not continually elaborating them? But in spite of the inner necessity that prompts them to prefer a super-mundane formula they, too, are deeply rooted in the workaday-world conception of reality.

Nothing, for instance, is more thoroughly ingrained in the minds of many American Indians than the fact that a supernatural warrant must be obtained for any undertaking of importance no matter how practical its nature. The Indian will tell you simply enough that if a deity has bestowed his power upon an individual in a vision and permitted him to go on a warpath, he may do so. Yet if one visualizes concretely the hazardous nature of such an enterprise in a small tribe, it is but natural to assume that any community allowing a young man to risk his own life and possibly that of others on the strength of communication in a dream, must be profoundly imbued with a religious spirit. Unfortunately this whole picture is wrong. It changes as soon as we obtain fuller details about the matter. Then we discover that no individual is ever allowed to proceed on even a private war party unless his dream-experience has been communicated to the chief of the tribe or else to some highly respected elder. Such men are always exceedingly devout. They certainly may be expected to take religious sanctions at their face value. Yet it was just these custodians of the tribal tradition who were most careful to see that the practical aspects of the situation did not militate too markedly against success. If, in their opinion, the undertaking was un-warranted—whether because they thought the leader too inexperienced, the possibility for adequate prepara-tion unfavorable, the strength of the enemy possibly too great, or what not—they refused to give their sanction and forbade it. Quite naturally they couched this prohibition in a religious phraseology. "The spirits have not blessed you with sufficient power" is the Winnebago formula, for instance.

The intense belief in the existence of the spirits and of their direct participation in the affairs of man is not to be questioned, any more than is the acceptance of the magical. But this in no way interferes with their full realization of all the facts involved in any given situation. In other words, though primitive man may describe life in a religious terminology it is not to be inferred that in the vast majority of cases he regards a purely mundane happening as due to super-natural agency. This is indicated clearly by the great care taken among many tribes not to demand impossible tasks from their deities. One does not ask rain from a cloudless sky during the dry season, nor security against capsizing in a canoe when foolishly setting out during a terrific storm.

Primitive man, in short, does not consider the deities or a magical rite as conditioning reality but as an accessory to it, as constraining it. Both the deity and the rite are aids for the proper functioning of a series of habitually connected individual or social events. The religious and magical content seems the all-important factor to us who are mere spectators; to primitive man they are, as we have said, simply aids, stimuli for the attainment of a goal.

Thus viewed the facts of primitive life take on a new psychological orientation. The attainment of a goal, the clear realization of a specific objective, becomes the main factor. Everything else is either completely slurred or regarded as secondary. Even rites, beliefs, motor activities, may all become functionless and accidental. Primitive man may not in our sense of the term provide for the morrow but he attempts something perhaps far more important—he bends all his energies, inward and outward, toward ensuring the success of his objective on the morrow. With this determination steadily before him he completely identifies himself with the goal to be obtained. He prepares for it, previsions it, preënacts it, and pre-attains it. Select any example at random—a war party among the Winnebago. In a dream communication from the spirits he ascertains the necessary number of moccasins and the necessary amount of food to be consumed on the expedition; he is told how many men he is to take along and how many of the enemy he is to kill. His divine certificate is then closely scrutinized by experienced elders and if it is accepted, then in the ceremony preparatory to his actually starting out he previsions his enemy. He destroys his courage, deprives him of his power of running, paralyzes his actions, and blunts his weapons. Thus protected and his enemy correspondingly weakened and constrained, he proceeds to the attack.

All these facts are admirably and convincingly illustrated by a very unusual document obtained by the late Mr. Russell from the Pima Indians of Arizona.[1] It represents a speech given by the war chief urging the people to go on the warpath against the Apache. I shall give it in full:

Yes, my poor brother-in-law, this land was covered with herbage. The mountains were covered with clouds. The sunlight was not bright and the darkness was not dense. All was rolling before our eyes. It was thought that the time had come for considering these things in council, my brothers. Then wood was gathered and a fire kindled, the flames of which burst forth, reaching to the sky and causing a portion of the earth to fold over, disclosing the underside where a reddish mountain stood. After these things had happened the enterprise was decided upon.

---

[1] Frank Russell, "The Pima Indians," 23d *Report of the Bureau of American Ethnology,* p. 357.

Then my breast was tightened and my loins girded; my hunger was appeased; sandals with strings were made for my feet; my canteen was made ready. I went about the country, from mountain to village, beneath the sheds and trees, offering all an opportunity to join me. Returning home I thought I saw my brother when I was in a trance. I tried to grasp him and my arms embraced nothing but myself. I somehow caught in my palm what I thought to be this power; turning this over I found it to be but a creation of my imagination, and again I was disappointed. I was unkempt and rough and my tears moistened the land.

The plan occurred to me to ask Nasia, the old woman magician, for aid. Thinking that I saw her I ran toward the eastward and finally reached her. I said, "Yes, you who make the bows of the Apache like a *kiaha* and crush his arrowheads, you who paint triangles and curves on the *kiaha* bottoms with the arrow foreshafts of the Apache dipped in his blood, you who twist the hair of the Apache and tie your *kiaha* with it." Thus I addressed her and she gave me a bundle of power which I grasped under my arm and ran with it to my home.

I thought of Vikaukam and prayed for his aid. When I finally reached him I said, "Yes, your house is built of Apache bows and bound with their arrows, you use his bowstrings and sinew to tie these withes. You use Apache headdresses and moccasins to cover your house. Within it you have square piles of Apache hair. At the corners of the piles cigarettes give off wreaths of smoke resembling white, black, glittering, purple, and yellow blossoms." Thus I spake and he gave me power which I carried away beneath my arm.

I thought of South Doctor and finally prayed to him. I said to him, "Yes, you who can make the Apache bow as harmless as a rainbow, his arrows like the white tassels of grass, his arrow shafts like soft down, his arrowheads like thin, dry mud, his arrow poison like the water fern upon the pools, his hair like rain clouds."

Thus I spake and he gave me power which I grasped under my arm and journeyed westward with four slackenings of speed. The home magician gave me a seat of honor. The cigarette smoked and I took it and, drawing in a cloud of smoke, I prayed to Old Woman Magician, saying, "Yes, you make the Apache bow like a game ring, you crush his arrow shafts and make headbands of them, you split his arrow foreshafts, color them with Apache blood, and make game sticks of them; his arrowheads you make like pottery paddles, you make a girdle of Apache hair."

Thus I spake and he gave me his power, which I caught under my arm and ran home, with four slackenings of speed. The home magician gave me a seat of honor. The cigarette smoked and I took it and, drawing in a cloud of smoke, breathed it forth in the direction of the enemy. The power grew and shone on and on until it slowly disclosed the enemy. The Pima magician desired that the earth move, the trees take on their leaves, the land be softened and improved, that all be straightened and made correct. The place was one where food was increased and they were gathered about it. Their springs were made larger and they were gathered about them. Their game was gathered together. Some of the enemy were in the west and they said, "We know that harm may come to us

if we go to that place, but we will not heed our own mis-
givings." They started on their journey and camped on the
way. In the morning they arose and continued, reaching
their friends' camp during the day, where they saluted
them. In the distant east were other enemies who heard
that their friends were gathering. When they heard of it
they said, "We know that harm may come of it if we go
to that place, but we must go." They started on their
journey and camped once before arriving and saluting their
friends. They took the sun's rays and painted triangles on
their blankets.

While this was happening among them my young men
were preparing to fight. They rushed upon them like flying
birds and swept them from the earth. Starting out upon
my trail I reached the first water, whence I sent my swiftest
young men to carry the message of victory to the old people
at home. Before the Magician's door the earth was swept,
and there my young men and women danced with headdresses and flowers on their heads. The wind rose and,
cutting off these ornaments, carried them to the sky and
hung them there. The rain fell upon the high places, the
clouds enveloped the mountains, the torrents descended upon
the springs and fell upon the trees.

You may think this over, my relatives. The taking of
life brings serious thoughts of the waste; the celebration
of victory may become unpleasantly riotous.

This is a reality at white heat and it is in such a
heightened atmosphere that primitive man frequently
lives. Since it is so frequent and accustomed an at-

mosphere, he is generally calm outwardly, although this varies from time to time and moments occur where pandemonium seems to reign. When, therefore, we see his life obviously permeated with religious beliefs and with rites and rituals at every step, we assume that all this emotional intensity is due to the religious and magical background in which he is enveloped. And here it is that many observers and investigators commit what is a fundamental error of interpretation; first, by assuming that there exists, in the minds of most natives, a cause and effect relation, and second, by stressing the wrong end of what constitutes, in each tribe, the habitually determined sequence of acts and beliefs. We can easily agree with Professor Lévy-Bruhl when he contends that any analysis of this sequence is, strictly speaking, nonexistent or, at least, rare, without nevertheless following him farther along his argument. In his famous work *Les Fonctions Mentales dans les Sociétés Inférieures* he implies that no primitive people are capable of logical differentiation or of a logical selection of data. He is certainly in error on this point as the subsequent chapters of this book will abundantly demonstrate. But he errs in an equally fundamental way when he unconsciously assumes that every analysis must be the work of the rational faculties.

Lévy-Bruhl is by training and nurture too much of an intellectual to appreciate how adequately sensations, emotions, and intuitions may determine a selection, and how such a selection can be on a par with a so-called rational analysis. For him any such selection implies a prelogical mentality and is not a true or correct analysis. Be this as it may, it is this non-intellectual analysis that is typical of much of primitive thought. But another element must not be forgotten, namely, that the selection is in its turn predetermined by being oriented toward a socially and individually determined goal. This goal, it may be said, is to fix what is to be interpreted as real. It thus follows that reality becomes largely pragmatic. What happens is true. So markedly developed is this pragmatic test for reality that even when the event that occurs is more or less definitely contradictory to the specific cultural background, it carries conviction. Let me illustrate the nature of this pragmatic test of reality by two examples.

An Indian of my acquaintance, in order to be favorably received by his relations, made a consciously dishonest claim of having been blessed by certain deities. By virtue of this blessing, he claimed, he was in a position to cure a young cousin who was ill. After having been entertained lavishly he left and promptly forgot all about the incident. A few months afterward his aunt met him accidentally and thanked him profusely for all that he had done for them and he discovered, to his unfeigned surprise, this his false claim had worked! Now what was his immediate inference? Let me quote his own words: "When I heard this I was surprised, not being certain whether I had been blessed or not!"

The second example concerns the same individual. He and a friend determined that they must secure the coveted war honor of killing an enemy. To embark on a war party, however, according to the ideas of his tribe, it was necessary to receive some warrant from the deities. Such a blessing he had not received. In spite of this he and his friends sought out an enemy and killed him. When he returned home he told his father about his exploit and among other things indicated that he had really been unqualified to undertake such an expedition. It is clear that the young man seemed somewhat puzzled about his success. Yet the outstanding fact for him was that he had been successful, that he had killed the enemy and secured the coveted war honor. It is this *fait accompli* that determines the reality. Not being devout, the young man did not trouble himself to state his success in religious terms. But the father was devout and, since the young man had succeeded, this implied that he had been in communion with the deities, if not precisely in the orthodox manner, at least to the extent that the deities had inspired the deed.

It may then be correct to say that while, strictly speaking, primitive man does not think of a·cause-and-effect sequence, he does predicate causes as such and effects as such; that the medicine-man and thinker deal with causes as such and sometimes with a real cause-and-effect relation, whereas the average man deals with effects simply.

If now we turn to the most insistent desire of primi-

tive man—long life, success, and happiness—this sense
of an objective world distinct from supernatural causa-
tion obtrudes itself even more strongly. Deities do
not control the success or lack of success of the normal
events and happenings of life. It is only at crises that
their aid is solicited. We can do no better than to
quote what an Indian told the writer in an autobiography which he wrote down and wherein he embodied the system of instruction current in his tribe:
"Help yourself as you travel along the path of life.
The earth has many narrow passages scattered over it.
Some day you will be journeying on a road filled with
obstacles. If then you possess the means for strengthening yourself you will be able to pass through these
passages safely. Indeed if you act properly (i.e. circumspectly) in life, you will never be caught off
guard."

Nothing more practical than this can well be imagined. Here we have a viewpoint thoroughly pervaded and saturated by a profound appreciation of
the realities of life. Nor is the statement quoted above
that of a practical man. It is, on the contrary, that of
an eminently religious individual, one who had occupied a prominent position in all the rituals of the tribe
and who had been accustomed to frame every act, no
matter how trivial, in a religious terminology.

This aspect of primitive man's perception of the external reality of life is a very salient feature of his
outlook. It can be easily accounted for. His envisaging of life and of the social world is firmly rooted in

two basic facts, in his conception of the relationship of the individual to the social group and his truly profound, all-embracing, and unsentimental knowledge and intuition of human nature. His intense realism expresses itself in an overwhelming craving for success and in an intense pursuit of every form of social prestige, while his intuitive understanding of human nature in all its manifold ramifications can be seen in the attitude he takes toward the expression of personality.

I think every one competent to judge will admit that in primitive communities free scope is allowed for every conceivable outlet. No moral judgment is passed on any aspect of human personality as such. Human nature is what it is and each act, emotion, belief, unexpressed or expressed, must be allowed to make or mar a man. It is each man's inalienable right—he would indeed be unfair to himself if he did not make use of it—to seek the approbation and respect of other individuals and of the community, even if this right be abused and exaggerated. No false modesty should be allowed to deter him. But there is an important corollary. If by the exaggeration of this craving a man comes into conflict with the world and with social realities, he will personally suffer and, what is far more reprehensible and dangerous, he may involve others in the consequences of his personally initiated self-seeking. If, for example, among the Winnebago Indians, a man in his insatiable desire for prestige completely overestimates his own powers and loses all sense of proportion, he is held strictly accountable for any harm that may result to others through his action. Should he embark on a warpath that is unauthorized and take with him members of the tribe, he is responsible for their safety, and if they are killed he is subject to the same treatment as if he had murdered them. The point of view is this: a man may risk his own life if he wishes. It is his own concern if he is willing to risk the unpleasantness of ridicule and disapprobation. He is exceedingly stupid to take such risks but that again is his own affair. To involve others in the dangers attendant upon an exaggerated prestige hunting, however, is a crime.

This prestige hunting is simply an outgrowth of a ruthless realism. It is possibly the fundamental fact in primitive life everywhere. The type of prestige sought differs, of course, from tribe to tribe. Much is sacrificed for its attainment. Playing such a rôle in their lives, it should not strike us as strange that religion and magic are found associated with it. In the autobiography quoted above we find the following passage: "Some people are acquainted with medicines used when they are in a crowd. If they employ it there, people will then be enabled to single them out and they will be considered great and important." The hunger for glory and for the respect of one's fellow men is literally overpowering. "Act properly," a man is told, "so that when you die your name will be held in respect and men will frequently talk of you and say, 'Ah, that man, he indeed possessed great

power!' " Another individual told me that when he
was young his father used to spur him on to fast by
telling him that if he did then he would become like
one of those Indians famous in story.

Now much of all we have mentioned differs in no
way from what holds among ourselves. The distinction between them and ourselves is that they recognize this will-to-power—for such it is—as a fundamental element of the human soul and refuse to pass
any moral judgment upon it. It is neither a virtue
nor a vice, although it may, in turn, become the one
or the other.

I have dwelt upon the desire for glory and prestige
hunting at such length because we encounter it so
obtrusively in aboriginal tribes and because its abuses
are there so patent and lead to so much conflict. If
these abuses are more rampant and if they are treated
more leniently there than among us, this is due to the
insistence upon unhampered self-expression. Every
man and woman seeks individuation—outer and inner
individuation—and this is the psychological basis for
their otherwise bewildering and unintelligible tolerance
of the fullest expression of personality. Limitations to
this expression naturally exist but these, we shall subsequently see, flow directly from an intense and clear-
cut appreciation of the realities of life and from an
acute sensitiveness to group reactions. If one were put
to it to sum up primitive man's viewpoint in a single
sentence it would be somewhat as follows: "Express
yourself completely but know yourself completely and

accept the consequences of your own personality and of your actions."

It would be asking too much to expect that the majority of people will accept this statement of primitive man's attitude toward life without demanding very adequate proof. That I hope to be able to give in the course of this book.

Now this whole conception of reality as pragmatic, this idea of a free scope for self-assertion, seems to belie all that we have always been taught by sociologists and numerous ethnologists about the tyranny of the group, and about the complete lack of individualism found in primitive communities. Indeed, according to a theory still largely accepted, the details of a religious rite, of a bit of sympathetic magic, etc., do not vary appreciably from individual to individual. The little change that exists is insignificant and imperceptible. People who hold this view go even farther. They deny that there is any variation in subjective attitude.

There is considerable justification for such a view superficially. It appears offhand to be corroborated by the apparent absence of any revolt against the type of government. Who, it might be contended, ever heard of a person attempting to alter the clan organization? Nor can anyone deny the monotony of the ritual performances, the ceaseless repetition of actions and of words so characteristic of primitive life. Then too, at ritual dances, the group seems to be acting as a unit and all individual consciousness to be merged into a vague superconsciousness. Since group activities of some kind or another fill so much larger a place in their life than among us, what more natural than to assume that this reflects a real lack of differentiation? And so sociologists have insisted that just as superstition and magic hold primitive man in a vise of fear and helplessness, so does an inexorable group-tyranny restrict and fetter all individual initiative. But, they contend that even were this group-compulsion to relax for a moment and allow the indiscriminate and free expression of individuality, there would be no individuality to express. It is with this assumption of the nonexistence of anything but a corporate consciousness that the vast majority of investigators begin. Primitive cultures, according to them, represent a stage in the evolution of civilization in which only the "group-mind" existed. The firm and inflexible chain that at such a stage holds people together is fear—fear of the unknown, fear of the natural phenomena they have not succeeded in controlling, and fear of each other. Deviation means ruin and destruction; ruin as punishment which the group will inflict, and ruin through utter inability to cope with a new environment alone.

Taking the magical religious trappings with which everyday life is invested at their face value, taking literally even the actual statements of many native informants and the descriptions given by the generality of ethnologists, there is ample ground for the above view. Granted our predominating intellectualistic outlook—leaving on one side mere prejudice and ignorance

—what we know of primitive life would superficially imply such an interpretation. But this is true only superficially and many ethnologists, particularly in America, have long known this, though for some inexplicable reason have never embodied it in their monographs.

Wherein does the error lie? It lies in this: in our unjustifiably equating the primitive group with the group as we know it among ourselves, and in our refusing first to examine what constitutes social reality for primitive man. Social reality is to him something unique and definitely distinct from the individual and no more emanates from him than does the external world. It is coexistent with the individual, both constraining and in its turn being constrained by him. As soon as we realize this, and that much of the religious and magical background is secondary, at times even being an inert accretion that but represents the external dress of a will-to-action, then the true interaction of the group and the individual becomes apparent at once. Far from cramping and fettering him—be it on the chase, on the warpath, at ceremonial enactments, etc.—this background then serves as a means of doubling the concentration of mind and body, of increasing a tenseness of nerve and muscle, of evoking a sense of personal power and well-being. It gives him what he most desires in life, prestige and a heightened sense of existence.

All that we know of primitive man when we come to know him at all intimately and are able to look below the surface, bears this out. Individualism, what might, in fact, be called "personalism," everywhere runs riot. Whether it be in the South Seas, in aboriginal Asia, Australia, Africa and the two Americas, the atmosphere that pervades each community is always the same—a ceaseless pitting of man against man, endless bickerings, jealousies, envies, hatreds, a delight in the discomfiture of others. This is, of course, the negative side, the one generally most clearly perceptible to outsiders and for that reason most definitely dwelt on by the casual observer. Old books of travel and adventure are replete with descriptions of the terrible atmosphere of hatred, fear, and jealousy which pervades a primitive community. If all they said were true life would be unbearable if not unthinkable. Wherever we find such a description, whether in some old work or in some recent study by a gentleman ethnologist or government administrator, we can be certain that it represents only one aspect of life just as it does among ourselves. There is a positive side, too, expressed in romantic and devoted friendships, in love, reverential family affection, in kindness, generosity, and pity, in the highest of all virtues, respect for individuality.

Consequently what we must always bear in mind is this medley of contacts, this friendly and unfriendly impingement of personality upon personality. All official restraint in the free expression of individuality is absent. We are here in the presence of that exceedingly unusual phenomenon, a clear-cut realistic and

unsentimental perception of life and of the nature of
human contact. The rapidity in the alternation of
love, hate, appreciation, and envy seems to bespeak
an emotionally unintegrated personality. Such is the
generally accepted view. Even so open-minded an
observer as Dr. C. K. Jung seems to accept it. Dr.
Jung quotes with approval, from a source not indicated, the following example: "A Bushman had a little
son upon whom he lavished the characteristic doting
affection of the primitives. . . . One day he came home
in a rage; he had been fishing and had caught nothing.
As usual the little fellow ran eagerly to greet him. But
the father seized him and wrung his neck upon the spot.
Subsequently of course he mourned for the dead boy
with the same abandon and lack of comprehension as
had before made him strangle him." [2]

No greater distortion of the actual facts could possibly be imagined. And yet Dr. Jung obtained this
example from what purported to be a first-hand account, and similar examples often fill reputable descriptions of a tribe. They all illustrate the unconscious bias that lies at the bottom of our judgment
of primitive mentality, the unconscious assumption
of the lack of differentiation and of integration to be
found there.

We know that this lack of stability and integration
is a basic assumption in all evolutionary theories of
cultural development. This is, however, emphatically
not the case with Jung and others who take his atti-

---

[2] *Psychological Types*, p. 295.

tude toward primitive mentality. Some other explanation must be sought. What makes for error in our interpretation is a certain mistiness of vision due to that sentimentality from which the northern European finds it so difficult to free himself. Now what saves primitive man from emotional anarchy is the fact that he is truly envious and jealous, a lover and a hater; that he means all he says, but means it for just that passing moment or hour, as the case may be, in which these feelings actually represent his attitude, and for no longer. He may have a theory of conduct but he bases no ethical judgments upon his kaleidoscopic emotional reactions. He has thus fairly adequately solved one of the most difficult and baffling problems in the world, of balancing repression with expression of personality and, at the same time, attaining to a true integration.

CHAPTER IV

CONSERVATISM AND PLASTICITY

IN the preceding chapter our interest was centered mainly upon the individual. We were able to demonstrate that in the contact of individual with individual free scope was permitted for personal expression. Is it indeed very plausible then that in group activities primitive man should suddenly become transformed into an automaton incapable of self-realization and prohibited from indulging in change? The layman and the scholar free from theoretical bias can be led to such an interpretation, it seems to me, only because he is in large measure dominated by what takes place in the enormous centers of population so characteristic of the great civilizations of Europe, Asia, and Africa. Man there has undoubtedly become an automaton.

Many sociologists have been led to make this assumption for other reasons: first, as a reaction against the extreme individualistic interpretations of culture still largely current among most people in England and America; and second, because of their strong evolutionistic bias. This made it necessary for them to suppose that primitive peoples have not freed themselves to any appreciable extent from the tyranny of the group.

From Tylor to Hobhouse they have consistently contended that in primitive communities there can be no differentiated individualism. In arriving at this conclusion, it must be freely admitted, they have been aided and abetted by certain defects, sometimes conscious, sometimes unconscious, in the generality of published ethnological monographs on specific tribes.

Now we are not primarily concerned with this problem at all. What we desire is to discover the nature of the attitude of a primitive tribe toward the group and group activities and how we are to explain the impression of uniformity and the absence of variation which many experienced ethnologists get. The whole question has been somewhat obscured by the rather uncritical manner in which investigators have transferred to primitive society the theory of the relationship of the group to the individual current among ourselves. This transference is, I contend, quite misleading; for, as pointed out in the previous chapter, the individual and the group are in primitive society strictly incommensurable units, each with a separate and independent existence. We have nothing even remotely comparable to primitive man's sense of an objective social world, a world which is just as real as the external world and which is conceived of as being just as independent of the individual as the external world is. The social reality he predicates has existed from all time and is, in his eyes, as old as the external world of the senses. Like the external world it is never static but always dynamic, taking on varying forms and appearing under different aspects. Yet in spite of this dynamic character it is always the same, a unique and unalterable social world. An individual may sin against varying parts of it without incurring dangerous consequences but if he sins against any fundamental aspect he must be prepared either to dissociate himself entirely from this world or die.

Possibly we have here one of the reasons for the absence of consistent skeptics or unbelievers and for the nonexistence of revolts against the real structure of society. A consistent skeptic and critic would feel it incumbent upon him to withdraw from his tribe either to face death in the wilderness or to found a group of his own. He would in normal times never think of attempting to force the group to his way of thinking, because of his feeling that the group and the individual are entirely distinct entities, interlocked at certain points and constraining each other at others, yet sufficiently autonomous as units to resist any complete submergence of the one by the other. Ample leeway is allowed but the essential configuration of either unit must not be tampered with. What the real and essential nature of this social configuration consists of and furthermore what the nature of primitive man's understanding and intuition of this is, it is well-nigh impossible to determine; certainly it will for many decades elude the abilities of a Western European investigator to describe. The best he can hope to do is to describe its external details. The interrelations of its component parts are quite beyond him. Yet it is just this,

I feel, that gives the social configuration its true significance for the members of the tribe.

Let me give a few examples. Among the Winnebago a rigid clan organization prevailed until fairly recently. As far as I could find out, deviations of a rather important character have always existed and have always been tolerated. But the moment any one negated some feature felt to be basic he was forced to secede. Secession among the Winnebago, as in fact among many tribes, is by no means uncommon. In the semi-legendary accounts that have been preserved, the causes are generally given as personal ones and they often are of a most trivial kind, at least to our way of thinking. We will not, I feel certain, be going far wrong in discounting these accounts and in assuming that in almost all cases a very profound revolt lurked at the bottom of the secession. The following very illuminating illustration bearing on this point was obtained from the Winnebago:

A young man fell in love with a girl belonging to a clan into which he was not permitted to marry. Nothing that his parents or the older people said seemed to have any influence upon him. Marry the girl he would in defiance of all clan regulations. In desperation the father resorted to the following very subtle plan. Among the Winnebago there exists a very curious and interesting custom which forbids a member of any other clan to ask for water in the lodge of a member of the bear clan. To do so is considered an unpardonable affront and an unforgivable breach of good manners. Should any one, however, presume to ask for water it is refused, but every other demand is granted. The father in this case deliberately committed this affront and when the water was refused and he was asked to make some other request, he asked for the hand of the daughter of the owner of this house, it so happening that members of the bear clan were eligible as mates for his son. The son apparently had to consent and the revolt was broken. Now it is quite obvious that the first offense is, from our point of view, a hundredfold more heinous than the second, the latter being to our feeling largely a matter of etiquette. I should have assumed offhand, without questioning, that the Winnebago attitude would be the same as ours. And yet here we have the undoubted and incontrovertable fact that the young man refused to secede in the first instance and did in the second.

The preceding illustration shows how a custom which to us appears trivial and unimportant played a fundamental rôle in this man's understanding and intuition of the social configuration of his tribe and effectively prevented his revolt. In sum, he was quite willing to break one part of the social structure, such as marrying within his own phratry, but not another. In the second example, we shall see that even where a departure from what the external observer would regard as the fundamental structure of society is more fundamental, the basic break, to the native, consisted in an apparently trivial detail.

My second illustration is again chosen from the

Winnebago. Among them about thirty years ago a ceremony was introduced which deviated in many significant ways from the normal Winnebago type. The tenets of this new religion were from the very beginning diametrically opposed to the old Winnebago cultural background. The new faith naturally encountered tremendous antagonism among the older members of the tribe and, although understood, was definitely disapproved of. Yet what completely placed it outside of the pale for certain individuals was not the introduction of some new belief or rite, nor the denial of the efficacy of the older rites and of the whole sacerdotal system, but the reversal of the customary manner of making the ceremonial circuit in entering the ceremonial lodge. This constituted, for many, the real sin against the social configuration.

Now all this has a distinct bearing on our understanding of the rôle played by the group. Many investigators have not always taken the trouble to find out what primitive peoples themselves implied by the group, what it actually meant to them. They have equated it with our own ideas, and blandly wiped out everything else.

Take the whole question of the assumed uniformity in custom and rite. Yet wherever we obtain detailed information about rituals, magical rites, etc., we soon discover that much of the predicated stereotyped uniformity and absence of variation completely vanishes, just as it does in the case of a myth. And the variation in former times must have been much greater than it is to-day, for in these unfortunate times investigators must perforce content themselves with fragmentary information, and a good deal of merging of discordant customs and information has taken place and produced a fictitious uniformity. Sociologists and ethnologists have been aware of this for some time. If it has made comparatively little impression upon many of them, the reason is to be sought in the fact that there has always existed a tacit assumption that there is but one true version of a myth, one true version of a rite. Where deviations or variants were present this was to be ascribed to errors due either to forgetfulness or ignorance, or to general inert degeneration. Perhaps the following examples will suffice to illustrate the assumptions which at times underlie the work of even the professional ethnologist. One investigator told me that in an attempt to obtain what he regarded as an ideally accurate account of a certain ceremony he had the half dozen or more individuals reputed to know most about it hold a conference and come to some agreement as to what was the proper manner of giving the rite. Many deviations and even contradictions were found to exist but these were all ironed out to the observer's satisfaction and the description thus obtained published as the one and only correct version. In another case it was proposed in all seriousness that different versions and fragments of certain myths should be combined together into the true version.

We are justified then in insisting that part of the uniformity postulated of a rite or a myth is due to the utter inadequacy of the ethnological record and that this, in turn, is not always or predominatingly due to unfortunate circumstances, but to tacit or expressed assumptions of the investigator. The most cursory glance suffices to show that we are indeed not here dealing with an inert degeneration but with the free play of participants and story-tellers. In view of what has been pointed out in the previous chapter this is of course exactly what we might have expected. Where a society is so permeated with a thirst for prestige and naïve self-glorification as is that of primitive man, it would be quite ridiculous to imagine that these traits would not find expression in theoretically unorthodox ways.

Yet I do not want to seem unfair in my strictures. To the outsider the procedure at a ceremony does not change; the general tenor of the speeches remains the same, the rites retain their prescribed sequence, and the tradition within the tribe continues that there is no change. Many investigators noticing this have rather hastily drawn the inference that there is no change and that the individual was merged in the group. Now the correct state of affairs, as far as I can determine it, is this: change and deviation occur abundantly and are recognized, but there also exists, among certain very important individuals in each tribe, a tacit theory of immutability. This theory has been developed, it is safe to say, by the priest and the thinker and is only inconsistently shared by the average man. It is this theory that ensnares so many ob-

servers into the belief that there is a correct version
for every rite and myth and that as soon as this is obtained we shall have an adequate description of the
mental and emotional attitude of the whole tribe.

This theory of immutability to which primitive man
gives repeated utterance and to which he subscribes, at
least to the extent of not too insistently or too obviously deviating from the path of his fathers, applies
not only to group but to purely individual activities
likewise. The most outstanding and familiar of such
activities are the various rites connected with sympathetic magic. These all belong intrinsically to a motor
level and the cultural trappings associated with them
are for the most part inert and functionless survivals.
Yet here where we might expect unlimited deviations
and variations we find the least. We cannot ascribe
this exclusively to motor inertia or to a vague fear of
untoward consequences. Part of it is to be explained by
the fact that primitive man's theory of immutability
holds with far greater vigor for these magical rites
than for any other activities and that it finds a definite
and clear-cut expression in formulæ which, in their
turn, are supposed to be immutable. When, however,
we leave the domain of magic, even the theory of immutability will not suffice to explain the actual uniformity either in group activities or in those personal
activities that are performed in the presence of others.
To account for this we shall have to take into consideration a far more potent and archetypal social reaction—
the fear and horror of ridicule.

In one sense the fear of ridicule is merely the obverse side of prestige hunting, and prestige hunting is at bottom but a defensive mechanism against ridicule. Into the purely psychological aspects and implications of this whole question we cannot enter here, for our main concern is with the manner of its evocation and with primitive man's sensitiveness to it. Stated broadly we may say that every mistake, every deviation from accepted opinion, every individual and purely personal interpretation, every peculiarity and eccentricity, may call forth ridicule. It is ridicule and not indignation and horror that assails a man who attempts to change a detail in a ceremony, to tell a story in some new and original manner, or who acts counter to some definitely accepted belief and custom, and it is the same fundamentally ill-natured laughter that greets him when he becomes unwittingly the victim of some untoward accident. To avoid it a man will go to any length. He may even commit suicide in consequence of it. "If you travel in the road of good people," say the Winnebago, "it will be good and others will not consider your life a source of amusement." Even the deities are not exempt from this horror of ridicule. Among the Winnebago there exists a delightful story of a man who dared to state that he disbelieved in the powers of the most terrifying and holiest of the Winnebago deities, and who in public expressed his contempt for him. A short time later, the deity in question appeared to the skeptic and pointed his finger at him, an action that was supposed to bring immediate death. The man stood his ground and did not budge and the deity—Disease-Giver was his name—begged the man to die lest people make fun of him!

The fear of ridicule is thus a great positive factor in the lives of primitive peoples. It is the preserver of the established order of things and more potent and tyrannous than the most restrictive and coercive of positive injunctions possibly could be. As a conserving force it takes its place by the side of primitive man's sense of a social world distinct from the individual, and his theory of the unchangeableness of group phenomena. But whereas the latter two are specifically group expressions, the fear of ridicule appertains exclusively to the individual as such. It is every individual's personal balancing wheel. Though we generally see only its superficial repercussions as individual impinges upon individual, as a matter of fact it really represents each man's tacit assessment of himself, each man's sense of inferiority, each man's profound discomfort with any happening, whether caused by him or not, which disturbs the psychic unity towards which he is unconsciously striving. His feelings of personal worth and personal dignity are being outraged when he is the subject of ridicule and he reacts to it instinctively, instantaneously, and with an intuitive recognition of its importance.

Where there are such checks and balances, it is perhaps but natural to assume considerable merging of the two kinds of social reality always present to the consciousness of primitive man—the group and the individual. And yet this is precisely what does not take place, a fact we cannot too frequently stress. The unusual degree of integration found in primitive culture—and that there is integration to a much greater degree and in a far more complete manner than among us no person at all conversant with the facts will deny—this integration is not due to any identification of the individual with the group or of individual with individual, but to the existence of a larger configuration in which the individual and the group are separate and distinct units.

CHAPTER V

WE have tried to make it clear that the older theory, according to which only a group consciousness existed in primitive communities, is wrong and that in the interests of truth and clear thinking it had better be consigned to that already impressive limbo of rejected ideas which have grown out of the uncritical and superficial application of the evolutionary theory to the history of civilization. Individualism is present everywhere, we have seen, even to the point of degenerating into what I have called "personalism." There is, however, a possible objection to the above point of view. It might justifiably be claimed that much of the individualism discussed in the preceding chapters was non-significant and that real individualism, real freedom from the shackles of group-tyranny and group-thinking, can be demonstrated only when it can be clearly proven that freedom of thought exists. To this point we must therefore turn. It can best be approached by a discussion of the significance of variants.

That far-reaching variants in the manner of giving a ceremony or of telling a tale exist we all know, but a relatively small number of investigators have ever taken the trouble to inquire just wherein the full implication of this variation lay. Explanations like inert degeneration or forgetfulness will no longer do. The only method of throwing any light on the problem is to obtain the same information from different individuals with whose temperament one is acquainted. With this object in view, I obtained different versions of the same myth from three individuals. Two of them were brothers and had learned the myth from their father. The differences between these versions were remarkable, but the significance of the differences lay in the fact that they could be explained in terms of the temperament, literary ability, and interests of the story-teller. But we are interested here not so much in accounting for the origin of variants as in discovering the attitude of the group toward these variants. What we would like to know is why they disapprove of them, for that the older and more conservative people do frequently disapprove of them is beyond discussion.

Now there can be no question that, to a far more marked degree than among us, to be different from other people and to have differences of opinion and interpretation did in primitive communities call down upon an individual sarcasm and ridicule. But it is equally true that if one felt strong enough to stand the chaff and unpopularity and that the prestige value attached to the deviations or peculiarities definitely outweighed the disadvantages, then one could be certain of one thing, that no prosecution or persecution would take place. If a man chose to disbelieve in the efficacy of the spirits, apart from the ridicule to which he would unquestionably be subjected, this led to nothing worse than a shrug of the shoulders for his idiocy and un-called-for bravado. Essentially this was considered a matter of private concern although it probably would mean worry and concern to friends and relatives.

In the preceding chapter we gave an instance of a daring skeptic questioning the powers of a great deity. Ridicule, sarcasm, perhaps even horror, were the response from the community, but no censure was passed on his fundamental criticism of the accepted religious beliefs of the tribe. We find the same reaction to-day in connection with a new religion that is sweeping over the Winnebago and which preaches the destruction of all that is holy in their past. Scorn, ridicule and abuse are hurled against the rebels but no crusade is organized against them because of their innovations. One of the old conservative members of the tribe who hated these innovators with all the intensity of a reactionary summed up their case as follows: "This medicine (the new religion) is one of the four spirits from below and for that reason it is bad. These spirits (from below) have always been longing for human beings and now they are getting hold of them. It is said that those who use this medicine claim that when they die they will only be going on a long journey. But I say that this is not the truth, that in fact those who eat this medicine destroy their soul and that when death comes to them, it will mean extermination. If I spit on the floor the saliva will soon dry up and nothing will remain of it. So will death be for them. I might, it is true, go out and preach against this doctrine but it would be of no avail for I certainly would not be able to draw more than one or two people away from these spirits. Many, indeed, will be swallowed by this religion; they will not be able to help themselves in any way. The bad spirit will unquestionably seize them." There is not a word here of a forceful suppression, of using the agencies of government to persecute the innovators, not a word against their right to do and think as they chose. It is simply their foolishness that is deplored.

The right, then, to freedom of opinion is never for a moment questioned. As further illustrations let us take the following. On one occasion I remember a thunderstorm coming up from the east, a region which, according to the Winnebago, was not inhabited by those mythical birds to whom thunder and lightning are attributed. A Winnebago commenting upon this thereupon boldly announced that some thunderbirds did live in the east, in spite of the conception to the contrary. His belief, I feel quite positive, did not obtain general credence. But no one attempted to attack him because of his heretical views. He was free to believe what he chose and take the consequences.

The same attitude is shown with regard to divergent versions of some of the more important myths of the tribe, the sacred ones, those referring to the origin of the clans, of death, of future life. In one instance when I obtained a very markedly divergent version of the most sacred myth of the tribe, the informant, in reply to my question as to why his version differed so much from the others, answered rather irritatingly, "That is my way of telling the story. Others have different ways." That was all. No judgment was passed.

There are certain investigators who have been convinced that a multiplicity of variants exists in every tribe and who then very cleverly turn the spit around and insist that primitive people are not capable of constructing any coherent system of thought, that general formulations, for instance, are quite beyond them. It has frequently been contended that primitive man was unable to give an objective formulation of his culture. This, I think, is a quite unjustified and erroneous assumption. It is true that few coherent systems of beliefs have been obtained. But they do exist for those who wish to look for them, although they are confined, as among ourselves, to a very limited number of people. They are not frequent because in the intellectual atmosphere we have just described, where the unhindered and free expression of thought was the order of the day and was regarded as a purely private concern, system-mongering or a systematic theology, for instance, was quite useless. It could be and was attempted, but it carried no validity, brought no prestige. It remained the expression of a particular man or, at best, of a particular group. Take the Winnebago again. There a well-formulated system of teaching existed. But this system was considered simply a more emphatic and codified warning of the older people to the young not to take unnecessary risks, to be warned in time and to go fully clothed and protected upon the road of life. This systematic formulation bestowed upon the deities no additional efficacy nor did it endow them with a more lasting immortality.

This brings us thus to the very core of the question, namely, that among primitive people freedom of thought was closely and intimately bound up with the whole significance of thought. Now thought among primitive people has a function different from that which it possesses among us. It gives validity to one special kind of reality, the reality of their subjective life. "I think, therefore that which I think exists," such is the motto of primitive man. True enough, it establishes only one kind of reality but it is an important one and one that bears directly on the whole question of his tolerance of complete freedom of expression. A man's personality must not be interfered with. If by expressing it he destroys himself, that is his own affair.

But all that we have said above refers to only one aspect of the tolerance of difference of opinion. The other one is more fundamental and perhaps more difficult for us to understand. However real his subjective life may be to him, however definitely he may feel that thought establishes its own reality, we would be hopelessly wrong in imagining that primitive man believes that thoughts, ideas, opinions, etc., bear any relation to the facts of social experience. What he practically says is that it makes no difference whether a man thinks so or so. The social reality is not altered by it. This is clearly what the old man whom I quoted on page 31 was trying to express.

Nor need I add that the freedom of thought encountered here is not due to any secondary emancipation from the shackles of traditional dogmatism, as among us. It is due to the recognition of personality and the right of personality to expression, and due to the clear perception of a lack of contact between thoughts, ideas, and opinions on the one hand and the social realities on the other. The life of thought does not dominate and tyrannize over even the most intellectual of primitive people as it does over some of the least intellectual among us.

This significance of thought in our own civilization brings us naturally to the question of the influence of the written thought, the word. To Western Europe and the peoples of the Mediterranean, accustomed for thirty centuries to an alphabet, the written word has assumed something of a magical charm. In the beginning was the word, i.e., the *written word*. In its manifold repercussions this worship of the written word finally included the unwritten word and then extended itself till it ended in the deification of thought. Thus the word and thought became things in themselves, living and real entities, instead of retaining their old function of merely giving validity to certain realities. In Hebrew mythology the letters of the alphabet dispute with God as to who is to have the honor of beginning the Pentateuch and we need hardly refer to the tremendous significance attached to meaningless vocables in Egyptian and Greek papyri.

Now this is not at all true for primitive peoples. Much if not all of the magical quality and potency possessed by the mere word and by thought among us is derived from its connection with the written script. This is quite intelligible. Granted a dynamic and ever changing world, then the written word with its semipermanence and its static character was a much desired oasis. For the development of the technique of thinking it was of the greatest importance. But culturally and psychologically it possessed even greater significance, for it completed the victory of the visual-minded man over his competitors. From that time on, at least for the literate man, the main verities were to become visual verities. The word and thought were to become either identified with the ultimate and unique reality or predicated as its cause, and the world was to be conceived of as a projection of the thought of the creator. All along this line primitive man takes issue with us.

I would be the last to deny that primitive man attaches importance and power to mere thinking or to magical formulæ. The fact is patent. All I wish to emphasize is that he does not believe that thought does more than validate the reality of his subjective life. It does not touch the two great realities which apart from his personality concern him most: the reality into which he is born and the reality with which he is born.

At birth he is ushered into both, the reality of the phenomenal world and the social world. Now what primitive man seeks is the means for discovering the nature of these two realities, and the methods for ensuring their normal and adequate functioning. Anything that will help him in this quest is valuable and acceptable. Thoughts, feelings, intuitions, etc., can and do enhance and constrain an already existing reality; they are, in this rôle, to be recognized as an important adjunct.

Very frequently, indeed, one finds primitive man claiming to have been able to achieve certain results through the insistence and perseverence of his thoughts. I myself was once informed by an Indian that he had always been so successful on the hunt because he *used* his thought. Now concretization of thought is common enough among primitive people just as is the concretization of the emotions. Never, however, did thoughts lose their primary character of proofs of reality. No such apotheosis of thought and of the word was possible as among us, because these were at all times regarded as simply one of the various mechanisms for appreciating the existence of certain things, one of the means, we have seen, for establishing their validity. The distortion in our whole psychic life and in our whole apperception of the external realities produced by the invention of the alphabet, the whole tendency of which has been to elevate thought and thinking to the rank of the exclusive proof of all verities, never occurred among primitive people.

Much was thereby inevitably lost and it is conceivable that what many profound thinkers consider the true differentiation of the subjective from the objective toward which "civilized" man has been laboriously and inconsistently striving for the last five thousand years, was in consequence rendered impossible for them. Yet much also was gained, or better retained, for the false overvaluation of the visual sense brought in its train a too exclusive preoccupation with the purely objective world, on the one hand, and a distortion of a purely subjective element like thought, on the other, by ascribing to it objective validity. Primitive man was spared both of these things. Thoughts and words were recognized as integral and concomitant elements in every act and their import was never slurred or forgotten. But that is all. Especially was this true in the relations of man to man and of man to the social group. In this way he became a much better psychologist than we are and was enabled to see the social world and the phenomenal world in a much truer perspective than we do. How true this is the subsequent chapters will, I hope, demonstrate.

CHAPTER VI

O N no subject connected with primitive people does so much confusion exist in the mind of the general public and have so many ill-considered statements been made as on the nature of their behavior to one another. The prevalent view to-day among laymen is that they are at all times the plaything of their passions, and that self-control and poise are utterly alien to their character, if not, indeed, quite beyond their reach. We have seen in fact that even so open-minded and sympathetic a scholar as Jung apparently still accepts this view (cf. page 39). That an example like the one used by Jung should in all good faith be given as representative of the normal or even the abnormal reaction of a primitive man to a given emotional situation, shows the depth of ignorance that still exists on this subject. Now quite apart from the manifest absurdity involved in the belief that any parent in a primitive group would wreak his rage at his lack of success in hunting, in this murderous fashion upon the first object that came within his reach, even if it be his innocent and beloved child, there are a hundred and one reasons that would have deterred him, even had he been the uncontrolled animal the illustration assumes him to have been. However, let that pass. The illustration has its uses, for it permits the contrast between the generally accepted belief and the true nature of the facts to emerge all the more definitely. Actually the situation is quite different.

Briefly stated, the underlying ideal of conduct among most primitive tribes is self-discipline, self-control and a resolute endeavor to observe a proper measure of proportion in all things. I am well aware that in some tribes this is more definitely expressed than in others and that not infrequently certain excrescences in their ceremonial life seem to contradict this assertion. Yet I think most field ethnologists would agree with me. Since in the face of so formidable a body of opinion apparently to the contrary, incontrovertible evidence will be demanded of me to substantiate so broad and explicit a statement, I shall confine myself in my presentation of the facts to a tribe which I know personally and where the material which I use can be definitely controlled. The data upon which I rely come from the Winnebago Indians of Wisconsin and Nebraska and are to be found in two monographs published by me. Only statements made by the Winnebago themselves in accounts either actually written by themselves or contained in verbatim descriptions of the rituals obtained in the original Winnebago are used in order to obviate all inaccuracy.

I can think of no better method of introducing the subject than by quoting appropriate passages from the Winnebago texts secured and then discussing them in the light of the knowledge they throw upon the system of ethics enunciated and, more specifically, upon the type of self-control implied. For facility of reference I shall number these passages:

1. It is always good to be good.
2. What does life consist of but love?
3. Of what value is it to kill?
4. You ought to be of some help to your fellow men.
5. Do not abuse your wife; women are sacred.
6. If you cast off your dress for many people, they will be benefitted by your deed.
7. For the good you do every one will love you.
8. Never do any wrong to children.
9. It is not good to gamble.
10. If you see a helpless old man, help him if you have anything at all.
11. If you have a home of your own, see to it that who-ever enters it obtains something to eat. Such food will be a source of death to you if withheld.
12. When you are recounting your war deeds on behalf of the departed soul, do not try to add to your honor by claiming more for yourself than you have actually accomplished. If you tell a falsehood then and exaggerate your achievements you will die before-hand. The telling of truth is sacred. Tell less than you did. The old men say it is wiser.
13. Be on friendly terms with every one and then every one will love you.
14. Marry only one person at a time.

15. Do not be haughty with your husband. Kindness will be returned to you and he will treat you in the same way in which you treat him.

16. Do not imagine that you are taking your children's part if you just speak about loving them. Let them see it for themselves.

17. Do not show your love for other people so that people notice it. Love them but let your love be different from that for your own.

18. As you travel along life's road, never harm any one or cause any one to feel sad. On the contrary, if at any time you can make a person feel happy, do so. If at any time you meet a woman away from your village and you are both alone and no one can see you, do not frighten her or harm her.

19. If you meet any one on the road, even if it is only a child, speak a cheering word before you pass on.

20. If your husband's people ever ask their own children for something when you are present, assume that they had asked it of you. If there is anything to be done, do not wait till you are asked to do it but do it immediately.

21. Never think a home is yours until you have made one for yourself.

22. If you have put people in charge of your household, do not nevertheless act as though the home were still yours.

23. When visiting your husband's people, do not act as if you were far above them.[1]

---

[1] All these passages, with the exception of 3, 18, 19, and 20, come

Obviously we are here in the presence of a fairly well elaborated system of conduct. To those who consistently deny to primitive man any true capacity for abstract thinking or objective formulation of an ethical code—and their number is very large both among scholars and laymen—the injunctions given above would probably be interpreted as having a definitely concrete significance. That is, they are not to be regarded as attempts at generalization in any true sense of the word but merely as inherently wise saws and precepts of a practical and personal application. Now there is sufficient justification for such a view to warrant our discussing it before we proceed any further.

A number of the precepts given avowedly allow a concrete practical and personal application. In 5, for example, we are told, "If you abuse your wife you will die in a short time. Our grandmother Earth is a woman and in abusing your wife you will be abusing her. Since it is she who takes care of us, by your actions you will be practically killing yourself." To precept 10 is added the following: "If you happen to possess a home, take him (the old man) there and feed him for he may suddenly make uncomplimentary remarks about you. You will be strengthened thereby."

---

from *Crashing Thunder: the Autobiography of an American Indian*, edited by Paul Radin; 3 comes from the myth given on pages 79 ff. of this book, and the others from the 37th *Report of the Bureau of American Ethnology.*

We thus do indeed seem to obtain the impression that a Winnebago in being good to a helpless old man is guided by motives secondary to those implied in the precept as quoted. And what follows would seem to strip our apparently generous precept of whatever further altruistic value still attaches to it, for there it is stated that perhaps the old man is carrying under his arm a box of medicines that he cherishes very much and which he will offer to you. Similarly in precept 11 we find, "If you are stingy about giving food some one may kill you." Indeed I think we shall have to admit that in the majority of cases none of the Winnebago virtues or actions are extolled for their own sake, and that in every instance they have reference to and derive their validity from whatever relation they possess to the preponderatingly practical needs of human intercourse. "Don't be a fool," precept 5 seems to imply, "and treat your wife badly, because if you do, you'll run the risk of having the woman's protecting deity, the Earth, punish you." I should not even be surprised if, in concrete instances, the moral was further emphasized by giving examples of how men were punished who had abused their wives. We are fairly obviously told to be guided by the practical side of the question, i.e., take no risks and get the most out of every good action you perform.

Now all this sounds extremely cynical and practical. But we must be fair and not too hasty in drawing our inferences. First of all it should be asked if the Winnebago in actual practice give the impression of always being guided by egotistical and ulterior motives, and second it should be borne in mind that if we can really prove that the ideal of human conduct is on a high plane, we need not concern ourselves needlessly with the apparent nature of the motives prompting individual acts. As a matter of fact primitive people are much less guided by consciously selfish and ulterior motives than we are, not because of any innate superiority over ourselves in this regard but because of the conditions under which they live. But, quite apart from this consideration, ought we in fact to lay undue stress on illustrations following what is clearly a general principle? Are we not after all, in our illustrations, merely dealing with a statement of what happens when some general principle of the ethical code is transgressed, and not primarily with an explanation of the principle? I do not feel, therefore, that even those instances which seem superficially to corroborate the prevalent assumption of primitive man's inability to formulate an abstract ethical creed, actually bear out, when more carefully examined, the contention of its advocates.

Now the question of the capacity of the Winnebago to formulate an ethical code in a fairly abstract fashion is of fundamental importance for the thesis of this chapter and that is why I am laying so much stress on it; for if it were not true our precepts would have to be regarded in the nature of mere proverbs and practical folk wisdom, as nothing higher indeed than crystallized maxims of conduct.

There are, however, in our list certain precepts where the abstract formulation is undeniable, where, in fact, reference to the particular context in which the precepts occur not only shows no secondary concrete significance, but, on the contrary, a reënforcement of their abstract and general connotation. In precept 1 the full statement is this: "If you hear of a person traveling through your country and you want to see him, prepare your table and send for him. In this manner you will do good and it is always good to do good, it is said." Similarly in precept 2. Here it is in the course of a speech delivered at a ceremony that the phrase occurs: "what does life consist of but love?" "All the members of the clan have given me counsel," the speaker says, "and all the women and children have pleaded in my behalf with the spirits. What love that was! And of what does life consist but of love?"

Here we have no concrete practical implications. The statements are meant to be taken as general propositions. They are very remarkable enunciations and we may legitimately draw from their existence the inference that even in so-called "primitive" tribes, certain individuals have apparently felt within themselves the same moral truths that are regarded as the glory of our great moralists, and that they have formulated these truths in general terms.

So much for the actual formulation. What, however, does this Winnebago creed tell us about the ideal of conduct itself? Does it teach us that love and forbearance are to be practiced for their own sake and is the love of which they speak identical with or even comparable to our idea of love?

When a Western European speaks of love, forbearance, remorse, sorrow, etc., he generally understands by these terms some quality belonging to an individual and for the possession of which he is to be honored and praised. We do not ask whether the love or the virtue in question is of an intelligent nature, whether it does harm or good, or whether we have any right to it. Who among us would speak of an individual not being entitled to his remorse or sorrow? We assume that the mere expression of remorse and sorrow is somehow ethically praiseworthy. If we see a man of manifestly weak character but of a loving disposition, even if his actions are inconsistent with a true love for his fellow men, insist that he loves them, while we may condemn him, we are inclined to overlook much in recognition of his enunciation of the principle that love of mankind is the highest ideal of life. In much the same way do we look upon any manifestation of sincere remorse or sorrow. We simply regard love, remorse, sorrow, etc., as inalienable rights of man, quite independent of any right, as it were, he may possess to express them. In other words, the Western European ethics is frankly egocentric and concerned primarily with self-expression. The object toward which love, remorse, repentance, sorrow, is directed is secondary. Christian theology has elevated them all to the rank of virtues as such, and enjoins their observance upon us because they are manifestations of God's, if not of man's, way.

Among primitive people this is emphatically not true. Ethics there is based upon behavior. No mere enunciation of an ideal of love, no matter how often and sincerely repeated, would gain an individual either admiration, sympathy, or respect. Every ethical precept must be submitted to the touchstone of conduct. The Winnebago moralist would insist that we have no right to preach an ideal of love or to claim that we love, unless we have lived up to its practical implications. That is the fundamental basis of all primitive education and is unusually well expressed among the Winnebago. "When you are bringing up children," runs the injunction to a young mother, "do not imagine that you are taking their part if you merely speak of loving them. Let them see it for themselves; let them know what love is by seeing you give away things to the poor. Then they will see your good deeds and then they will know whether you have been telling the truth or not." An exactly similar attitude is taken toward remorse. "If you have always loved a person, then when he dies you will have the right to feel sorrow." No amount of money spent upon the funeral of a person with whom you had been quarreling will make amends.

But it is not merely love, remorse, etc., to which you have no right as such. You have equally no right to the glory attendant upon joining a war party unless it is done in the right spirit. In the document from which most of our statements have been taken—the autobiography of a Winnebago Indian—a man is represented as being about to embark on a war party because his wife has run away from him. "Such a man," the author insists, "is simply throwing away his life. If you want to go on the warpath, do not go because your wife has been taken away from you but because you feel courageous enough to go."

In consonance with such an attitude is the differentiation in the degree of love insisted upon. Love everybody, it is demanded, but do not love them all equally. Above all do not love your neighbor as you love those of your own blood. "Only if you are wicked," the injunction says, "will you love other people's children more than your own." The injunction certainly says that we must love everybody, but this must be humanly understood, and humanly understood you cannot, of course, love every one alike. The Winnebago would contend that such a statement would be untrue and that any attempt to put it into practice must manifestly lead to insincerity. It would, moreover, be definitely unjust in that it might make for the neglect of those whom primarily you ought to love most. Here the difference between the attitude of primitive man and that of Western Europe is most clearly brought out. According to primitive standards you deserve neither credit nor discredit, neither praise nor condemnation, for giving expression to a normal human emotion. It is the manner in which, in your relations to the other members of the tribe, you *distribute* this emotion and the degree to which it is felt by others to be sincere, that calls forth respect and admiration. It is wicked to love other people's children as much as your own; it is wicked to love your wife to the detriment of your family and yourself; it is wicked to love your enemy while he is your enemy. An excellent illustration of this conviction—that it is fundamentally wicked and unintelligent to make the expression of even a socially commendable emotion like love an end in itself—is contained in the following passage taken from the autobiography quoted above:

When you get married do not make an idol of the woman you marry; do not worship her. If you worship a woman she will insist upon greater and greater worship as time goes on. It may be that when you get married you will listen to the voice of your wife and you will refuse to go on the warpath. Why should you thus run the risk of being ridiculed? After a while you will not be allowed to go to a feast. In time even your sisters will not think anything of you. (You will become jealous) and after your jealousy has developed to its highest pitch your wife will run away. You have let her know by your actions that you worship a woman and one alone. As a result she will run away. On account of your incessant annoyance she will run away from you. If you think that a woman (your wife) is the only person you ought to love, you have humbled yourself. You have made the woman suffer and have made her feel unhappy. You will be known as a bad man and no one will want to marry you again. (Perhaps afterwards) when people go on the warpath you will join them because you feel unhappy at your wife's desertion. You will then, however, simply be throwing away your life.

A complete insight is afforded by this example into every phase of Winnebago ethics. You are to love your wife, for instance, but it is to be kept within personally and socially justifiable limits. If not, the whole adjustment of an individual to his environment is disturbed and injustice is eventually done to every one concerned—to his family, to his wife, and to himself. Marked exaggeration and disproportion would, from a practical point of view, be unthinkable in a primitive community. The result, in the hypothetical case we discussed above, is clear: loss of life and suicide, and possibly even the dragging of innocent people into your calamity—those, for instance, who are going on a warpath properly prepared spiritually.

The psychology expressed here is unimpeachable. To have analyzed the situation so completely and so profoundly and to have made this analysis the basis of social behavior is not a slight achievement, and this achievement is to be evaluated all the more highly because the Winnebago was predominantly a warrior culture. The objectivity displayed is altogether unusual, the husband's, the wife's, the tribal viewpoints, all are presented fairly and clearly.

CHAPTER VII

THE IDEAL MAN

IN the preceding chapter we were afforded a glimpse into primitive man's idea of right and wrong. We saw that it hinged largely on his analysis of and attitude toward the individual and toward personality, a subject which, in my opinion, has been misunderstood by most students of primitive life. We pointed out that the purely egotistical expression of an emotion or an instinct was regarded as ethically and socially reprehensible. Yet it must not be inferred from this that no such expression existed or that, in its minor aspects, it was as rigorously condemned as the example, given in the previous chapter, of the dangers attendant upon idolizing one's wife, might lead us to suspect. On the contrary the direct expression of human frailties was accepted as inevitable, something to be regarded as neither admirable nor the reverse. The desire for self-assertion, the right to be admired, the right to swagger and boast, to glory in one's achievements, these are all definitely to be sought. No one is to hide his light under a bushel. This is very concretely expressed among all primitive peoples by their magical "medicines." Among the Winnebago there is a certain Paint Medicine which makes its possessor rich and beloved by all. One enviable medicine can even be used when its possessor is in a crowd in which he would normally be completely submerged, and then "people will notice only him and will consider him a great man." Such an ambition is not considered as in the least culpable. True, you run the risk of being laughed at, but that is a risk you take under all circumstances. Apart, then, from the fear of ridicule, you may indulge in all the normal cravings you wish. If a man chooses to begin an account of his life—as in the autobiography to which so much reference has already been made—by informing the reader that just before his birth his mother was told that she was about to give birth to a man who would not be an ordinary individual, comment upon it is unnecessary.

You have, in short, a right to indulge in any action that does not involve harm or danger to some one else. You may accordingly indulge in as much gossiping as you desire to and make as many slanderous and sarcastic remarks about other people as you dare. Primitive people are indeed among the most persistent and inveterate of gossips. Contestants for the same honors, possessors of the sacred rites of the tribe, the authorized narrators of legends, all leave you in little doubt as to the character and proficiency of their colleagues. "Ignoramus," "braggart," and not infrequently "liar" are liberally bandied about.

The first impression an ethnologist receives is likely to be quite bewildering. It is not at all to be marveled at then that under these conditions some observers have drawn the conclusion that not love, kindliness, and forbearance, but envy, slander, and hate are the dominant atmosphere of a primitive community.

It does not, however, require a long sojourn among them to realize that the unkind and slanderous remarks so frequently bandied about do not engender feuds and that often the principals concerned are on very good terms. The explanation of this interesting phenomenon is not to be sought in any suppression or sublimation, but in the unconscious acceptance of a theory of freedom of expression for normal human feelings and a refusal to regard expression of opinion as implying anything beyond the significance it happens to possess at a particular moment. Such remarks are, in other words, not to be taken as representing final or generalized estimates which are to be implicitly assumed as applying whenever one speaks of a colleague or competitor. What it comes to at bottom is simply this: that every individual has the same right to indulge in slander, gossip, outbursts of conceit, jealousy, etc., that he has to give vent to the more respectable emotions. Once having given this naïve relief to his sensitiveness, jealousy, or what not, he forgets all about it, not, however, in the manner of a child who forgets because he can be easily distracted, but because he attaches no ethical evaluation to the expression of such emotions.

Primitive people thus accept the expression of all human emotions as normal. But they go much farther; they frankly accept the fact that this expression is specifically different in different individuals. Each man, woman and child stands by himself. To use psychoanalytical terminology, there is no *identification*. It is this absence of identification that explains primitive man's capacity for seeing human relations and understanding human conduct so objectively. Now this respect for and acceptance of personality brings with it an insistence upon individual responsibility.

The respect for personality is shown in a number of ways. For instance in the example given on page 74, the husband in his increasing love and jealousy for his wife is represented as watching her all the time, and herein is seen a definite infringement of her individuality. Even where the corporate interests of the tribe are involved, as in the case of the tribal hunt or the tribal warpath among the Dakota Indians, the personality of the members of the expedition is still respected. On such occasions the interests of the joint undertaking demand a definite restriction of personal liberty. Were a man to transgress the rules then set up, his tent would be burned and his personal property destroyed. If, however, he submitted to this treatment without resistance, then subsequently he would be given a new tent and new property equivalent to, if not slightly higher in value than, that which had been taken from him.

This respect for individuality is extended to the children as well. We saw on page 72 that a child was not supposed to accept a mother's professions of love as having any intrinsic meaning unless her conduct harmonized with them. This assumption, that a child has a personality and is not simply to be identified with its parents, is well illustrated by two incidents witnessed by the author. On one occasion, wishing to purchase a pair of child's moccasins which he had seen in a certain house, he approached the father of the child on the matter but was told that the moccasins belonged to the child. When pressed, the father agreed to ask the child—I believe it was about five years old—whether he cared to part with them. The whole transaction took place in a perfectly serious manner. There was not the slightest flippancy about it. The child refused and that ended the matter.

On another occasion a very small child, about two or three years old, managed to creep into a ceremonial lodge while a very sacred ceremony was in progress. I watched the scene very carefully, inquisitive to see what would happen. No excitement ensued nor was there any scolding and loss of temper as would have inevitably been the case among us. Within a very short time and in a manner very difficult to describe— so subtle and full of understanding was it—the child was removed without any offense to its dignity and with no shriekings or commotion. Such examples, I feel certain, can be multiplied indefinitely by experienced and observant ethnologists. I presume that it is this same respect for the child's individuality that has led, among the Winnebago at least, to the belief in the ineffectualness of corporal punishment, or of admonition. "If you have a child," the injunction runs, "do not strike it. If you hit a child you will merely put more naughtiness into it." It is also said that women should not lecture their children, that they merely make them bad by admonition.

The respect for individuality has another side and this side has led to the doctrine that each man alone is responsible for his own conduct. Parents can only inculcate an ideal and possibly describe the means for its accomplishment. They can do no more. "If you do all we have told you," a Winnebago child is told in effect, "you will lead a happy and prosperous life." "When the Indians have a child whom they love very much, they preach to him so that he may never become acquainted with the things that are not right, and that he may never do any wrong. Then if, later in life, he does any wrong he will do so with the clear knowledge of the consequences of his action."

According to the Winnebago ethical ideal, then, a person must rely upon himself, and it behooves him consequently to prepare himself properly for the battle of life. Life, as the Winnebago are always fond of putting it, is not a broad, straight path but a road full of narrow passages and it is the task of every individual to safely surmount these. Only in this way can he hope to obtain the two things that men prize most in the world—happiness and prosperity, and the esteem of their fellow men. The deities alone can provide you with the adequate means for this, and it is essential, therefore, to get into *rapport* with them as soon as possible. But—so the Winnebago theory demands—the deities help you only to help yourself and they aid you only upon definite conditions. These conditions, we shall soon see, throw a most illuminating light upon Winnebago ethics. They are well known and frequently discussed by the moralists and devoutly religious people in the tribe. The ordinary man may very well say that the simple act of prayer by itself suffices; the moralists would never subscribe to any such doctrine. They insist upon a definite inward purification, a reverend and a humble spirit, persistent effort, strength of character, the saving grace of a sense of life's realities and, finally, a knowledge of oneself.

Let us turn to the first point, inward purification. How essential it is the following fasting experience of a Winnebago will show:

So that he might know the spirits, grandfather Djoben-angiwinxga fasted and thirsted himself to the point of death (i.e., refrained from drinking). He made himself pitiable in their sight. At first he fasted four nights and the Night-Spirits came to him, with mighty sounds they came. Soon they stood before him and spoke. "Human being, you have thirsted yourself to death and we are going to bless you for that reason. We who speak are the Night-Spirits." They blessed him with life and with success on the war-path. Then he looked at them and he saw that they were small birds and had fooled him.

Then once again was his heart sore. In despair he said, "Well, if I have to, I'll die fasting!" So he fasted again and once again he rubbed charcoal on his face and fasted for six nights this time. Then once again, from the east, did the Night-Spirits come. Then he looked at them and in his heart he wondered whether these were indeed the Night-Spirits. But they were not. He was being fooled. This time, however, instead of feeling sad, he said, "I don't care what happens: I am willing to die in order to get a blessing."

Then for the third time they fooled him.

He had, at first, thought during his fasting that just to spite the spirits he would fast again but now (as he prepared to fast for the fourth time) he rubbed charcoal on his face and wept bitterly. Both hands contained tobacco and he stood in the direction from which the Night-Spirits had come and, weeping, he put himself in the most abject condition.[1]

Here we see a man possessed of tremendous ambition, approaching his ordeal in a very matter-of-fact manner. After his first rebuff we see him exclaiming, "I will die but I shall obtain what I want." Yet all he can think of is to continue the externals—fasting and dabbing his face with charcoal. He receives a second rebuff but still learns nothing. Only after his third rebuff does he realize that his inward approach has been all wrong. Only then when "his heart ached to its very depths" does he attain the necessary inward purification.

---

[1] Paul Radin, 37th *Report of the Bureau of American Ethnology,* pp. 477-481.

Humility of spirit and seriousness of intention are thus regarded as the essential prerequisites in all undertakings. This is particularly true of all things connected with religion. Boasting, pride, conceit find no place here no matter how great the tolerance extended to them on ordinary occasions. Children are continually reminded of the importance of humility and it is constantly brought home to them by their elders. In the autobiography quoted before, there is an excellent illustration. The author of that document tells how a feast was given ostensibly for him and his brother, who were fasting at the time. "That night the feast was given. There, however, our pride received a fall, for although the feast was supposedly given in our honor we were placed on one side of the main participants." This same man himself states that during his fasting he had never really tried to render himself pitiable in the sight of the spirits, that he had never been truly lowly at heart.

The clearest demonstration of the worth of humility is naturally to be found in the prayers uttered at the various ceremonies. There humility and modesty have practically become ritualistic formulæ. "The small amount of life you have granted me," is the modest claim. In a similar humble spirit they say, "We shall perhaps be able to sing only one song but even if one knows only one song and takes great pains about singing it, perhaps it will suffice to propitiate the spirits."

The finest and deepest expression of this humility

before the deities and the world is, however, to be found in the prayer offered up at one of the funeral wakes. The ghost of the departed is represented as coming into the presence of the arbiter of the dead and she—it is a woman—asks him what he had been told to demand of her when he left the world. Thereupon he responds and says, "O great-grandmother, as I listened to my beloved relatives they said very little indeed. Four requests I was asked to make and the first is this: I was to ask for life, that the flames from the lodge fires might go straight upward. Yet they would be satisfied if at my departure the flames merely swayed to and fro." [2]

Seriousness of intention has in its turn developed into a definite theory of concentration. Frivolity becomes an unpardonable sin. The Winnebago have a verb which means "to concentrate one's mind" and this concentration of mind has come to be absolutely essential for every prayer and rite—for every undertaking, in fact. For the priest and thinker, failure simply signifies that this fixation of the mind upon the object to be obtained, to the utter exclusion of everything else, did not take place. A member of one of the main ceremonies of the Winnebago thus describes what is implied by this "concentration." "Not once did I speak; not once did I move around; not once did I change my position. Just as I had been told to sit so I remained sitting. Not once did I, by chance, permit my glances to wander from side to side. This was

---

[2] *Ibid.*, p. 153.

a holy ceremony and I was bashful in its presence." [3]
By the deities in turn this concentration is accepted
as an indication of complete sincerity and of true
perseverance.

The strength of character and wisdom which is insisted upon as the highest ideal of life is even more
convincingly illustrated by the symbolical interpretation of the Journey of Life as recounted by this same
tribe in its principal ceremony, the Medicine Dance.
The highest ideal of a devout member of this ceremony
was to lead an upright life, to go through life bravely
without a whimper, bearing slander and misrepresentation without stooping to correct them, and enduring
loss upon loss without discouragement. The myth in
question is so beautiful and the symbolism of so remarkable and elevated a kind that I shall quote it at
some length:

My son, as you travel along this road (the road of life),
do not doubt it. If you do you will be unhappy and you
will injure yourself. But if you do everything I tell you
well, it will benefit you greatly.

My son, the first thing you come to as you travel along
this road will be a ravine, extending to the very ends of
the world, on both sides. It will look as though it could
not possibly be crossed. When you get there you will
think to yourself, "Grandfather said that I was, nevertheless, to pass across." Plunge right through and you will get
to the other side.

---

[3] Paul Radin, "Personal Reminiscences of a Winnebago Indian,"
Journal of American Folklore, XXVI, pp. 293-318.

Now this ravine means that sometimes in life you will lose a child and thoughts of death will come to you. But if you pay attention to my teachings you will be able to go right on and find the road of the lodge on the other side. If you do not try to go beyond, if you get frightened and dwell upon your loss too much, this will be your grave.

After you have crossed the ravine you will see the footsteps of the medicine-men who have gone before you marked very plainly in the road. Step into them and you will feel good. Then as you go along, you will come to an impenetrable wood of stickers, thorns, and weeds. You will not see how you can possibly get around them and then you will remember that your grandfather said that you would be able to penetrate this brushwood too. So this, likewise, you will pass.

The impenetrable brushwood means death. Someone you have loved greatly, but not your wife, will die. You must try to get through this obstacle, not get frightened, and not dwell upon your hardship too much. Otherwise this will be your grave.

As you pass along the road, evil birds will continually din into your ears and will cast their excrement upon you. It will stick to your body. Now do not brush it off and do not pay any attention to it. If you paid attention to it you might forget yourself and brush it off. That would not be right; life is not to be obtained in this manner.

The evil birds have the following meaning. The fact that you have joined the medicine lodge signifies that you would like to lead a good life. Now as soon as you have joined the lodge, the work of evil tattlers will begin. They will say that you have done things contrary to the teachings of the lodge. Perhaps a bit of bird's excrement will fall on you. What of it? Don't brush it off without thought. Some people might even claim that you had said that the lodge was no good. However even then you must not forget yourself and blurt out, "Who said that?" and get angry. Keep quiet and hold your peace.

As you go along, you will come to a great fire encircling the earth and practically impossible to cross. It will be so near that it will scorch you. Remember then that your grandfather had said that you would be able to pass it. Plunge through it. Soon you will find yourself on the other side and nothing will have happened to you.

Now this great fire means death. Your wife will die. Go through this as well as you can and do not get discouraged. This fire will be the worst thing that you have to go through. You will have been living happily and then, without warning, your wife will die. There you will remain with your children. Bear in mind, however, what your grandfather said and plunge straight through. On the other side you will find the footprints of the medecine-men.

After a while you will come to tremendous perpendicular bluffs which hardly seem surmountable. Think again what your grandfather said and you will then soon find yourself on the other side of these bluffs and quite safe.

These bluffs mean death. As you travel along the road of life you will find yourself alone. All your relatives, all your loved ones, are dead. You will begin to think to yourself, "Why, after all, am I living?" You will want to die. Now this, my grandson, is the place where most encouragement is given for it is here most needed. This is the most difficult of all the places you will come to. Keep in the footsteps of the medicine-men and you will be safe. The teachings of the lodge are the only road; they alone will enable you to pass this point safely.[4]

Nothing higher than this can possibly be preached. No manlier, more profound, and wiser envisaging of life has come from the mouths of the world's great moral teachers. Nor is the influence of these ethical principles on character formation to be dismissed too lightly on the plea that, after all, they represented an ideal only and that they had but little practical bearing. That we are dealing with an ideal rarely lived up to goes without saying; that, however, it had no appreciable influence would be manifestly unfair to assume. Of one ceremony a Winnebago told me, "This ceremony molded me. I paid the most careful attention to it. I worshiped it in the best way I knew how. I was careful about everything in my life. A holy life it was I sought. Most earnestly did I pray to be reincarnated. This ceremony was made with love." [5]

But inward purification, a humble and a contrite heart, strength of character, etc., these are all, let me again stress it, not to be regarded as virtues in themselves. They are evaluated as virtues because they

[4] *Crashing Thunder*, pp. 105 ff.

[5] "Personal Reminiscences of a Winnebago Indian," *Journal of American Folklore*, XXVI, pp. 293-318.

are, literally speaking, the best and most adequate preparation for the proper understanding of life's realities and of one's own powers. Happiness is obtained by the proper relation of man to the deities and to his fellow men, and the first was interpreted, among the Winnebago at least, as being simply another way of expressing his relation to his personal values. Embraced within these was his understanding of his own capacities.

We have pointed out before that complete freedom in the expression of the normal human egotistical emotions was permitted without hindrance. But, it will be justly contended, are not boasting, prestige hunting, desire for power as such, conceit, jealousy, etc., in direct opposition to the religious-ethical ideal just described? Quite definitely so. Indeed, I am fairly well convinced that the religious-ethical is meant to be a direct challenge and criticism of the purely mundane ideal. We should be careful not to fall into an obvious error here due to our Christian ideals. The sage's and the ordinary man's viewpoint are opposed, not because the one is morally superior to the other, not because the one is good and the other is bad, but because the one is more likely to help in the attainment of that very object so ardently desired—happiness and prosperity. This, the Winnebago and probably all primitive peoples would contend, the ethical-religious ideal is more likely to do because it emphasizes the cardinal fact of life, the sense of proportion which alone saves man from destruction and misery.

It is the sense of proportion that dominates all primitive life in spite of the superficial impression to the contrary. The exaggeration and license apparent in many rites, ceremonies, and customs prove to be, when more carefully studied, adventitious and do not touch the core of the matter. It might even be said that they are felt to be in conscious opposition to the guiding principles of conduct. Individuals who do not observe the proper sense of proportion have very clearly a recognized place in the life of the people, particularly in their religious life, but such individuals rarely become the standards to be followed. I remember very well a Winnebago commenting upon the religious frenzy of a certain participant in a ceremony, who in his ecstasy danced until he fell exhausted to the ground. "It is good," he said, "to have some people like that but it would be very bad if most people were like him."

It is thus the insistent admonition of the wise men and of the experienced elders that man learn the limits imposed by nature, and above all that man learn the limitations to his own powers. Neglect of this brings one into collision with reality, and a collision with reality means lack of success and often death. We shall, in the subsequent chapter, see how our failure properly to understand and sense the limits imposed by reality and our failure to intelligently evaluate our own capacities are at the bottom of the Winnebago conception of tragedy and doom. The methods the Winnebago, at least, take to understand both realities are effectively depicted in their fasting experiences.

Fasting among them begins at the age of five or six and lasts till eleven or thirteen. It is naturally, in view of the extreme youth of the faster, entirely controlled by the parents or grandparents. Many a gift of the deities is rejected by a wise and solicitous father or grandfather because it is beyond his idea of the child's capacities. He does not, of course, always put it that way. The rejection is in fact generally couched in a religious phraseology. Sometimes the father will say, "It is too sacred"; at other times, "The spirits are trying to deceive you." As an instructive example let me give the fasting experience of a young girl to whom a very sacred deity had appeared, but a deity whose gifts often entailed death. In answer to her father's question she relates how the deity had come to her.

"In four days he told me he would appear to me. 'The day on which I appear to you will be a perfect day. Now whatever you wish to make for yourself you may. You will never be in want of anything for you can make whatever you wish out of my body. With all this I bless you for you have made yourself suffer very much and my heart has been torn with pity for you. I bless you with life and with the right to transmit this blessing to your descendants.'

"All this, father, the spirit said to me."

"Daughter, it is not good," answered the father, "the spirit is trying to deceive you. Do not accept it. He will never bestow upon you what he has promised."

"All right, father, but let me at least give him offerings. I will not accept his blessings because you forbid it."

Then after four days she took her offerings to the place where she was to meet the spirit. "(My father) said you were not a good spirit," (the girl said). "He is right," answered the spirit, "for one side of my body is not good; yet the other side is. I was created in that manner."

Then the woman looked toward the lake and saw a tree standing in the water. This the spirit climbed and around this he wrapped himself. Then he took a tooth and shot the tree and knocked it down. "This is what you would have been able to do," said the spirit to her. "Everyone would have respected you greatly and you would have been able to cure weak and nervous people. But you would not listen to what I promised you. You refused it." [6]

In another fasting experience, the gift is definitely rejected because it is too great. The father tells his son, "My son, this is really too great. If you accept this blessing you will not leave any human beings alive. You will always want to go on the warpath." [7]

Let us now turn to the formulation of their doctrine of man's relation to his fellow men. This is most clearly expressed in the insistence on moderation and proportion, inward and outward, in the consideration for the comfort of others, and in the refusal to inflict one's own troubles upon one's neighbors. "Never overdo anything," a father counsels his son.

---

[6] 37th *Report of the Bureau of American Ethnology*, pp. 302-304.
[7] *Ibid.*, pp. 299-300.

Perhaps their ideal, however, is best seen in the definition of what constitutes an upright and a virtuous man. This same informant in another passage describes his brother-in-law in the following fashion: "He was a good man; no one did he dislike; never did he steal; never did he fight." In the semi-historical account of the origin of the most famous of the Winnebago rituals, the Medicine Dance, the founders are described as looking around for new members to initiate. And whom do they select? Good men, i.e., those who are righteous, wise, and kind-hearted. And as youth is unstable, young people are excluded from the ranks of the truly virtuous. As the tale states, the founders never selected a young man but one who was slightly beyond middle age.

This picture of the ideal man would not be complete, however, unless one other trait be added, namely that of forgetting one's self in the interest of others. This ideal is given in their demands on what the chief of the tribe ought to be. "He must be a man of well-balanced temper, not easily provoked, of good habits. If he sees a man or a woman or a child pass by he is to call to them and give them food to eat, for these are his brothers and sisters." [8]

It goes without saying that people who have arrived at ethical ideas as elevated as the above would have laid particular emphasis upon self-control, particularly in its bearing on the possible injustice and discomfort which the lack of it inflicts upon one's fellow

---

[8] *Ibid.*, p. 320.

men. While it is true that every person has a right to self-expression, this self-expression must not be such as to cause discomfort to other people, and it most emphatically must not involve other people in one's misfortune. Even when some one in one's family has died, a situation where one might expect a lenient and sympathetic attitude toward any expression of grief, restraint is enjoined upon the mourner for two characteristic reasons; first, because no one has a right to inflict his personal sorrows upon others and second, because it is so utterly useless. At one of the funeral rites of a Winnebago the mourner, a woman, was addressed as follows:

"My sister, it is claimed that it is best for a person not to weep, that a widow should not mourn too much, for then people will make fun of her, and also for the fact that, having children, she must for their sake look forward to life. Now there is nothing amusing in what I am going to say (although it may sound so) that, namely, we should not cry on such an occasion as to-day, but, on the contrary, keep up a good spirit. I do not mean that I am glad that my brother-in-law has died. But if you were to weep, some one might come and say to you that it behooves you more to show him your teeth than your tears—that you should smile.

"And again it is said that one should not cry, for when a body is laid in the ground then there is no more hope of its ever returning to this earth again." [9]

---

[9] *Ibid.*, p. 150.

At this same ceremony one man arose and addressed the visitors to the following effect: "It is said that we should not weep aloud and you will, therefore, not hear any of us making any utterings of sorrow. And even although we weep silently we shall smile upon all those who look at us. We beg of you all, consequently, that should you find us happy in mood, not to think any the worse of it." [10] Additional examples are hardly needed.

With this demonstration of intelligent self-control the system of ethics is complete. As embodied in the precepts and the behavior of the moralists among primitive people, it teaches the highest type of conduct that man can attain to anywhere—the right of every man to happiness and to freedom of expression in consonance with his particular capacities and temperament; the recognition of the limitations imposed upon this freedom of personal expression by human relationships; and, finally, the full responsibility each man must assume for his actions. That such a code, from its very nature, was never fully lived up to will be manifest to all. Indeed what we witness is the constant conflict between the principle of full self-expression and the ideal virtues such as self-control, moderation, and true self-knowledge. But this conflict, too, was recognized and in its turn came to be the basis for a very interesting formulation, by the more philosophically inclined, of the tragic sense of life.

---

[10] *Ibid.*, p. 151.

CHAPTER VIII

THE PHILOSOPHY OF LIFE: FATE, DEATH AND RESIGNATION

IN the two previous chapters we were able not only to demonstrate that among primitive people moralists and moral philosophers were to be encountered but we were actually able to see them at work—enunciating ethical maxims, constructing systems of morality, even indulging in the discussions of quasi-philosophical niceties for their own sake. General principles were formulated in abstract and logical terms. The time-honored contention that primitive man cannot think abstractly is thus shown to be another of those superficial generalizations left over by the crude evolutionary assumptions of the eighteen-seventies. For a final and definitive refutation of this hoary contention I refer the reader to Chapters XIII and XV. We frankly admit that only a few people in each community were capable of abstract thinking and that a still smaller number were interested in the formulation of ethical creeds. But the same holds, of course, for ourselves, only that among us the terminology of abstract thought has become far more generally disseminated.

We have thus seen that the higher natures among primitive people can have a true moral sense and an intuitive insight into right and wrong. That they can also possess true wisdom, that they can envisage life in a critical and half-pessimistic manner, that they can face fortune and misfortune objectively and with equanimity, that they can in fact accept life in all its realities and still enjoy it, for that the reader is not prepared any more than is the ethnologist who discovers it. And yet there is no escaping recognition of the fact, for it is borne in upon him in numerous songs, speeches, myths, and proverbs and is to be encountered in every tribe in the world. It is to proving this contention that I shall devote the following two chapters.

In order to disarm all criticism and to make out as authentic a case as possible, I shall select my data almost exclusively from the direct evidence given by natives in their own language and only resort to quotations given in the words of investigators when that is absolutely necessary. In this way I hope to escape all those possibilities of error and unwitting misrepresentation and distortion, favorable and unfavorable, which are likely to lurk even in the work of the most careful and experienced ethnologist.

It is the essence of every truly profound attitude toward life that it understand, or at least seek to understand, the nature and limitations of human demands upon God, upon life, upon one's fellow men, and upon one's self; and that these demands and limitations be accepted with equanimity. Strange as it may seem to us and irritating as it may be to our pride, we shall

have to confess that greater progress was made toward
the attainment of such an ideal among primitive peoples than among us. Nor was this attitude confined
simply to a few individuals among them. On the contrary it appears to have had a very extensive dissemi-
nation. Naturally its formulation in poetry and philosophy was the work of a few.

Among us the recognition of the truth of human
nature drives us into pessimism, cynicism, or sensation-
alism: the full realization of the limitations of man
and the insignificant rôle he plays in the world and the
universe, drives many, on the other hand, to seek refuge
in religion. In both cases the problem is not faced.
Ridiculous as it may seem on a superficial view, it yet
does remain a fact that primitive peoples do and have
faced the problem far more frequently and far more
consistently than the people of Western Europe. That
they did not always succeed is clear and the existence
of doctrines like fatalism, particularly in the Malay
area, represents as definite a failure as our pessimism.
Fatalism may, however, be an imported attitude in the
Malay region due to the influence of Mohammedanism.
Yet even if this interpretation be wrong, this doctrine
is not common among primitive people.

What is life? This is naturally the first question
that every philosopher and moralist, primitive and
civilized, seeks to answer. Let me give the answer of
a Ba-ila philosopher as contained in the legend of how
an old woman sought God in order to find an explanation for certain bitter aspects of life:

She was an old woman of a family with a long genealogy. Leza, "the Besetting-One," stretched out his hand against the family. He slew her mother and father while she was yet a child, and in the course of years all connected with her perished. She said to herself, "Surely I shall keep those who sit on my thighs." But no, even they, the children of her children, were taken from her. She became withered with age and it seemed to her that she herself was at last to be taken. But no, a change came over her; she grew younger. Then came into her heart a desperate resolution to find God and to ask the meaning of it all. Somewhere up there in the sky must be his dwelling. She began to cut down trees, joining them together and so planting a structure that would reach heaven. Finally she gave up in despair, but not her intention of finding God. Somewhere on earth there must be another way to heaven! So she began to travel, going through country after country, always with the thought in her mind: "I shall come to where the earth ends and there I shall find a road to God and I shall ask him: 'What have I done to thee that thou afflictest me in this manner?'" She never found where the earth ends, but though disappointed she did not give up her search, and as she passed through the different countries they asked her, "What have you come for, old woman?" And the answer would be, "I am seeking Leza." "Seeking Leza! For what?" "My brothers, you ask me! Here in the nations is there one who suffers as I have suffered?" And they would ask again, "How have you suffered?" "In this way. I am alone. As you see me, a solitary old woman; that is how I am!" And they answered, "Yes, we see. That is how you are! Bereaved of friends and husband? In what do you differ from others? The Be-setting-One sits on the back of every one of us and we cannot shake him off!" She never obtained her desire: she died of a broken heart.[1]

This is a facing of the problem of life. The old woman is decisively reprimanded: "Yes, life, the Besetting-One, sits on the back of all of us and we cannot shake him off. What cause is there for pessimism, what cause is there for optimism? If you kick against the pricks you die." The old woman did not obtain her desire and she died. We shall see later on that this also is the essence of primitive man's idea of tragedy—a kicking against the pricks, whether it be a failure to recognize the true nature of the world in which you live, or your own nature or that of your neighbor.

This then is the Ba-ila answer. It neither blinks the problem like Job nor falls into the two extremes of Leibnitz and Voltaire. The Ba-ila refuse to believe that we are either living in the best possible of worlds or in the world of Candide unless it be of the mature Candide, when he had begun to cultivate his garden.

The same idea is voiced by the Ewe of West Africa when they say, "The world is stronger than everything else and that is why we say that the world is God." The Winnebago, on the other hand, liken life to a road

---

[1] C. W. Smith and A. M. Dale, *The Ila-Speaking Peoples of Northern Rhodesia,* II, pp. 197*ff.*

with narrow passages through which no person unaided by the deities can pass without running the risk of tragedy. Yet a man must recognize the limits to the aid the deities can give. To fail to do so, to try to force their hand, means ruin. The Winnebago possess not a few stories of such attempts to coerce their deities into bestowing upon men powers that are in conflict with the world, with ultimate reality. Few are as poignant as that given on page 203 *ff.* where a young boy cannot, even in thought, face the idea of death and demands of the gods immortality. They grant him a happy, prosperous, and long life but he persists in his request and so he must die.

But the critical insight into life, the inexorability of fate, and the philosophic acceptance of human nature in all its aspects comes out most clearly in the remarkable proverbs that form so integral a part of the literature of the African Negroes, the Polynesians, and the Malays, to a consideration of which we will return in Chapter X.

It has been frequently contended that all primitive people assume that no death is ever a natural one and that the only kind of speculation they ever indulge in is to discover who has caused death. Both these contentions are quite wrong. The inevitability of death and the inexorability of fate are frequently mentioned in both song and proverb, at times with courageous acquiescence, at times with petulant complaint, at times with melancholy sadness. It is the first of these notes that runs through the following five poems:

I

Sky and earth are everlasting,
Men must die.
Old age is a thing of evil,
Charge, and die!

Crow, Montana

II

I feel no fear
When the Great River Man
Death speaks of.

Ojibwa

III

The odor of death,
I discern the odor of death
In the front of my body.

Ojibwa

IV

Sing me a song, a song of death,
That I may guide it by the hand.
Sing me a song of the underworld.
Sing me a song, a song of death,
That I may walk to the underworld!

Thus speaks the underworld to me,
The underworld speaks thus:
"O beautiful it feels in the grave,
"O lovely is the underworld!
"But yet no palm wine you can drink."
Therefore I take you by the hand
And journey to the underworld.

Ewe, Western Africa

V

FAREWELL TO LIFE

(Sung by two youths as they were led by their enemies to death.)

Oh, how love has bound my heart
And kept me slave on this side of the river!
Oh, that a priest would enchantments use
And rid me of the love I feel!
How soon the tattoo-lines of Mata-ora
Would mark my face! But Tu-ki-rau
Has not left those to drive away
Those sycophants of northern race.
My voice annoys my ears
And grieves my heart; and when
I, near to my home, stand erect,
Fast fall the teardrops
From my weeping eyes.

Maori, New Zealand

How completely it can overwhelm them comes out
clearly in the following:

I

O how it strikes us full in the face,
Death!
O how completely does it crush us,
O what pain!

Ba Ronga, Southern Africa

II

Ye he he ya! It deprived me of my mind
When the moon went down
At the edge of the waters!
Ye he he ya!

Ye he he ya! It deprived me of my breath
When the mouse-dancer began
To gnaw on the water!
Ye he he ya!

Ye he he ya! It deprived me of my mind
When Modana the uttering he began,
Of the cannibal cry
On the water!

Kwakiutl, British Columbia

The theme of the inevitability of death pervades
the proverbs and poetry of practically every tribe.
I must content myself with only a few examples here.
"It will arise as surely as the stomach," i.e., death
is inevitable, says the Ba-ila proverb. "Death has no
heifer," i.e., it comes to all, the same people say. You
are warned to be careful, to be circumspect: "Rejoice
circumspectly, son of my master, the enemy has come,"
i.e., be moderate in your exultation for Nemesis is
bound to overtake you. Remember, they insist, that
the powers of the universe are unconquerable, or, as
they put it, "When you exult, God sees you." It is in
a somewhat similar strain that the Apache warns his
people after a successful war expedition: "The taking
of life brings serious thoughts of the waste; the celebration of victory may become unpleasantly riotous."
The Tlingit philosopher says rather sadly, "I always
think within myself that there is no place where people
do not die." The same spirit pervades the following
philosophic dirge of the Ewe of West Africa:

Death has been with us from all time;
The heavy burden long ago began.
Not I can loose the bonds.
Water does not refuse to dissolve
Even a large crystal of salt.
And so to the world of the dead
The good too must descend.[2]

In the same tribe there exists a song in which a mother is kindly but firmly reprimanded for weeping too much over the death of her only child:

Large is the city of the nether world
Whither kings too must go
Nevermore to return.
Cease then your plaint, O mother of an only child!
Your plaint O cease, mother of an only child!
For when did an only child
Receive the gift of immortality?
So be it, mother of an only child,
And cease your wail, and cease your wail![3]

The whole gamut is run from mild complaint to denunciation in the poems here quoted:

I

O deaf son who wouldst not hearken;
I spread before thee life and death.
But thou wouldst bind around thee
The old used mat of death.
I alone was left, a solitary one,
A cast-off plank of the
House of the god Tane.

Maori, New Zealand

---

[2] Johann Spieth, *Die Religion der Eweer*, p. 236.   [3] *Ibid.*

II

Alas! this is the turning over,
The severing of the link of life.
The turning over that you
May join the many,
The multitude,
The *ariki* gone before.
Ascend the road
To heaven.

Mangaia, Polynesia

III

(*The singers approach.*)

A great thing we desire to do,
A *kposu* song, an *adzoli* song,
To sing we shall begin:
Awute here lies dead,
He now lies on his bier.
Death did announce himself to him.
O dead friend, lying on your bier,
Return once more, your bonds to loose!

(*The deceased appears and speaks.*)

You all now know
Within my body the word has perished,
Within Awute speech has died.
Who was't destroyed it in my body?
'Twas death dragged it away;
A warrior snatched it from my body.

(*Death appears and speaks.*)

Now my turn it is to sing!
I came and thundered,

I had my lightning flash upon the tree
And threw him down!
Come let us go!
Footsteps I hear, people are approaching.
An evil brother does announce himself;
Inopportune he comes.

Ewe, Western Africa

IV

Solo

Alas, Pangewi!   The case is hopeless,
The canoe is lost!

Chorus

O god Tane, thou didst fail me!
Thou didst promise life;
Thy worshipers were to be as a forest
To fall only by the axe in battle.
Had it been the god Turanga—
That liar!   I would not have trusted him.
Like him, you are a man-eater!
May thy mouth be covered with dung:
Slush it over and over!
This god is a man after all!

Solo

Plaster him well, friends.   Ha!   Ha!

Chorus

Dung is fit food for such gods!
We parents are in deep mourning
Like that first used by Tiki.
We mourn for our beloved first-born.

Oh, that one could stir up the gods,
And cause the very dead to awake!
Yonder stands thy weeping mother.
Thy spirit wanders about, One-makenu-kenu,
Inquiring the reason
Why his poor body was devoured by the gods.
Fairy of the axe! Cleave open
The secret road to spirit-land; and
Compel Vatea to give up the dead!

Solo

Puff, Tiki, a puff such as only ghosts can!

Chorus

Wait a moment.

Solo

Puff, puff away!

Chorus

A curse upon thee, priest Pangewi,
Thou hast destroyed my boy.

Mangaia, Polynesia

At times the attitude may change completely and
we find a spirit of pure Epicureanism. Thus in a
strain strangely reminiscent of Omar Khayyám, the
Tlingit lover sings:

"If one had control of death, it would be easy to
die with a wolf woman. It would be pleasant." Or,
"We all must die sometime, so of what use is anything?" [4] Frequently death is faced with a philosophic

---

[4] J. R. Swanton, "Tlingit Myths and Texts," 39th *Report of the
Bureau of American Ethnology*, p. 415.

calm and resignation worthy of Socrates. Elsdon Best relates how an old Maori is suddenly stricken ill and as his aged wife begins to lament he reproves her, saying, "Do not lament. It is well. We have trodden the path of life together in fair weather and beneath clouded skies. There is no cause for grief. I do but go forward to explore the path." [5]

So, too, do the following poems envisage death and, what is even more difficult to bear, tribal and cultural extinction:

I

The tide of life glides swiftly past
And mingles all in one great eddying foam.
O heaven now sleeping! Rouse thee, rise to power;
And thou, O earth, awake, exert thy might for me
And open wide the door to my last home,
Where calm and quiet rest awaits me in the sky.

Maori, New Zealand

II

The minor stars now westward troop in majesty;
The satellites of Rehua go on in drowsy mood
The path they ever went;
But Ue-nuku-kopaku the bent, the decrepit god,
By them shall be sustained.
But what may it avail since he, Wari-a-hau,
Rushed reckless to the battle front,
Nor heeded that the great, the people's power,
The guardian and protector had succumbed.

---

[5] "Spiritual and Mental Concepts of the Maori," *Dominion Museum Monograph No. 2* (Wellington, New Zealand), p. 13.

No aid had he to grapple
With the fierce, the unrelenting Tu,
Nor rays of light were seen on Wai-tawa peak,
Where all the mighty men of Ngatitu
In silence lay, with Rangi-a-te-amo there.

Seek, seek, the guardian power and rouse it now to act,
Before our great canoe o'erturn and all is lost.
I'll deck me with the white crane's plume
As gentle sea breeze wafts the prized young *totara*
And near the staff of Hine-tapeke will stand,
Whilst spray from Rotu-ehu comes and dims the eyes
Of those your younger brothers in this world.
Turn ye and look towards the peak on Rangi-toto seen,
All distant and alone;
And know the lizard god, the unknown one,
Has now forever left his home and westward gone,
On ocean's foamed white-crested waves.

And yet we still in silence sit
Nor ask the aid of those illustrious visitors,
Who from a distance by propitious gales have come to you;
Whilst in your presence lie the corpses, the slain, the fish
    of Tu,
The ancient ancestors of those of Tuku and of Hika-e.

O, gently blow, ye breezes of the land,
But rouse to deeds of daring none, O active soul of man!
I dreamt and in my dream I felt the chill of snow
Grate through my trembling frame, as in the nights of omen
    ill,—
Those *tamatea* nights of dread,—
The signs of which are seen in the midnight clouds.

O thou beloved!
I grieve my want of that to cover thee—

The beauteous mat brought from the east
To hide thy now cold frame.
O couldst thou once again arise
And at the day-dawn speak,
Then wouldst thou chant
The incantation of Pou-awhi and Wharangi
Of Awatea-roa, Manuka and Whakatane—
Tell the power by which thy ancestors and Wai-ra-kewa,
Learnt the path across the moaning ocean-road
To this our home.

Maori, New Zealand

III

I silent sit, as throbs my heart
    For my children;
And those who look on me
As now I bow my head
May deem me but a forest tree
    From distant land.
I bow my head
As droops the *mamaku*
And weep for my children.
O my child! So often called,
    "Come, O my child!"
Gone! Yes, with the mighty flood.
I lonely sit 'midst noise and crowd.
    My life ebbs fast.
My house is swept clean, clean swept,
    Swept for ever.
The shining sun has nought to gladden now,
And yonder peak oft gazed upon
    In days of joy,
Now prompts the sigh to heave
With feelings chill as coldest air
    Of frosty south.

But I still bow me in my house
And ponder in despair.
My heart shall then forget
The deeds of man.
Oh, was it theft that makes the moon to wane?
Or was it theft that makes the avalanche?
And was it they who caused my children's death?
The hosts of God uplift their power on us,
And now annihilate us, like the *moa* extinct.

Maori, New Zealand

Here there is no blinking at death. And this refusal to be terrified, this warning against undue resentment or unmeasured wailing, is to be evaluated all the
higher because, for the thinker at least, there is no
paradise or happy hunting ground where the difference
between the living and the dead is wiped out. To the
philosopher, be he Maori, Winnebago, or what not, the
land of the dead is a place from which no one returns
or if he does return, it is never as the same person.
The Maori definitely call the spirit-land "the realm,
from which none return to the upper air." The ordinary man may identify the life after death with unlimited joy and with the fulfillment of all his wishes;
the thinker apparently refuses to be deceived. As an
old Maori said in speaking to Elsdon Best of the dead,
"Never more shall we see them unless when sleep
comes and our *wairua* (spirits) go forth to meet them.
But that is only a spiritual seeing. We cannot touch
them. The living come and go; they meet and greet
each other; they weep for dead friends and sympathize

with each other. But the spectres of the dead are silent and the spectres of the dead are sullen. They greet not those whom they meet; they show neither affection nor yet sympathy, no more than does a stump. They act not as the folk of the world of life." And the Masai of East Africa give voice to a similar sentiment in their proverb, "Life and death are not alike."

CHAPTER IX

MEN AND WOMEN

IN a preceding chapter we had occasion to speak of primitive man's marked tolerance for every form of personal expression no matter what it was. All he demanded was that there be no railing against fate or society if an exaggerated expression of one's personality entailed suffering, misfortune, or even death. This being accepted he had both sympathetic forbearance and respect for every man's individuality in all its multiform and often kaleidoscopic manifestations. The *comédie humaine* possessed an unusual degree of fascination for him. He was a past master in the art of describing man in all his moods, as lover, hater, actor, and what not. Fortunately he has left us in his song-poems and myths an unusually good and complete record of his accomplishments in this respect. The myths are too long to quote and require too specialized a knowledge to be of any real value to a layman and I shall therefore confine myself entirely to the poems. In these poems are found expressed practically every human emotion, from the most light-hearted teasing and flirtation to inconsolable sorrow and unquenchable hatred. Instead of giving my own inference from these poems I intend to let the reader draw his, and with that object in view I shall devote the rest of this chapter to a fairly extensive and representative number of these poems. I have grouped them under various headings, hoping in this manner to show both the scope of primitive man's interests, his psychological insight and understanding of human nature, and the formal excellence he frequently attained in the expression of this insight.

FLIRTATION

I

Your body is at Waitemata
But your spirit came hither
And aroused me from my sleep.

O my companions, detain my *huia*
That the cord of my palpitating
Heart may again be mine.

Go then, O water of my eyelids,
To be a messenger to the
Huia feeding on my life.

Tawera is the bright star
Of the morning;
Not less beautiful is the
Jewel of my heart.

The sun is setting in his cave,
Touching as he descends the land
Where dwells my mate,
He who is whirled to
The southern waves.

Go to Tuhua, to the wilderness;
At Wharekura, to carry
Nothing but the paddle in
The basket of grass;
That's all you've got for your pains.

Maori, New Zealand

II

SHE AND HE

Who will marry a man,
Too lazy to till the ground for food?
The sun is the food for
The skin of such a one!

Who will marry a woman
Too lazy to weave garments
Tongarire is the food for
The skin of such a one!

Maori, New Zealand

III

THE HABITS OF WOMAN

I don't like the habits of woman;
When she goes out,
She *kuikuis*,
She *koakoas*,
She chatters;
The very ground is terrified
And the rats run away:
Just so!

Maori, New Zealand

IV

The wicked little Kukook, hah hayah used to say.
I am going to leave the country
In a large ship.
For that sweet little woman
I'll try to get some beads
Of those that look like boiled ones.
Then when I've gone abroad
I shall return again.
My nasty little relatives,
I'll call them all to me
And give them a good thrashing
With a big rope's end.
Then I'll go to marry
Taking two at once;
That darling little creature
Shall only wear clothes of the spotted sealskins
And the other little pet
Shall have clothes of the young hooded seals.

Eskimo

LOVE

I

Love does not torment forever.
It came on me like the fire
Which rages sometimes at Hukanui.
If this beloved one is near to me,
Do not suppose, O Kiri, that my sleep is sweet.
I lie awake the livelong night,
For love to prey on me in secret.
It shall never be confessed lest it be heard by all.
The only evidence shall be seen on my cheeks.
The plain which extends to Tauwhare:

That path I trod that I might enter
The house of Rawhirawhi.
Don't be angry with me, O madam; I am only a stranger.
For you there is the body of your husband;
For me there remains only the shadow of desire.

Maori, New Zealand

II

Fragrant the grasses of high Kane-hoa;
Bind on the anklets, bind!
Bind with finger deft as the wind
That cools the air of the bower.
Lehua blossoms place at my flower;
O sweetheart of mine,
Bud that I'd pluck and wear in my wreath,
If thou wert but a flower!

Hawaii

III

THE DESERTED HUSBAND

Come back from Toa, O Aitofa,
O my beautiful erring spouse!
As the rapid flow of the current at Onoiau,
And as the swollen torrent from the valley,
So flows my yearning heart after thee,
O Aitofa, have compassion on thy lover, lest he die!

The promontory of Tainau has become beautified by thee.
The husband will fear, will shrink, will faint at the reap-
    pearance,
At the return of the love of the cherished wife,
Of that face so bright and beautiful.
Look whichever way he will she seems to be down there still.

The moon sinking into the western shades is the image of the
    husband,
The image of Moanarai at the moment.
As a great cloud obscuring the sky is his grief,
The grief of the husband mourning for his estranged wife,
And like the sky darkened by its rising is my distress for her.

Alas for me! Alas for me! my little wife,
My darling has gone astray!
My little beautiful wayward spouse,
My friend who made my heart brave,
My friend in the storm, has been stolen away.
A wreath of the *fara* tree, a garland of pandanus blossoms
    I have gathered for thee,
O Aitofa, and lo, thou art flown!

Ah, woe is me! Is it thus that thou shouldst treat me?
Lo, thou art drifting away over the ripples in the Aoa
    shallows,
Thou art passing the fragrant vale of Vavaara,
And leaving Mt. Rotui, the upper jaw of Hades behind thee.
Thou hast forsaken thy favorite bathing place with its
    clear water,
And thy gardenia bush that blossoms without ceasing.
Alas for thee, Aitofa! Thou art a little toy canoe that
    the wind carries away.

Alas for my anguish and the rage of my heart!
Ah me! I despair and think of suicide,
I am possessed with frenzy. Alas for us both!
The mind of the husband gives back the effort to win back
    thy love.

Alas for my darling! Thy fair face is lost to sight;
There is no benefit from the home.

A piercing thorn to me, a pretty thorn art thou.
What is my fault for which thou art vexed,
For which thou hast disdained me?
Why hast thou cut the cord of love and deserted me,
An evil-working woman?

As a long continued storm is my anger,
At the throbbing within, within me.
My bowels yearn, my heart flows out after thee.
I am chilled with lingering affection for thee; O Aitofa,
    return!

Here is a bunch of red feathers for thee,
Here is a wreath of scarlet feathers for thee,
Here is a necklace of beautiful pearls for thee,
Here is thy home.
I am Moanarai thy husband.

Tonga, Polynesia

IV

Thou Hast Deserted Me, My Prince

Oh, thou my spouse,
Thou hast deserted me, my prince,
Me, the lonely one;
A deserted cow I stand,
A deserted buffalo
Without a comrade.
Now that my husband has deserted me
Now I am poor who once possessed a spouse.
My father,
The great, the illustrious,
The great, he who walked resplendent,
The mountain Si Manabun, that easily caves in;

He who arose dext'rously like the sun
And set with difficulty!
At night they often summoned him, my father,
And in the morning, too, they called for him.—
O thou bear on the road!
Thou tiger at the gate!
And now thou art fallen, fallen! Father, prince,
Spouse.
Oh, my father,
Thou who hadst bones that never grew tired,
Hands that never rested.
Never enough can I bewail my spouse,
My father, to whom the world was friendly.
Aye, ever must I think of him, whene'er I raise my eyes!
When I remember how he went to the mart,
There where the traffic flourishes,
Oh, then I cannot clearly see the world,
So plenteously the tears do fall:
When I recall the misery extreme,
That racks my frame—
The thought that I have no spouse!

Batak, Sumatra

V

ANXIETY

Oh, my sweet offspring,
Oh, do not attempt
To leave me, a rice pod!
Let me for thee be buried in the earth.
My father must continue to live,
To live in the midst of the world.
If you were to die,
Ah, I would be like a hen who has been allowed to fly away,
Like a horse that is freed.

My little offspring desires to leave me,
To leave me, one born out of time,
Me, who resemble an oft-fired earthen pot,
Like an iron utensil.
Oh, yes, indeed, I am pulled from above,
I am thrown in all directions like a lid
When I recall to my mind your lips
That could not yet frame answers
To its mother's words,
She who now stands alone!
I would drown myself if you died,
Drown myself in the river Si Tumallam,
If you were thrust into the depths,
Into the deep abyss
That we cannot ascend.
I shall endeavor
To make a twisted cord—
The road to death.

Batak, Sumatra

VI

FAREWELL FOREVER

Oh, the pain now gnawing at my heart
For loss of thee, my own beloved!
How oft along the white seacoast
With joyous heart I voyaged on
To our own home, to Ko-iti;
And saw as Ra, at even, set, the ruddy clouds,
Those tattoo-marks thy old progenitor
Pa-wai-tiri on heaven drew!

But death is nothing new.
Death is, has ever been, since Mawi died of old.
The Pata-tai laughed aloud

And woke the goddess dread
Who severed him and shut him up in gloom.
So dusk of even came on
And Ti-wai-waka flew and lighted on the bar
O'er which is cast all refuse
From hearth and home of man.

Then, then, for thee that evil came.
The priest no meet incantation made
Nor sacred water laved
In offerings propitiatory for thee.
Not so in ancient times thy ancestors would act—
But now I moan thy loss of power,
The impotence displayed by Ka-hae,
The ignorance now shown in all the world.
Farewell—farewell forever—yes, farewell.

Maori, New Zealand

VII

FAREWELL TO MY NATIVE LAND

There far away is the tide of Honipaka (a hill).
Alas! thou, Honipaka, art divided from me.
The only tie which connects us
Is the fleecy cloud drifting hither
Over the summit of the island
Which stands clearly in sight.
Let me send a sigh afar to the tribe,
Where the tide is now flowing—
The leaping, the racing,
Skipping tide.
Oh! for the breeze, the land breeze,
The stiff breeze.
That is my bird,
A bird that hearkens to the call,

Though concealed in the cage.
Oh! for the wind of Matariki!
Then will Te Whareporutu
And the great Ati-awa
Sail swiftly hitherward.
So ends my song of love.

Maori, New Zealand

VIII

Forever Severed Is Our Love

Her praise is ever heard—
'Tis praise of kindness.
I am shorn of all and live in silence,
Friendless and alone.

O heaven outspread!
With fortitude inspire my heart,
That not forever I with tears lament for her, my spouse.
Stir up my inmost heart to deeds of daring,
That my calamity may be forgotten.
Has Merau, goddess of extinction, died,
That I forever still must weep
Whilst day on day succeeds and each the other follows?
Grief on grief?
Now gathers all my woe and floods my heart with weeping;
Agony I dread, and now I shrink with fear of even one
    drop of rain.
At eventide, as rays of twinkling stars shine forth,
I weep, and on thee gaze, and on their shining courses.
But oh! for naught in space I float.
Oh, woe is me!
Who now like Rangi am, from Papa once divided.
Now flows at flood the tide of keen regret;
And, severed once, forever severed is our love!

Maori, New Zealand

IX

Tell it to the west,
Tell it to the south,
And to the north also;
Look at the stars above
And glance at the moon.
I am as the tattooed tree.
Say who is thy beloved
And let the scent of
The mokimoki plant
Give forth its sweetness
And foster those desires,
That in the midst
Of waving plumes
I may a listener be.

Maori, New Zealand

X

Just as the eventide draws near
My old affection comes
For him I loved.
Though severed far from me,
And now at Hawa-iki
I hear his voice
Far distant; and
Though far beyond
The distant mountain peak,
Its echoes speak
From vale to vale.

Maori, New Zealand

XI

Methinks it is you, leaf plucked from love's tree,
You, mayhap, that stirs my affection.
There's a tremulous glance of the eye,

The thought she might chance yet to come:
But who then would greet her with song?
Your day has flown, your vision of her—
A time this for gnawing the heart.
I've plunged just now in deep waters:
Oh the strife and vexation of soul!
No mortal goes scathless of love.
A wife thou estranged, I a husband estranged,
Mere husks to be cast to the swine.
Look, the swarming of fish at the weir!
Their feeding grounds on the reef
Are waving with mosses abundant.
Thou art the woman, that one your man—
At her coming who'll greet her with song?
Her returning, who shall control?

Hawaii

XII

Up to the streams in the wildwood
Where rush the falls Molo-kama,
While the rain sweeps past Mala-hoa,
I had a passion to visit
The forest of bloom at Koili,
To give love-caress to Manu'a,
And her neighbor Maha-moku;
My hand would quiet their rage,
Would sidle and touch Lani-huli.
Grant me but this one entreaty,
We'll meet 'neath the omens above.
Two flowers there are that bloom
In your garden of being;
Entwine them into a garland,
Fit emblem and crown of your love.
And what the hour of your coming?
When stands the sun o'er the *pali*,

When turns the breeze of the land,
To breathe the perfume of *hala*,
While the currents swirl at *Wai-pa*.

Hawaii

XIII

How will the coming July morning be,
I wonder?
My mind is very weak at the thought
Of being unable to see my sweetheart.

Tlingit, Alaska

XIV

If one had control of death,
It would be very easy to die with a Wolf woman,
It would be very pleasant.

Tlingit, Alaska

XV

What are you saying to me?
I am arrayed like the roses
And beautiful as they.

Ojibwa

XVI

Look where the mist
Hangs over Pukehina.
There is the path
By which went my love.

Turn back again hither
That may be poured out
Tears from

My eyes. It was not I
Who first spoke of love.
You it was who first made advances
To me when but a little thing.
Therefore was my heart made wild.

This is my farewell of love to thee.

Maori, New Zealand

XVII

Set, O sun, in the mists of your cave,
While the tears flow like water from my eyes.
I am a forsaken one since you have gone,
O Tarati. Now is vanishing from the sight
The point of Waiohipa,
And the cliff of Mitiwai is fading away like smoke.
Beneath that cliff is the god of my love.
Have done, spirit, the work of intrusion.
Now that you are absent in your native land,
The day of regret will, perhaps, end.

Maori, New Zealand

XVIII

A loon I thought it was,
But it was
My love's
Splashing oar.

To Sault Ste. Marie
He has departed.
My love
Has gone on before me.
Never again
Can I see him.

Ojibwa

XIX

Although he said it.
Still
I am filled with longing
When I think of him!

Ojibwa

XX

Come,
I am going away.
I pray you
Let me go.
I will return again.
Do not weep for me.

Behold,
We will be very glad
To meet each other
When I return.
Do not weep for me.

Ojibwa

XXI

LULLABY

Here is little Rangi-tumua, reclining with me
Under the lofty pine tree of Hine-rahi.
And here am I, my little fellow,
Seeking, searching sadly through the thoughts that rise.
In these days, my child,
For us two no lofty chiefs are left.
Passed are the times of thy far-famed uncles,
Who from the storms of war and witchcraft
Gave shelter to the multitude, the thousands.

Maori, New Zealand

XXII

Old Love

A storm from the sea strikes Ke-au,
Ulu-mano sweeping across the barrens;
It sniffs the fragrance of upland *lehua*,
Turns back at Kupa-koili;
Sawed by the blows of the palm leaves,
The groves of Pandanus in lava shag;
Their fruit he would string 'bout his neck;
Their fruit he finds wilted and crushed,
Mere rubbish to litter the road—
Ah, the perfume! Pana-ewa is drunk with the scent;
The breath of it spreads through the groves.
Vainly flares the old king's passion,
Craving a sauce for his meat and wine.
The summer has flown; winter has come;
Ah, that is the head of our troubles.
Palsied are you and helpless am I;
You shrink from a plunge in the water;
Alas, poor me! I'm a coward.

Hawaii

XXIII

A Lament

Here I sit through summer's long night,
My heart is always beating for my beloved.
Come near me, my daughter, and keep by my side;
Thou art ever restless when I nurse thee.
Obstruct not my vision while gazing inland
At the approaching canoe and the cloud drawing near
Its edge, as it rises by Haumapu.
Thy ancestors lived and remained with me;
But they are driven downwards to Paerau.

O Toko and thy party welcome here!
I am afflicted with a disease from afar.
I must haste to hew down
The thicket of spears at Tahoraparoa;
That my spirits may be soothed,
Which are excited for my land.

Mangaia, Polynesia

XXIV

The bright sunbeams
Shoot down upon
Tauwara, whose
Lofty ridge veils thee from
My sight, O Amo, my beloved.
Leave me that my eyes
May grieve, and that
They may unceasingly mourn,
For soon must I descend
To the dark shore—
To my beloved who has gone before.

Mangaia, Polynesia

XXV

WHITHER HAS SHE GONE?

Solo

Whither has she gone?

Chorus

She has sped to Avaiki,
She disappeared at the edge of the horizon,
Where the sun drops through.
We weep for thee!

Solo

Yes, I will forever weep
And ever weep for thee!

Chorus

Bitter tears I shed for thee;
I weep for the lost wife of my bosom.
Alas, thou wilt not return!

Solo

Oh, that thou wouldst return!

Chorus

Stay; come back to the world!
Return to my embrace:
Thou art as a bough wrenched off by the blast!

Solo

Wrenched off and now in Avaiki—
That distant land to which thou art fled.

Mangaia, Polynesia

XXVI

LAMENT FOR A CHILD

Kachila, blood of my blood, let me think of thee!
Perhaps, thinking of you, the whole world will hear of my
    grief.
These little hair-ornaments, let them be thrown into the
    river
That the crocodiles may wear them.
O dear, my child!

Ba-ila, Southeastern Africa

XXVII

LOVE SONG OF THE DEAD

You are hard-hearted against me,
You are hard-hearted against me, my dear;
You are cruel against me,
You are cruel against me, my dear.
For I am tired waiting for you
To come here, my dear!
Different shall now be my cry for your sake, my dear.
Ah, I shall go down to the lower world, and cry for you
    there, my dear!

Kwakiutl, British Columbia

XXVIII

THE ABSENT ONE

I know not whether thou has been absent:
I lie down with thee, I rise up with thee.
In my dreams thou art with me.
If my eardrops tremble in my ears,
I know it is thou moving within my heart.

Modern Aztec, Mexico

XXIX

WE MUST PART

Many are the youths indeed,
But thou alone art pleasing to me;
You, O chief, I love.
But we must part
And long will be the time!

Oglala, Sioux

SATIRE

I

THE STRIFE OF SAVADLAK AND PULANGITSISSOK

Savadlak speaks:

The south, the south, and the south yonder,
Where settling on the midland coast I met Pulangitsissok,
Who had grown stout and fat with eating halibut.
Those people from the midland coast they don't know
    spearing,
Because they are afraid of their speech.
Stupid they are besides.
Their speech is not alike,
Some speak like the northern, some like the southern,
Therefore we can't make out their talk.

Pulangitsissok speaks:

There was a time when Savadlak wished that I would be a
    good *kayaker*,
That I could take a good load on my *kayak!*
Many years ago some day he wanted me to put a heavy
    load on my *kayak*.
(This happened at the time) when Savadlak had his *kayak*
    tied to mine (for fear of being capsized).
Then he could carry plenty upon his *kayak*,
When I had to tow him and he did cry most pitifully.
And then he grew afeared,
And nearly was upset
And he had to keep his hold by help of my *kayak* string!

Eskimo

II

I behold you, land of Nunarsuit,
The mountain tops on its south side are wrapped in clouds.
It slopes toward the south,
Towards Usuarsuk.
What couldst thou expect in such a miserable place!
All its surroundings being shrouded with ice.
Not before late in spring can people from there go travelling.

Eskimo

III

She

When I think of you, I am weeping as I go!
When I go along the bluffs, I am weeping as I move.

He

O Niagiwathe, do you say that to me?
My grandmother you are: so I feel and am annoyed!

Ponka, Nebraska

IV

No One Desires You

Refuse me as much as you wish, my dear!
The corn you eat at home, why 'tis made of human eyes!
The goblets that you use, they are of human skulls!
The manioc roots you eat, they are of human shin bones!
The potatoes you do use, they are of human hands!
Refuse me as much as you wish!
No one desires you!

Ba-Ronga, Southeastern Africa

V

THERE ARE PLENTY OF MEN

I had a dream last night:
I dreamt my husband took a second wife;
So I took my little basket and I said before I left,
"There are plenty of men."
Thus I dreamt.

Lkungen, British Columbia

VI

O messenger, thy words are wind!
Me, the glorious tree, me thou deceivest,
For were not these thy words:
"When thou canst see the pupils of the sun,
Entwine thy way in secret to the woods?"
And when I came
Verily it was mine to scold and to upbraid thee.

O most deceitful art thou; cobold, frog arboreal,
So dost thou seem reflected in the pool!
Barely, indeed, hadst thou begun in growth
When death almost constrained thee,
For ever were thy eyes twisted and turned, a flirt,
Whenever thou didst walk and promenade!
Thou art become most apt in coquetry!

Buin, Melanesia

VII

Thou art the bird who at the dawn doth walk!
Did you not to the chief's enclosure come
And say to me:
"Give me glass pearls in quantity
And then we too will after, sport in love"?

Well, then, if thus so great your lust for pearls,
Why cocoanuts do you not smoke for Dick?
These he would gladly take and give you wares in turn,
Many the glass pearls he too has for you.
Truly I am the tree magnificent and you the tree of blood
Which the dead spirit spies when first he looks.
When for your son the chief did make a feast,
Why e'en at that time, standing you howled for pearls!
"O give me," you did say, "that I therewith
May gird them as a dress upon my limbs
Whene'er I walk abroad."

Buin, Melanesia

HATRED

I

Go, sir, companionless
To be set up as a spectre above Waiwetu.
Yes, laugh on, sir;
Take care your feet return not quickly.

I have no blood left for you to drink.
I am exhausted in celebrating the greatness of your fame.
Who shall sing your death to the world?
Shall it be the mist above Tirchanga?
Shall it be the mist gathering round Kaihinu?
Yes, better let it be so, sir.

O that this were your brain!
This stone that lies by the food-fire!
So would I devour it with thorough satisfaction.

Maori, New Zealand

II

Portentous lightning flashes on the mount,
An omen of disaster—and for whom?
Nay, 'tis the withdrawal in dark death of stately plumes
Of those our foes, who glut our hungering throat.
For Pango is my fierce desire,
That I in full revenge may drink the brains
From out thy skull, O Tuku-uru-rangi!

Who shall feel the lover's jewel of *pounamu*
Upon the sinuous shores of Wairau?
May evil take the cooked head, nameless one, Te Roha!

My precious one was dragged away
And from the flood withdrawn
Whilst following heedlessly the *weka* path,
The path of war besides the moss-grown trees:
Yet who would deign to eat that grayhead in this world?
In vomit would it be cast forth!

Away with thee, O *ariki!*
That these my teeth may gnaw thy skull,
May crush its parasites,
Whilst I on brains of Wahaka-piko glut—
O my food! A parasite am I, an eater too, of brains—
An eater, too, of thee, O Horu!
Stricken and crushed the fragments fly.

Maori, New Zealand

III

O the saltiness of my mouth
In drinking the liquid brains of Nuku
Whence welled up his wrath!
His ears which heard the deliberations!

Tutepakihirangi shall go headlong
Into the stomach of Hinewai!
My teeth shall devour Kaukau!
The three hundred and forty of Te Kiri-kowhatu
Shall be huddled in a heap in my trough!
Te Hika and his multitudes shall boil in my pot!
Ngaitahu (the whole tribe) shall be
My sweet morsel to finish with!

Maori, New Zealand

LULLABIES

I

Why dost thou weep, my child?
The sky is bright; the sun is shining;
Why dost thou weep?
Go to thy father: he loves thee,
Go tell him why thou weepest.
What! Thou weepest still?
Thy father loves thee, I caress thee:
Yet still thou art sad.
Tell me, then, my child, why dost thou weep!

Balengi, Central Africa

II

Hush thee, child!
Mother will bring an antelope
And the tidbit shall be thine!

Kiowa, Oklahoma

III

Baby swimming down the river:
Little driftwood legs,
Little rabbit legs.

Kiowa, Oklahoma

IV

Sleep, sleep, sleep!
In the trail the beetles
Carry each other on their back.
Sleep, sleep, sleep!

Zuni, New Mexico

V

It is hanging
In the edge of the sunshine.
It is a pig, I see,
With its cloven hoofs;
It is a very fat pig.
The people who live in a hollow tree
Are fighting,
They are fighting bloodily.
He is rich.
He will carry a pack toward the great water.

Rabbit speaks:

At the end of the point of land,
I eat the bark off the tree;
I see the track of a lynx.
I don't care; I can get away from him.
It is a jumping trail—
Sep!

Ojibwa

VI

Don't sleep!
Your paddle fell into the water, and your spear.
Don't sleep!
The ravens and crows are flying about.

Kwakiutl, British Columbia

VII

Don't sleep too much!
Your digging-stick fell into the water, and your basket.
Wake up!
It is nearly low water.
You will be late down the beach.

Kwakiutl, British Columbia

VIII

On the hillside I was running,
My knee I skinned, I skinned.
The red-headed wolf, the red-headed one,
Farther off he cannot ease himself.
His face it itches,
At all times does he kill.
Yellow with fat he becomes;
The dog gets full: he smokes.

Crow, Montana

IX

You were given by good fortune to your slave,
You were given by good fortune to your slave,
To come and take the place of your slave!
O tribes, now hide yourselves!
I have come to be a man and my name is Hellebore!
The cedar withes are twisted even now, that I shall pass
Through the mouths, through the heads that I obtain in war,
For I am true Hellebore!
Princes' heads in war I'll take when I come to be a man,
And then I shall have your names, as my father he has done,
He who now has your names for his own!

Kwakiutl, British Columbia

X

You need not think that the smoke of your house in the
middle of Skedans will be as great as when you were
a woman (in your previous existence).
You need not think that they will make such a continual
noise of singing in Skedans Creek as they used to when
you were a woman (in your previous existence).

Haida, British Columbia

XI

Whence have you fallen, have you fallen? Whence have
you fallen, have you fallen?
(i.e., how did you come to us?)
Did you fall, fall, fall, from the top of the salmonberry
bushes?

Haida, British Columbia

MISCELLANEOUS

I

THE OLD WARRIOR

Mighty, mighty, great in war,
So was I honored;
Now behold me old and wretched!

Oglala, Sioux

II

The Sioux women
Pass to and fro wailing.
As they gather
Their wounded men,
The voice of their wailing comes to us.

Ojibwa

III

I do wonder
If she truly is humiliated—
The Sioux woman—
Whose head I have cut off?

Ojibwa

IV

They are talking about me
Saying, "Come with us."

Is there anyone
Who would weep for me?
My wife would weep for me.

Ojibwa

V

On the day of my death
Let it rain in torrents;
Let everyone become aware
That a great man has passed.

Ewe, West Africa

VI

The Great Magician

Know, when the towns did call me,
I came at their behest—
They knew they had called me, the magician.
Indeed they knew the great magician.

Ewe, West Africa

VII

THE PEOPLE ALWAYS CALL ME

I have arrived, you see:
The people always call me.
Always they desire me,
Me, the great shaman.

I have arrived, you see:
Kings, too, they do call me,
Always they desire me.

Ewe, West Africa

VIII

FRIENDSHIP

Friend, whatever hardships threaten
If thou call me,
I'll befriend thee;
All-enduring, fearlessly,
I'll befriend thee.

Oglala, Sioux

IX

ENVY

No child does one lend me!
Only a morter will they lend me!
Ah, if I were an eagle,
Ah, if I were a hawk,
Then would I carry one away!

Ba-Ronga, Southeastern Africa

X

THE TEMPTRESS

Listen ye clans!
That rottening wood, this woman, scours the path!
Her many-tongued apron she let fall
And said to me, "O do thou pick it up
That I may have oblivion of my husband.
Happy, thy food will I prepare for thee,
Yet do thou keep discreet nor wag thy tongue.
Thy land that will my people plant for thee;
Your pigs, these too, my people they will feed
And then within the hall they will prepare them.
Why, hadst thou then no word of all the wealth
Which they, my people, garnered?"

(And thus the man) "Once in another place
Didst thou speak evil of thy spouse.
And now dost hunger for the leaves of love,
Wailing, forever wailing, yearning for me.
When thou didst weep for me
Then didst thou say, 'Carry me to thy home,
Carry me quickly to another town,
Return we may thereafter.' "

O coco-sap what shall I, Parrot-planter,
Give thee as gift?
Upon the road I heard thee: "Follow me
When to another village we have come
Rest thou content upon my skirt of love,
And having rested joyful will we twitter."

Buin, Melanesia

XI

The Persistent Wooer

Spite in my soul, I still pursue your trail!
Aye, when some day you, widowed, shall stand there,
Willingly will I lead you to my home.
I was still young
When by command you went
To this your spouse.

Spite in my soul, I still pursue your trail!
Aye, when within the bath of death he stands,
Then shall you give me of your apron fringe
One piece, that I may bind it on my arm.
Your spouse, stunted in growth, appears.
Tell him I pray, "Forged is the deadly spear
Which from another's hand, shall strike him down."

Buin, Melanesia

XII

Song Written by a Man Who Was Jilted by a Young Woman

Oh, how, my ladylove, can my thoughts be conveyed to you,
    my ladylove, on account of your deed, my ladylove?
In vain, my ladylove, did I wish to advise you, my ladylove,
    on account of your deed, my ladylove.
It is the object of laughter, my ladylove, it is the object of
    laughter, your deed, my ladylove.
It is the object of contempt, my ladylove, it is the object of
    contempt, your deed, my ladylove.
Oh, if poor me could go, my ladylove! How can I go to you,
    my ladylove, on account of your deed, my ladylove!

Now, I will go, my ladylove, go to make you happy, my
   ladylove, on account of your deed, my ladylove.
Farewell to you, my ladylove! Farewell, mistress, on
   account of your deed, my ladylove!

RETORT TO THE PRECEDING SONG

O friends! I will now ask you about my love.
Where has my love gone, my love who is singing against me?
I ask you, who walks with my love?
Oh, where is my love, where is the love that I had for
   my love?
For I feel, really feel, foolish, because I acted foolishly
   against my love.
For what I did, caused people to laugh at me on account of
   what I did to you, my love.
For I am despised on account of my love for you, my true
   love, for you, my love.
For you have said that you will live in Knight Inlet.
Oh, Knight Inlet is far away, for that is the name of the
   place where my love is going.
O Rivers Inlet is far away, for that is the name of the place
   where my love is going.
For he forgot of my love, my true love.
For in vain he goes about trying to find some one who will
   love him as I did, my love.
Don't try to leave me without turning back to my love,
   my love.
Oh, my love, turn back to your slave, who preserved your
   life.
I am downcast, and I cry for the love of my love.
But my life is killed by the words of my love.
Good-by, my love, my past true love!

Kwakiutl, British Columbia

XIII

Love Song of Taskedek Whose Lover Had Gone to Japan

You are hard-hearted, you who say that you love me, you
  are hard-hearted, my dear!
You are cruel, who say that you are lovesick for me, my
  dear!
Where are they going to take my love, my dear?
Where are they going to take my dear, that causes me to lie
  down sick, me, the slave of my dear?
They will take my dear far away!   I shall be left behind,
  my truelove, for whom I pine, who keeps me alive,
  my dear!
They will take my dear out to sea far away!   There the one
  is going for whom I pine, my master, for whom I am
  lovesick, my dear!
I wish I could go to you, my master, that I might make you
  happy, my dear, for I think you long for me, for my
  love, my dear.
I wish I could go to you, my dear!   I wish I could make
  you dream that you embrace this one whom you love,
  my dear, the one for whom I pine, my dear!
I wish I could go to be your pillow, my dear!   I wish I
  could go to be your feather bed, my dear! the one for
  whom I pine, who keeps me alive, my dear!
Now farewell, my truelove, for whom I pine, who keeps
  me alive, my master, my dear!

Song of Menmentleqelas in Answer to the Preceding Song

Stop, friends, and let us listen to the song that my dear sings
  for me, the one whom I am leaving so cruelly.

Stop, friends, and let us listen to the weeping of my dear,
my truelove, my dear!

Whence, O friends! comes the sound of the one who is crying
for me, my truelove, my truelove, my dear.

O friends! she whom I left behind is crying for me, my truelove, my truelove, my dear.

Don't long for me! For you I am working, my truelove,
for whom I pine, my dear, my truelove, my dear.

Don't cry for me! I am working for you, my true mistress,
my lady, my truelove, my dear.

Don't long for me! I am coming back, my dear, my truelove, my dear.

Don't cry for me! I am paddling toward you, my dear,
my truelove, my dear.

Song of Same When Taskedek Had Deserted Him

You are cruel to me, you are cruel to me, my dear!

You are hard-hearted against me, you are hard-hearted
against me, my love!

You are surpassingly cruel, you are surpassingly cruel
against me, for whom you pined.

She pretends to be indifferent, not to love me, my truelove,
my dear.

Don't pretend too much that you are indifferent of the love
that I hold for you, my dear!

Else you may be too indifferent of the love that I hold for
you, my dear!

My dear, you are indifferent of the love I hold for you,
my dear!

My dear, you go too far; your good name is going down,
my dear!

Don't try hereafter to follow me, my dear!

Don't hereafter cry for me, my dear!

Does not this make sick your heart, my dear?

Friends, do not let us listen any longer to love songs that
    are sung by those far away!
Friends, it might be well if I took a new truelove, a dear
    one.
Friends, it might be well if I had a new one for whom
    to pine, a dear one.
I wish she would hear my love song when I cry to my new
    love, my dear one!

Kwakiutl, British Columbia

CHAPTER X

APHORISMS ON LIFE AND MAN

IN the preceding chapters we found primitive man
giving expression to a fairly definite philosophy of
life which was characterized by a very unusual degree
of objectivity. In the present chapter we shall try to
show that this same objectivity was applied to the
analysis and evaluation of character. Much of this
analysis is best and most adequately expressed in the
aphorisms and proverbs current among all primitive
peoples, although they have taken on a more precise
literary form and assumed greater importance in
Africa and Polynesia than in other parts of the world.

Nothing seems to have escaped the discriminating
and discerning insight of the native philosopher and
sage. Every corner of the human soul, every angle in
human relationships is disclosed and illuminated in
a manner that would have done justice to Stendhal.
Here as in the poems quoted in the preceding chapter
we have man in all his aspects, his loves and his hates,
his arrogance and his pettiness, his affectation and his
simplicity. If the foibles seem unduly emphasized
that is, after all, the nature of proverbs and aphorisms.
Sometimes it is a warning or a moral lesson that is
conveyed. Generally, however, we are treated to irony

and sarcasm. But no discussion can better bring home to the reader the full implications of all that is contained in these aphorisms and what wisdom and psychological insight must have gone to their making, than an actual perusal of them. I shall, therefore, even at the risk of overburdening the reader, quote a representative number from a few regions.

BA-ILA PROVERBS

1. Wisdom comes out of an ant heap.
2. A wise man ran on without eating it, a fool coming behind ate it (i.e., the wise in their own conceits often miss the good things of earth).
3. O man, don't try to teach your mother, try others.
4. Get grown up and then you will know the things of the earth.
5. The pig died in the trap (against which it had been warned).
6. Annoy your doctors and sicknesses will come laughing.
7. The prodigal cow threw away her own tail.
8. It is the prudent hyena that lives long.
9. A man knows his own woe.
10. The god that speaks up is the one that gets the meat.
11. You may cleanse yourself but it is not to say that you cease to be a slave.
12. That which is rotten goes to its owners (i.e., only a few remember the dead).
13. When a chief's wife steals she puts the blame upon the slaves.

14. When a dog barks the fame belongs to the master of the village.

15. They spurn the frog but drink the water (i.e., they don't like to find a frog in their drinking water but they will drink it after the frog is removed).

16. Mr. No-Fault ensnared a snake in the road (and then left it to bite passers-by).

17. There is no chief who eats out of an *impande* shell (i.e., the shell may show his wealth but when it comes to eating the chief must eat like ordinary people, out of a dish).

18. An ax shaft is made out of an ordinary piece of wood (i.e., an ordinary person can be made of great use but, on the other hand, he is not essential).

19. Build rather with a witch than with a false-tongued person, for he destroys a community.

20. A living tortoise is not worn as a charm (i.e., whether you see it or not, you must not speak evil of a living man).

21. Better help a fighting man than a hungry man, for he has no gratitude.

22. The old thing pleases him who married her.

23. What is ugly to other people is fair in the sight of the child's mother.

24. While you are away from home visiting, your own people know all about you (i.e., whatever you do it is sure to come out).

25. The work of a chief doesn't prevent one from hunting out one's own fleas (i.e., if you are working for a

chief that does not hinder you from minding your
own affairs).

26. The man at home in thought is not to be deceived by
much porridge (i.e., you can't retain a homesick man
by offering him plenty to eat).

27. A river that would not be straightened has bends in
it (i.e., you lie on the bed you make).

28. You shave me with a blunt razor (i.e., I have been
deceived by promises).

29. I threw a stone into an ant heap (i.e., I have done
something foolish and it is beyond repair).

30. He has the kindness of a witch (i.e., he is overkind).[1]

While there is clearly what might be called a definite
family resemblance between all African proverbs, still
each tribe has its own style and all are at one in the
light they throw upon the African Negroes' insight into
human nature. Thus, for instance, the Baganda of
Rhodesia and the Masai are as prolific as the Ba-ila in
their pithy comments, friendly, unfriendly, and neutral, on that strangest of all things, man.

Baganda Proverbs

1. A grumbler does not leave his master, he only stops
others from coming to him.

2. The stick which is at your friend's house will not
drive away the leopard (i.e., it is of no use in an
emergency).

---

[1] E. W. Smith and A. M. Dale, *The Ila-Speaking Peoples of Northern Rhodesia*, II, pp. 311 ff.

3. A borrower only seeks you in order that he may borrow and not to repay you.

4. The god helps you when you put forth your running powers.

5. He who has not suffered does not know how to pity.

6. He who passes you in the morning, you will pass him in the evening.

7. You have many friends as long as you are prosperous.

8. Let me cut the difficult knot, as the wizard did at Bubiro (i.e., settle the question).

9. You appear and pretend to like me, as the orphan child is loved while still mourning for its father.

10. When I remember it I laugh because it is not I who am concerned.

11. When it is not your mother who is in danger of being eaten by a wild animal, the matter can wait until the morrow.

12. The beautiful woman is the sister of many (i.e., she has many admirers and many who claim to be related to her).

13. The despised person is ever present.

14. The heart is a market place (i.e., it chooses what it likes best, just as we do at a market).

15. Covered with shame like a child who has stolen from its mother.

16. He who takes by force is not apt to trap (i.e., gentleness and not force arrives at truth).

17. I had a number of friends before calamity befell me.

18. Risk is never absent from those who seek wealth.
19. The owner of the pot does not kill the potter.²

MASAI PROVERBS

1. The mouth which ate fat shall eat excrement and that which ate excrement shall eat fat.
2. The slayer of the enemy has become a coward and the poltroon has become a brave man.
3. Coal laughs at ashes not knowing that the same fate which has befallen them will befall it.
4. The firewood which has been cut ready for burning, laughs at that which is being consumed.
5. It is the same thing when a man is once there, whether he has been called or whether he has come of his own free will.
6. Everything has an end.
7. Events follow one another like days.
8. Behold the people you are passing. The man is there and the male, the woman and the female (i.e., all people are not alike and if you watch you will see that some of the passers-by are good and some are not).
9. We begin by being foolish and we become wise by experience.
10. A man does not know when he is well off; it is only when he is poor that he remembers the days of plenty.

---

² J. Roscoe, *The Baganda*, pp. 485-491.

11. When an event occurs only a part of the truth is sent abroad, the rest is kept back.
12. Bravery is not everything and however brave a man may be, two brave men are better.
13. The nose does not precede the rest of the body.
14. Warriors and cripples remain apart.
15. Don't make a cloth for carrying a child in before the child is born.
16. The zebra cannot do away with his stripes.
17. The bark of one tree will not adhere to another tree.
18. Persevering to accomplish an end and being able to do a thing are not the same thing; it is greater to persevere.
19. Nobody can say he is settled anywhere for ever: it is only the mountains which do not move from their places.
20. Broken pieces of a gourd cannot be fastened on to a cooking-pot.
21. Do not repair another man's fence until you have seen to your own.
22. It is better to be poor and live long than rich and die young.
23. Men may be partners, or may eat from the same dish, but they cannot tell what is passing through each other's minds.[3]

Passing now to the Polynesian proverbs we find certain marked differences in style although the problems are the same. Poetic metaphors and similes are

---

[3] A. C. Hollis, *The Masai*, pp. 238-251.

far more common, and, as might have been expected, a philosophic coloring pervades the formulation of the proverbs. Very frequently, too, the allusions are so local and specific that an elaborate explanation is necessary before an outsider can understand. I shall give selections from the Samoans, the Hawaiians, and the Maori.

SAMOAN PROVERBS

1. The hurricane and the calm are neighbors.
2. When the old hen scratches, the chickens eat beetles.
3. The brightness of the setting sun (is beautiful but will soon pass away).
4. Blessed is the moon which goes and comes again.
5. To stand on a whale and angle for minnows (i.e., to neglect important matters for little ones).
6. The crying of a dead trumpet (i.e., it makes a lot of noise but is dead).
7. The *ufu* (a fish) is sleeping and the *paipai* (a crab) is at rest (i.e., we have finished and there is no more to say).
8. The *aeno* (a crab) dies by its own claw (i.e., a man suffers the direct consequences of his own actions).
9. The crab and his legs had no consultation (i.e., to disclaim all responsibility).
10. Until the mountains fall; until the valleys are levelled.
11. First pluck the breadfruit which is furthest away (i.e., do the difficult thing first).
12. The roots may be in the forest but they will be

exposed in the roads (i.e., though supposed to be secret, the story will leak out).

13. Cleaning away stones because of faint-heartedness (i.e., a man who anticipates defeat is not likely to conquer).

14. Beaten by the mallet, beaten by the handle (i.e., to be beset by misfortunes on all sides).

15. The light weight of a burden when first lifted (i.e., do not imagine your work, life, etc., are all going to be light).

16. Let the sea determine as to the quality of the canoe.

17. The fishing may be without fish but doubting and suspicion will always have a catch.

18. The banana is plucked up but the sucker is planted. (The king is dead, long live the king!)

19. The plate of the drill rejoices in vain, for the point of the drill is broken. (This is used to express some insuperable difficulty. The family rejoices in the birth of a child but joy may be premature, for the child may die.)

20. One disease has gone but another has come.

21. Let the sinnet ring and the stand for the fishing rod go together (i.e., let your acts agree with your words).

22. The sun and the sea are nearing each other (said of approaching death).

23. The hilltops are near but the roads to them are long.

24. Often warned, the salt has now entered into his body (i.e., he is justly punished after many warnings).

25. The wisdom of a child but only a child (i.e., he does his best).

26. The many are the chiefs. (God is on the side of the strongest battalions.)

27. Don't go about thoughtlessly in the off months, because good times only last a few days.

28. The deaf man hears when he is tapped on the shoulders. (If you don't listen to advice, painful experience will teach you.)

29. No hole is made in the body by words. (Never heed what men say.)

30. Stones will rot but words never rot. (Anything may be forgiven but offensive words.)

31. A mouthful fallen from the mouth. (There's many a slip 'twixt the cup and the lip.)

32. O that all wishes were accomplished in fact! [4]

To the above I would like to add a few where the meaning has to be explained to be understood:

33. It is only the people of Neiafu who disparage the *to-elau* (the N. E. trade wind).

The explanation is as follows: It is said that two cripples in Neiafu grumbled continually against the northeast trade winds because they did not cause the coconuts to drop immaturely from the trees, as they were not able to climb for them. They preferred the west wind which caused the nuts to fall even though

---

[4] George Brown, "Proverbs of the Samoans," *Proceedings of the Australasian Association for the Advancement of Science*, 1913.

they were not ripe. This proverb is used to describe those who despise the good and prefer the bad or who prefer to have a worthless article like an immature coconut rather than have the trouble of getting a good one.

34. Let the blame be upon Vala.

Vala was the daughter of the chief Anufetele. The chief was standing at the council meeting one day and was making a formal speech to the meeting. His daughter Vala was seated on the ground quite near him. She whispered to him, "Dear elder, remove the gummy matter out of your eye." The old man thinking she was prompting him, repeated her words in his speech and the whole audience laughed loudly in derision. The girl again whispered to her father the words, "Wipe your mouth" and the old man repeated her words, at which there was again a burst of laughter and he sat down overwhelmed with shame. The application is that the blame be put on the guilty person. Anufetele was not at fault so much as Vala.

35. Has come again the offering of Mosopili which was too late.

Mosopili dwelt at Foaluga but his parents lived at Foalalo. His sister was very sick and a message was sent to inform him of the fact, and that she was likely to die, but he did not go to visit her. Again and again he was told of her illness but he still deferred his promised visit. At length he was told that she was dead, when he at once seized a *siapo* (native cloth) and ran down to Foalalo, but his sister was dead. He neglected to show his love for his sister while she was living and only tried to do so when it was too late.

36. The feather-blowing of Lavea.

Lavea was the head of a family at Safotu. Their family god was supposed to be present in the fowl and so they were, of course, prohibited from eating or injuring that bird. When Lavea and his family became professing Christians these customs were not observed and as a proof of the sincerity of his conversion, Lavea was asked to kill and eat a fowl and this he consented to do. He was, however, still very much afraid of the family deity and as a compromise he blew away the feathers as an offering to the god and ate the fowl.

This proverb is used to illustrate the folly of trying to be right with all sides; of a merely pretended allegiance; and that of retaining the best, and offering that which is of no value.

37. The body of Galue was bruised in vain.

Galue was a man who was very desirous of getting the best fine mat at a division of the property. He was so anxious for this that in order to show his good will and his respect for the family beforehand, he threw himself down on the stones and was much bruised. After all this, however, the mat in question was given to another man.

This proverb is applied to any one who fails to get something for which he has toiled or suffered.

HAWAIIAN PROVERBS

1. I will not be taken by an old taro leaf; give me the tender bud of the plant. (This is used by a young girl in disdain of an elderly suitor or one of low rank.)
2. Man is like a banana the day it bears fruit. (After the banana plant has borne fruit, it dies down and another takes its place.)
3. As the creeping dodder, creeping in Mana, so is love misplaced for the tree without foundation. (A parasite lover clings like the trunkless dodder.)
4. The wind of Ulupau woos a red blossom. (The fruitless advances of a young man to a maid.)
5. Gather the *pulu* below while the rain stays high above. (Make hay while the sun shines.)
6. The hardwood weeps when the smooth pebbles clash. (When people fight, the innocent suffer.)
7. When the *wiliwili* blooms then the sharks bite. (A young girl and her suitors.)
8. The little *hau* tree crowds the big one. (This is used when a small person crowds in or sits too close to a big person.)
9. Open the sluice gate for the fish to enter. (Advice of an elderly person to a boorish youth in order that he may correct his habits and gain friends.)
10. Like an angleworm is the prayer of the priest. (This refers to the twists and turns with which the magic incantation finds out its victim.)

11. Even little fishes make the mouth water.
12. Dead though the *taro* may be, the maggot lives on. (Though a person may think his past acts dead, yet they still live on.)
13. When the pandanus is ripe, the sea eggs are fat. (This refers to a parasite growing fat on the riches of a young person.)
14. The *akule* fish stays in deep water. (The burnt child dreads the fire.)
15. Not all knowledge is contained in your dancing school.
16. Do not mind if the lower part burns, but watch the upper lest it be overdone. (Do not mind the common people but watch the upper ranks upon whom everything depends.)
17. Continue to do good and heaven will come down to you.
18. Standing in the doorway of disappointment. (One who makes a long face over frustrated hopes.)
19. The puffed mouth is full of wind.
20. Blasphemy is a god that devours its own master.
21. Love is a mist; there is no mountain to which it will not cling.
22. The heads of the gods are hidden in the clouds.
23. I am a little stone but I can roll far.
24. A keeper who boasts of his tempestuous snare. (This refers to a boastful father whose daughter has disappointed him.)
25. Smite the waters with convolvulus, the waves will break. (A person who hits another will receive a blow in return.)

26. Heap up a pile, you carry the burden.
27. A fleet of small canoes will dash up the spray. (This illustrates wrath over trifles.)
28. Blow hither, blow hither, O wind of Hilo, put aside the little dish, grant me the big one! (This is said of an ambitious person.)
29. Feed men and they will obey.
30. Careless work with the hands brings unclean food to the mouth.
31. To obey is life, to disobey is death.
32. Tender are the little sins when the child is creeping; transient in childhood; obstinate in youth; hard to change in maturity; and fixed in old age.
33. One day only has the stranger. (He is a guest for one day, then he must work.)
34. It is living together teaches the meaning of love.
35. Delicious is a bundle of *taro* tops where there is love.[5]

Maori Proverbs

1. Though the grub may be a little thing it can cause the big tree to fall.
2. A spear shaft may be parried but not a shaft of speech.
3. The weaving of a garment may be traced but the thoughts of man cannot.
4. Son up and doing, prosperous man; son sitting, hungry man.

---

[5] "Hawaiian Stories and Wise Sayings," collected by L. S. Green and edited by M. W. Beckwith, in Publications of the Folklore Foundation, Vassar College, No. 3.

5. Did you come from the village of the liar?
6. The offspring of rashness died easily.
7. The women shall be as a cliff for the men to flee over.
8. Great is the majority of the dead.
9. The home is permanent, the man flits.
10. Outwardly eating together, inwardly tearing to pieces.
11. Man is passing away like the *moa*.
12. Will the escaped wood hen return to the snare?
13. Perhaps you and False-Tongue travelled here together?
14. Well done, the hand that roots up weeds!
15. A chief dies, another takes his place.
16. Passing clouds can be seen but passing thoughts cannot be seen.
17. The digger of fern root has abundance of food, but the parrot-snarer will go hungry.
18. Those who escape the sea god will be killed by those on shore.
19. It was not one alone who was awake in the dark ages.
20. The white heron eats daintily, the duck gobbles up the mud (i.e., a man is known by his tastes).
21. You cannot hew a bird-spear by the way (i.e., prepare carefully).
22. A raindrop above, a human lip below (i.e., dropping water wears away a stone, slander a good name).
23. The white crane whose flight is seen but once. (Angel visits, few and far between.)
24. Black and red united can do it. (The red-ochred chief and the charcoal-smeared slave united can do it.)

25. Food given by another is only a throat-tickler; but food gained by the labor of one's own hands is the food which satisfies.

26. Great is your going forth to war, small your return.

27. Deep throat, shallow muscle.

28. He who goes before gathers treasures; he who lags behind looks for them in vain.

29. Sir, bale the water out of your own mouth!

30. One day's beauty, a short-lived pleasure.

31. Food underdone is your own, fully cooked goes to others. (This is a warning against dawdlers.)

32. He who is a valiant in fight is a valiant apt to stumble. But he who is a valiant in cultivating food is a valiant who will abide—even to a natural death, worn out by old age.

33. Cold which is only skin deep, stealing warmth, is not worth a word of complaint.

34. The large chips made by Mr. Hardwood fell to the share of Mr. Sit-Still.

35. A crooked part of a stem of *toetoe* can be seen, but a crooked part in the heart cannot be seen.

36. O slave of two growths, shooting up, sinking down (i.e., a child grows up to be a man and afterwards descends to a second childhood in old age).

37. When the seine is worn out with age, the new net encircles the fish. (When a man grows old, his son succeeds him.)

38. Let him go on asking, his strength lies in asking questions.[6]

---

[6] Edward Treager, *The Maori Race;* Edward Shortland, *Traditions*

Only a cursory perusal of these proverbs is necessary to convince even the most skeptical that we are not dealing here with any vague group activity or folkway—that last refuge of the tired sociologist and ethnologist—but the personal envisaging of life by those individuals who in any group are concerned with and interested in formulating their attitude toward God, toward man, and toward society—the philosophers, the sages, and the moralists. These proverbs are merely offshoots of that more consistent and more ambitious formulation which we have discussed in some of the preceding chapters.

---

and Superstitions of the New Zealanders; and J. W. Stack, "Notes on Maori Literature," *Proceedings of the Australasian Society for the Advancement of Science,* 1891.

CHAPTER XI

THE TRAGIC SENSE OF LIFE

IN Chapter VIII we quoted the very profound tale of the Ba-ila woman who spent her long life seeking God so that she might ask him why he had afflicted her with so many misfortunes. Her more tough-skinned contemporaries assure her that God, fate, life, the Besetting-One, sits on the back of every one of them and that they cannot shake him off. But she will have none of their resignation and realism, and continues her search until death. Fate to her was clearly not some inevitable, non-personal, and non-discriminating force but an unjust personal agency inflicting pain and suffering upon her individually. Like so many other sensitive natures life was too much for her. She could not accept it as the vast majority of people do nor could she find any adequate explanation for it. Hence arose her terrible perplexity and bitterness.

But there are some temperaments who make terms with life in all its forms and who recognize that tragedy flows from the inward strivings and passions of man when he comes into conflict with the inevitable and irresistible forces of nature and society. As this clash of man and the world is often quite beyond the powers of any individual to foresee, control, or alter, there arises a feeling or an attitude toward life which may aptly be called the tragic sense of life. For Western Europe this has been well if somewhat pedantically described by the famous Spanish essayist, Miguel de Unamuno, in his work entitled *Del Sentimiento Trágico de la Vida.* Now this same attitude is also to be found among some individuals in primitive communities. At times it can lead to uncompromising and hopeless pessimism, at other times to a general theory in which the doom and disaster that so often follow in the wake of man are attributed to some human transgression, to some overstepping, whether it be conscious or not, of the limits imposed by each man's nature. In other words man is at fault.

As an example of the extreme pessimism into which it may develop—but a pessimism into which no criticism and fault-finding with fate enters—let me give the following very remarkable Maori poem:

Bow to earth and bow to heaven, whilst thou, O man! with craving hunger driven—weary, gaunt and near insanity, must wander aimless and alone, whilst death creeps nearer still, and to one focus draws that path of glory, honor, fame, and joy which youth had planned, and blots and blurs the whole; whilst, staggering, thou canst scarcely sweep aside the grass that grows along the path up to thy home.

How, coward and servile, gnawing hunger makes the soulless frame to stagger, when at dim eventide the reeling form oft seeks to eat the refuse *rori,* cooked and left by Parekorau.

How, crushed by shame, the once most noble self now dies within, as crouching thou drawest near, to see thy boyhood's home! No welcome greets with uttered words, or calls aloud thy name; but thou must onward pass, and in the path of Pu-hou go, and thence, yet still a starved one, come.[1]

From this unrelieved pessimistic expression of life's tragedy I should like to pass to a discussion of the tragic sense of life as it emerges in a number of myths of the Winnebago Indians and where doom is conceived of as due to human transgression.

Like the majority of American Indians, the Winnebago distinguish sharply between what might be called myths and realistic tales. Under "myth" is included everything regarded as having taken place in a distant past; under "tale" everything that has occurred within comparatively recent times. The word for myth means "sacred"; that for tale, "what is told"; i.e., what is considered as a real happening. It matters not how completely mythical the content of a story may be; as long as it is thought of as portraying an actual occurrence it is a tale. Stylistically a very interesting difference exists between the two, the former always having a happy, the latter, prevailingly if not always, an unhappy ending. The Winnebago themselves appear to be well aware of this trait of their myths as the following personal experience indicates.

While engaged in translating a text I must have un-

---

[1] J. C. Anderson, *Maori Life in Aotea*, p. 298.

consciously given my interpreter the impression of being worried about the fate of the hero of the particular story. He had been cut up into pieces and was being slowly boiled in a cauldron at the particular moment that my face apparently attracted the interpreter's attention, for he stopped short and said to me very kindly, "Don't worry. He isn't dead. They never die." Whether the Winnebago are equally conscious of the tragic ending of their realistic tales I had no means of determining; that, consciously or not, a definite selection of subject matter has taken place is quite evident, for otherwise the invariable tragic dénouement would be inexplicable. The impression conveyed is that they regarded life, the contact and pitting of man against man, of peoples against peoples, as leading inevitably to tragedy, an inference perhaps not so strange in a civilization where the highest ambition of man was to die on the warpath and where the most insistent pursuit of life was prestige.

Among many peoples has such a conflict, in fact, formed the subject matter of heroic myth and epic. We encounter it among the Polynesians, the Maya, and the Aztec and it underlies the theme of the *Iliad*, the *Chanson de Roland, El Cid* and the *Nibelungenlied*. In the *Iliad,* the *Nibelungenlied,* and the *Chanson de Roland* we know definitely that the conflict represented the legendary reflection of a real clash of peoples and civilizations and it seems extremely probable that the same explanation holds for the great epic tales of the Polynesians, the Aztec, and the Maya. Among the plains tribes of North America, likewise, where there has been an incessant and marked contact of different tribes and cultures, we find similar stress upon a tragic ending so that we may assume a certain degree of correlation between an epic or prose tale having a tragic ending, and definite historical clashes; it was indeed in this connection that man first sought and found a literary expression for the tragic sense of life.

In the following pages I shall discuss three Winnebago tales all ending tragically, and in all of which there exists from the beginning a definite presentiment of impending death. I shall attempt to show that this sense of impending misfortune is due to two distinct concepts of tragedy and doom, one implicit as in the *Iliad* and *Nibelungenlied*, the other explicit, embodying more or less a theory of how woe and death have come into the world. I shall try to demonstrate that in the tale of the "Traveller" we are, at bottom, dealing with the memory of some historical conflict or change analogous—although on a much smaller scale—to that which the *Iliad*, the *Chanson de Roland* and the *Nibelungenlied* depict; that the tragic dénouement reflects this cultural clash, exemplifying thus the implicit theory of doom, whereas the other two tales, and the secondary episode woven into the "Traveller," illustrate the explicit theory of doom.

The second theory, and with this we shall be principally concerned, ascribes tragedy neither to the inevitable and obvious conflict of individual with individual nor to the struggles of people with people but to the ceaseless conflict and strife, within each man, of his own passions, desires, and ambitions. More particularly is it ascribed to that irresistible craving which exacts from man and the world more than he is entitled to and more than his abilities and powers warrant—more, in fact, than he can adequately hope to cope with. The resulting tragedy is the penalty imposed by fate for any departure from the basic ideal of the Winnebago, that proportion be observed in all matters. It represents the price to be paid for any deviation from that fundamental sense of reality which ordains—as implied in the examples quoted—that an old man may not enjoy what is the prerogative of youth nor a youth hope to escape death. It is with both of these themes that the following Winnebago tales deal. As an ethical corollary to the last we find the doctrine that power desired for its own sake entails destruction not only for one's self but for others as well.

We have here three sources for a possible development of the sense of tragedy and doom. Now the idea of doom, although closely bound up with that of tragedy, contains one marked difference. Tragedy may and does result from accidental circumstances, whereas doom means more specifically the inevitable tragedy arising from the expression of certain ambitions, feelings, and desires which, though easily explicable, bring only ruin in their train. This holds true even though humanly speaking the situation in which the actions are placed allows little liberty of choice. Thus it would be well-nigh impossible for a devout old Winne-bago who has suddenly come upon what looks like an exceptionally holy lake, not to ponder upon the nature and the powers possessed by the spirits presumably in control of it; or to expect him not to visualize the good fortune of the youth whose happy fate it will be to fast there. It is only natural that he should thereupon think of his son as that happy youth. Yet in thus allowing his son to act as his surrogate he has sealed his son's doom. Similarly it is not to be supposed that a boy, goaded on by an overambitious and power-seeking father, should know how to observe proper and reasonable limits in his demands on life, nor can it be supposed that, unaided, he will possess sufficient discrimination to separate a pretended from a real benefactor.

Now this is the underlying theme of the tale of the "Traveller." Perhaps it is even too much to ask—this is the theme of the third tale—that a youthful faster who is filled with the praises of the powers of the spirits about to appear to him, should give up his demand for immortality. An inevitable and inexorable chain of events, all of them explicable from a human standpoint, impels these people onward and constrains them to their doom just as bitterly as in Greek tragedy. But here it is not an external crime with its inevitable punishment but an inner transgression, flowing from the very nature of human cravings followed by an inevitable retribution. And the sin committed is one difficult for erring man to guard against—that of attempting to attain something which is beyond human power.

I think that I am not lifting simple tales out of their proper context in making the above claims. Throughout the area inhabited by the woodland tribes of Canada and the United States, overfasting entails death. The Ojibwa believe that those who fast too long either die or are transformed into tenuous apparitions so light that the faintest human breath can blow them away. Among the Winnebago overfasting is popularly supposed to mean death. In the three tales to be discussed all that has been added is a motivation and an interpretation for this death. That defeat and death should be ascribed to some exaggeration, to some pardonable yet regrettable human frailty, is a motif exceedingly common in Winnebago mythology. Thus in one of the versions of the myth of the "Twins," the uncle of the heroes is defeated because he permitted himself to lose his temper. "The bad spirit," it there says, "was jealous of your uncle and provoked him till he lost his temper and then defeated him."

Humility, modesty, and a sense of proportion are the cardinal virtues whose practice is repeatedly urged upon young people. It should not be regarded as either strange or unusual that something in the nature of a true sense of the tragedy of life, or of a mystical groping for what lies beyond human power, should have developed among certain individuals. This it is that finds expression in these tales. I do not for a moment contend that either all or even a large number of the Winnebago were capable of so philosophical an outlook. For the vast majority death was simply a consequence of overfasting and thus may very well have been little more than a superstitious bogey; but this, of course, in no way excludes the existence of a more advanced attitude, shared by the few and found definitely inculcated in occasional tales and myths.

Let us now turn to tales themselves. I have selected three, one called "The Traveller," the second, "The Seer," and the third, "The Faster."

The hero of the first is nicknamed "Traveller" in satirical allusion to the fact that from his earliest infancy he never rested. He is the only son of one of the four great water spirits created by the supreme deity, Earthmaker, to hold the earth in position. To distinguish these primal spirits from most others, Earthmaker is supposed to have molded them with his own hands and it was thus their great boast that they were not born of woman.

From earliest childhood Traveller evinced interest only in visiting the remotest corners of the universe. While he was thus frittering away his time, a terrible fate was being prepared for his people. The thunderbirds, the hereditary and implacable foes of the water spirits, were planning to annihilate them. When, therefore, the young man returns from one of his journeys he finds his father utterly disconsolate, sitting with bowed head in a corner of the room. When asked the cause of his worry the father bursts out into bitter reproaches and sarcasm against his good-for-nothing

son and explains to him finally the fate about to overwhelm them all. The son is told that although a council of the water spirits is to take place that day it
seems quite clear that destruction is not to be averted.
Much to the father's surprise and indignation the son
immediately offers to meet the son of the chief of the
thunderbirds in single combat. At this the father jeers
but when he realizes how serious is his son's resolve,
his anger and sarcasm change to solicitude and he be-
seeches him that if he must go, he should at least wait
till his parents are dead so that they will not have to
bear the sorrow of his death. The young man, however, remains obdurate and prepares to put his plan
into execution.

The story then continues as follows:

Near the spot where Traveller stood was the center-pole
of the lodge. At its base appeared a hole and through this
he crawled, subsequently emerging on the other side under
the earth. He was then near his home. There he took what
he needed and immediately started out again. He again
crawled down through the base of the center-pole and continued travelling under the earth until he finaly came to
the mouth of the Mississippi. Up this river he proceeded
until he had passed its source and approached a hardly
noticeable dried-up spring. All that could be detected of
it was a moist spot. This spring originally had been the
door of a lodge standing there in former times. Then he
repaired it and placed guards at the entrance. The spring
was very pleasant to behold so he remained there.

Soon he noticed that a human being was fasting near by. When brought into his presence Traveller said, "Grandson, I am going to give you a blessing. You are the first one to receive one from me. Because you have made yourself suffer so much, because you have thirsted yourself to death, because you have made yourself so truly a compassion-inspiring a spectacle, you shall attain to the full length of years. You shall die of old age. Remember that a normal life is very short. I was not born of a woman's womb but Earthmaker molded me with his own hands."

The young man went away and then told his father of the blessing he had received. "My son, it is good. The water spirits are the greatest spirits in the world. You have had a good dream."

The young man fasted again and after four days and four nights of fasting the attendants of Traveller came for him again. When he was brought before Traveller the latter said, "Grandson, I am going to bestow my blessing upon you again because you have made yourself a com-passion-inspiring object with your weeping. I am one of the greatest spirits Earthmaker created and never before have I bestowed my gifts upon any one. But now that you have received them you must not fast any longer. All the spirits know that I have given you these gifts and no one else will say anything to you (i.e., give you similar ones). And, indeed, who is my equal? Who could give you a greater blessing than mine? So do not fast any longer. You shall never be in want of anything. Your lodge shall always be supplied with the things you need." Then the young man looked at the lodge and saw that it was filled with everything desirable. "All these," continued Traveller, "I bestow upon you."

The young man went away and told his father of what he had dreamt, and the father again said, "My son, that is a good dream. Fast again."

Then the young man fasted again for four nights and for four days, and at the end of that time the attendants of Traveller came after him again. When, as before, he was brought before the Traveller this one said, "Grandson, I have bestowed my blessings upon you already. I told you before that I had done so and I told you to stop but yet you persist. Everything that you can possibly desire I have bestowed upon you; all the things that human beings possess, all these I have given you."

Then the young man went away and told his father. "Now then, my son, it is good. I told you to fast again, and you have done it. Indeed, it is good. These water spirits are very great spirits. So fast, my son, again."

So the young man fasted again for four nights and once again the Traveller sent for him. "Grandson," he said, "stop fasting. I told you that long ago, but evidently I cannot make you understand. I knew, however, all the time that you were seeking that which I am now about to bestow upon you. Tell me, of what value is it to kill a person? Earthmaker did not create me for that purpose but I am, nevertheless, in control of great war gifts. The first time you go on the warpath you will be the leader. You will receive as your victim a man who possesses no weapons with which to defend himself. Go, for you will be victorious. The second time you go on the warpath, if you so desire it, you will have two men. The third time you will kill three men and the fourth time a whole village. And in addition I thought that it would not be necessary for you to make use of my body (for medicines), but now I have resolved to let you see my body. Tomorrow, at noon, you will see me and then may prepare medicines for yourself from my 'bones.' As long as the human race lasts so long will this medicine chest made from my bones endure. But remember when I say 'day' I mean what I call day and you call the middle of summer. And when I say my body is there I don't mean in that precise spot. My body is the water and wherever there is water there will you see me. When the time for you to come has approached I shall let you know. Grandson, I have given you my blessings and I want you to bring your relatives with you when you come to obtain your medicine chest. I shall see to it that the animals you desire shall emerge from the water. I shall feed you all. Now, grandson, what more can you want? So do not fast again and go home immediately. Remember, you must come back in the morning, that is, at noon."

The young man went home and told his father what had happened. "My son," said the latter, "this is good. You have dreamt for all your people. I thought this was going to happen and that is why I asked you to fast again." Then the father thanked the boy again.

The young man now stopped fasting. The people of the village were told of the promise made by the water spirit so they all moved to another place. When they got there they found many bears, otters, beavers, etc., and had plenty of food.

Now the summer came and the time mentioned by the Traveller was at hand. Then Traveller said to the youth, "Come alone and bring your offerings in a boat." The place where he was to go was called Big Lake (Lake Winnebago). The next morning at the appointed time the young man went there. He put all the necessary offerings into a boat and started out. About noon he seemed to notice something and as he looked attentively he perceived some drizzling rain. Then he heard a roaring sound and the earth shook. The roaring became very loud and there in the mist he suddenly saw a man smiling at him. Above the place where the man stood the colors of the rainbow were visible; eight rainbows, one above the other. Around this man's waist was wrapped four times the tail of a water spirit. The water spirit was unconscious. Neither of the two combatants (the water spirit and the thunderbird) was able to extricate himself from the other's grasp.

Suddenly the water spirit said, "Grandson, it is your fault that I have come to this. I gave you my blessing and I promised to show you my body. This person here, my enemy, heard it and came first. Grandson, he has caused me to suffer very much, so shoot him for my sake."

Then the thunderbird spoke, "Ah my younger brother, what this person has just said is untrue. My younger brother, he is your enemy, so shoot him for my sake for he has caused me to suffer very much."

Then Traveller replied, "Grandson, it is he who is telling you an untruth. If he is really such a good friend of yours, why did he never pay any attention to you? Indeed, he is not telling you the truth. He has not done for you what I have done. If he is your brother and is speaking the truth you would have known it long ago. So shoot him for me for he has caused me to suffer very much."

"My younger brother, he is not telling you the truth. He has not in reality bestowed any blessing upon you at all (i.e., in order to benefit you). He did it because he wanted you to come here in order to help him. We are, in truth, brothers and this one is your enemy. He never would really have given you anything. My younger brother, he has caused me to suffer, so shoot him for me."

Thus they kept on for a long time. Whenever the water spirit spoke the young man believed him and whenever the thunderbird spoke the young man believed him in turn. Finally he was convinced that the thunderbird was telling the truth and was just on the point of shooting the water spirit when the latter, realizing his intention, said, "Well and good, shoot me. In truth you do not know how to appreciate what I have done. This, too, remember, if you shoot me, that I am not the only water spirit in existence. Remember that water is my body. Never touch water, therefore, for it will be the body of a water spirit you are then touching and it will be a continual reminder to you of me. All the water spirits hear me. But you yourself will not escape anyhow." Frightened at this speech the young man shot the thunderbird.

"O my! O my! Younger brother! He did not conquer me fairly. Indeed, we have not been defeated fairly! Had I known that he was going to do this I, too, would have bestowed blessings upon you as he did. He has defeated me by treachery, younger brother. This, indeed, must have been his intention for he covered his tracks when he came here. Younger brother, he lied to you when he told you that he was one of the greatest spirits Earthmaker created. That is not true. He is only the son of such a one and he was born of a woman's womb. All that he has told you is untrue. Younger brother, since you have, however, done this you will not live much longer. Even now, on your return home, a large war party will come upon you and you will be the very first one to be killed. You have brought ruin upon all your relatives for they, too, will be slain."

That was all. The thunderbird was then taken under the water.

The young man's heart was filled with remorse but it was, of course, all of no avail for he had already shot the thunderbird. He went home and told his father what had happened. The old man talked excitedly, but there was nothing to be done about the matter any more. There was no help for anything now. Both started home and on their way they were attacked by a war party and all those who had been occupants of the old man's lodge were killed. Those not related to him escaped unharmed.

Let us now examine this extraordinary and dramatic tale. In the second and fourth paragraphs of the story, we have Traveller represented as bestowing upon the youth what is the normal blessing, one to which all people look forward and one that lay very well within the powers of any spirit to give. What first strikes us as strange is the manner in which Traveller makes his boasts and the deliberate falsehood of his claims. He here sins against two tenets of Winnebago ethics— never to boast and never to lie. At every ceremony people who recount their achievements are cautioned against exaggeration. "Always say a little less," the older people tell them. It is, indeed, quite obvious that the boasting and falsehood are here put into Traveller's mouth for a definite purpose, that purpose being to depreciate him. Stylistically, in Winnebago myths, such words foreshadow the defeat of the speaker. So, for example, in one of the versions of the myth of the "Twins," we have the uncle of the heroes and his enemy before they attempt the test which is to decide their fate, talking to each other as follows:

"You are not equal to me," they said to one another. "I am one of the greatest that Earthmaker has created," both of them said. Finally the uncle got angry and took his pipe. "I am one of the greatest that Earthmaker has created," he thought, and that is why he was not afraid to get angry.

Every Winnebago hearing this would assume that the man so speaking would be defeated. The same holds for the statements of Traveller in the opening paragraphs. All the sympathy of the Winnebago audience would from the beginning be against Traveller. The father, so the Winnebago might feel, should, however, have been suspicious from the first. The explanation of the unusual behavior of the father is to be sought in the fact that the depreciation of the Traveller is probably a secondary reinterpretation; and secondly

—and this is the important point—in the fact that the father is to be represented as a selfish and over-ambitious man.

Thus far all the transgressing has been done by Traveller. In paragraph 7 we have, however, the first suggestion of a new complication. There, in spite of Traveller's express statement to the youth that he was to cease fasting, the father tells him to continue. An interesting point is here involved. Up to this point Traveller has bestowed upon the youth only such powers as he really possessed. His transgression has consisted only in his boasting and in his falsehood. He apparently does not want to transcend his powers. The father, however, forces his hand. The whole burden of guilt is now transferred to father and son, and the Winnebago audience realizes instantly that they are dealing with an instance of a youth who has fasted too long. From the Winnebago point of view the sin which father and son commit is infinitely greater than that of Traveller, for the former have allowed themselves to be beguiled into a quest for power as such. The father has allowed his craving for power to overwhelm him and he is using his son as a surrogate for himself. The faster is obviously helpless between a dishonest spirit and a selfish, ambitious father. Yet something can be said for the father. To realize that a water spirit has appeared to his son, and not to desire those things almost always associated with the specific gifts in their bestowing—the opportunity of seeing the spirit himself and preparing medicines from his "bones"—that is asking the normal prestige-hunting Winnebago to exercise a well-nigh superhuman control.

Thus at the very outset we find an innocent boy caught between a cunning deity and the ambitions of a father, an old man tempted beyond endurance. Both of these facts are preliminary elements in the tragedy that is to unfold itself.

From another point of view, too, the second speech of Traveller in the fourth paragraph is interesting, for therein is contained the enunciation of the approved Winnebago theory of ethics by one of the spirits himself. "What more can a man want than I have bestowed?" he asks in substance. "You have received long life and the promise that all your wishes are to be gratified." What the normal, sensible Winnebago father would then have said is put into the mouth of the spirit: "Stop fasting now." The author of this version of the tale evidently wished to impress upon his hearers this important truth. Yet this does not in the least detract from the fact that it is put into Traveller's mouth because it is the latter's definite design to throw the guilt on to the human pair.

The motivation and plot elaboration are unusually good. Traveller is depicted as an exceedingly crafty and cunning individual. From the very beginning it is clear that the water spirits, unaided, cannot win and Traveller therefore plans to obtain human aid; so he binds son and father to him by catering to their will-to-power in such a manner, however, that all initiative ostensibly is placed in their hands. In making his claim to be one of the greatest spirits in the world he is, of course, throwing out a bait which few Winnebago would have refused.

Once they have taken the initiative, he can safely warn the boy to stop fasting, and protest, as he does in the eighth paragraph, against being coerced into bestowing upon him specific victory on the warpath, into showing himself in person, and in allowing medicines to be prepared from his "bones." By this time father and son are hopelessly enmeshed in their destiny. Traveller had obtained the one thing he desired, the gratitude of the youth, and on this gratitude is to depend his victory over the thunderbird. The skill of the motivation is particularly manifest in the way in which the ulterior purpose of Traveller is made to fit into the accepted Winnebago yearnings and ideals and into their concept of "sin." It was rather normal, though admittedly dangerous, for a Winnebago to attempt to obtain the final blessing of the water spirit; namely, the right to use his "bones." For Traveller to insist, therefore, that the faster should stop after one or two attempts and after he had received what hundreds of spirits could have given him, seems unreasonable. He gives the youth this right because he realizes that he would be disobeyed and that, in fact, his refusal would act really not as a deterrent but as an incentive to further efforts. "Blessings are not to be obtained easily," the Winnebago say. It is Traveller's purpose, as we have seen, to compel the young man to force the spirit's hand and to make the latter bestow upon him what he did not possess—the gift of specific victory over the enemy. The essential object is to obtain unflinching gratitude, and thus the boy receives long life, gratification of all wishes, the "bones" of the water spirit, and victory on the warpath, the last two gifts drawn, so to speak, from Traveller against his will.

In this whole scene everything is quite normal and it is in fact this normality that largely contributes to the pathos of the whole situation.

Reverting again to the narrative, we find nothing of real importance until we come to the very dramatic scene described in the twelfth paragraph. The water spirit and the thunderbird are there represented in mortal combat. Traveller, true to his rôle of the crafty deceiver, accuses the youth of having brought him into his present predicament because of the promise exacted that he would appear to him in person. He reminds the youth of the gifts bestowed and calls upon him to shoot the thunderbird. In other words, the youth is now to show his gratitude, and as payment for his culpability in Traveller's plight, to help the latter in his combat against the thunderbird. The thunderbird's answer in the thirteenth paragraph is the first intimation that has come to the unfortunate youth that deception has been practiced. Traveller's reply is quite unanswerable. In the fifteenth paragraph the thunderbird informs the boy that everything Traveller has said and pretended is false, that the whole purpose of the latter has been to entice him to the lake so that the youth could aid him. The young man is naturally in a frightful predicament. His instinct would, of course, be to help his supposed benefactor—yet he wavers. To those unacquainted with Winnebago beliefs this hesitation must seem unwarranted. It is entirely due to the fact that to-day the thunderbird is the favorite deity of the Winnebago and his honesty and virtues are considered self-evident.

The end of the story is a double and poignant tragedy, with the defeat of the most popular of Winnebago deities and the death of a youthful and innocent faster.

We must now turn to an entirely different aspect of this tale. Although Traveller is manifestly the hero, all Winnebago sympathy goes to the thunderbird and, were this regarded as a myth and not as a real happening, the audience would undoubtedly have expected the thunderbird to triumph. Heroes are frequently killed but their death is always temporary and they are eventually restored to life even if it takes a generation. Here no such thing happens. What is manifestly a myth in every essential particular, with the exception of the fasting experience, is put into the category of a tale, interpreted as a real happening, and given an unrelieved tragic ending.

The central facts we have first to elucidate are the victory of the water spirit and the transfer of what was presumably a myth to the category of a tale. The explanation of the victory of this particular water spirit is comparatively simple. It is a very old and still general belief that the oldest spirits in the world are those created by the Earthmaker to hold the world in position and to keep it from moving. These are four water spirits. Equally old was the belief that there are five worlds, one above the other, and that the central one is ruled over by a water spirit called Traveller. Traveller cannot be defeated because this would run counter to an accepted fact of Winnebago cosmology. His position is so secure that not even the famous hero-deities of the Winnebago, the Twins, in their reckless wanderings over the universe make an attempt to interfere with it.

It is evident, therefore, that Traveller cannot be depicted as being defeated. Why, however, is he drawn in such unfavorable colors? Why is he not the unblemished hero of the tale? Here, too, the explanation is fairly simple. Water spirits to-day are regarded by the Winnebago as either definitely evil or dangerous because of the twofold nature of the gifts they bestow. In some respects their gifts are regarded as the greatest within the power of any spirit to grant. A definite ambivalent feeling does, nevertheless, attach to everything concerned with them and on the whole the evil side is believed to predominate. But the myths and certain folk beliefs indicate quite clearly that this was not always so; that at one time the water spirit was as moderately benevolent as the thunderbird. The older conception of the nature of the spirits among the Winnebago also indicates a belief in the twofold classi-

fication of good and bad. The thunderbirds formed
no exception to this rule and in a number of myths the
bad thunderbirds are described in a very unfavorable
light. Under the influence of a marked tendency
toward systematization this old dual concept has been
abandoned and most spirits to-day are regarded as
either good or bad. The water spirits have been
largely put into the bad and the thunderbirds into the
good class. Traveller, therefore, as a representative
of the water spirits, had to be represented as evil.
This could only be done by so motivating the incidents
connected with him that they would appear in a most
unfavorable light. He is consequently depicted as a
boaster, a liar, and a deceiver. The attainment of the
position which he occupied and from which he could
not be displaced had to be attributed to the most
despicable of maneuvers entailing the death of an unfortunate human being. If he could not be hurled from
his predominant position in the tale he could at least
be transformed into the arch-villain of the piece. If
additional corroboration for this interpretation of his
rôle were really wanting it could be furnished by the
fact that this is the only myth or tale collected among
the Winnebago where the hero is a villain and yet
succeeds.

The villainy of the hero thus reflects a definite
change in the viewpoint of the Winnebago, a definite
historical event; namely, the displacement of one cult
by another. The tale we have before us is then nothing
more or less than a reinterpretation, in terms of a

predominantly thunderbird civilization, of a water spirit victory. The real hero had to be depreciated and the victim, the thunderbird, elevated to the position of hero, and it was this readjustment that rendered the tragic ending inevitable.

So much for the fate of the thunderbird. I take it that originally the aid of the human faster was legitimately obtained and that he was depicted as trying to get into *rapport* with one of the greatest of the spirits. With the exception of the specific gift of victory on the warpath—which in this form was associated, to my knowledge, only with the thunderbirds, the sun, and the evening star—the gifts bestowed are those expected from a water spirit. It was the change in the cultural background that necessitated the youth's death because he helped a water spirit, and it was the new attitude, also, that compelled such thoroughgoing changes in the motivation of detail upon detail of the actual fasting experience that it became transformed into an example of the inevitable dangers attendant upon over-fasting. The fasting experience, accordingly, takes on the appearance of a moral lesson and this explains why Traveller finds it necessary to point out to the youth that he must not demand more than an ordinary individual is entitled to. This is all secondary here. In the tales of the "Seer" and the "Faster," we shall see that these themes form the basic element in the plot. Yet, whether the reasons I have advanced for the motivation are true or not, the fact remains that in the present version the fate of the faster is sealed from

the very beginning; first, because he has been condemned to decide a conflict in which he had no concern, and, second, because he is coerced into transgressing certain cardinal elements of the Winnebago
moral code.

One point still remains to be answered. What is the
significance of the human faster? Why was it thought
necessary to have the time-old struggle between the
water spirits and the thunderbirds decided by human
agency? The calling in of a man to decide the conflict
of deities may be common in classical mythology but
it is extremely unusual in the mythology of primitive
peoples. Among the Winnebago the story of Traveller
is the only instance extant where such a theme, or
anything even remotely resembling it, occurs, and this
being so, I cannot but feel that some significance attaches to it. In my opinion the fasting experience was
not originally connected with the theme of this combat
of the water spirit with the thunderbird at all. That
theme is one of the most universal in North America
and only among the Winnebago and related tribes has
a faster become associated with it. He may have been
brought in originally in order to demonstrate the superiority of the water spirits over the thunderbirds, or
for various other reasons. In our version this episode
has clearly come to be the direct reflection of the larger
conflicts of the deities. It is thus the symbolical representation of the struggle for supremacy of two cults, of
two contending civilizations. The tragic dénouement
has, in this instance, essentially the same origin as that

of the *Iliad,* the *Nibelungenlied,* and the Quetzalcoatl myth of the ancient Aztec.

The second of my examples, the tale entitled "The Seer," is psychologically far more subtle than the first. As it is very short, I shall quote it in its entirety:

An old man once came upon what looked like a very holy lake. Its shores were steep and extended precipitously to the very top. Pine trees abounded everywhere. The old man stood watching the lake and then exclaimed, "This lake must indeed be very sacred and the various spirits who preside over it must be extremely powerful. *Would that I were young again!* Here, most assuredly, would I fast!" Thus he spoke. But then continuing he said, "But what am I saying? Have I not a son? *I shall make him fast here!"* So as soon as he arrived at his home he constructed a place for his son to stay and then besought him to fast.

All winter long the son stayed there and fasted. Whenever his father came to see him he told him that as yet nothing had taken place. Three years the boy fasted there and yet he did not succeed in dreaming of anything. When, however, during the fourth year, his father came to him, the son addressed him as follows: "Father, at last I have received a blessing. The spirit asked for four offerings, tobacco, feathers, a dog, and a white deer; for these he asked. And then he asked ·for a fifth, a human life." When the boy finished the old man expressed his gratitude. Then he named the day on which this was to take place (i.e., the offerings were to be made). "He who is in control of this sacred lake," continued the youth, "I shall behold, I

was told. To him it is that you are to bring your offerings."
The father felt very happy. He went home and it was a
marked day.

Then the offerings were taken to the lake. There everything appeared to be in a turmoil and there was a tremendous noise. Every few minutes objects would emerge from
the water. The old man standing there thought to himself,
"Now, this is the time. Now it is going to appear." But
then again he would think to himself, "No, perhaps not."
Many things appeared; indeed, everything imaginable, and
finally out of the lake there rose a burning log, smoking.
When the disturbance had completely subsided the two saw
stretched out on the shore a very white water spirit; one of
the kind that cannot be butchered with an ordinary knife.
So the old man made himself a knife of red cedar wood
and with this he proceeded to cut up the water spirit. Out
of its body he began to make weapons of all kinds. One
piece of the body he cut off in order to prepare a certain
kind of drink, another in order to make a war medicine.
Out of the blood he made a magical paint which would
enable him to kill an enemy even if the latter were resting
within his own tent. The Winnebago would love this medicine (he thought). There was nothing this medicine could
not accomplish. Then he made a bad medicine which would
prevent any person from making his (the old man's) heart
ache or from making fun of him. The medicine was of a
kind that if he wished to kill a man he would merely have
to decide upon the day and then the man in question would
perish. Indeed if he merely fixed his thoughts upon a particular man, that man would suffer. He could, with this

medicine, make a man crazy, or he could deprive him of his soul. If a man were very far away and he but uttered his name, if he were but to murmur, "Let him die!" that man would die.

These were the medicines he made. No good ones did he make; only bad ones.

Then they made their offerings to the water spirit and when these were over the old man said to his son, "My dear son, let me myself be the offering." But the son said, "No, father, when you have grown old and death has come to you, then you shall live with the water spirit; you and he shall be companions." Thereupon the old man replied excitedly, "My dear son, even if this were to happen this very minute, indeed I should be satisfied." "Father, when you die, here at this sacred lake you shall live. Here forever shall you remain, as long as the earth lasts."

Then they went home to their people. The old man immediately began to use his bad medicines. Wherever a child was to be discovered who was especially beloved, wherever people were to be encountered who were unusually popular, the old man killed them. Soon the water spirit appeared to the young boy and said, "What is this your father is doing? He is killing those who are most beloved, men and children. This is not good. Tell him to stop. Tell him if he refuses he will be transformed into a rock. Earthmaker did not create me for the purpose (to which your father is now putting me) and he would be displeased if this continued."

So the youth went to the father and begged him to stop, telling him that if he refused he would be transformed into a rock. But the old man replied, "My dear son, I have now become so accustomed to what I am doing that I cannot stop."

The next morning the old man did not move and when his son looked at him he saw that he had become transformed into a rock.

So much for the story. Certain things are quite clear. The water spirit has, in addition to the usual four offerings, demanded a fifth, a human life, that of the faster. To emphasize this demand we see death symbolized by the smoking log emerging from the lake to which the two men have gone to make their offerings. Now this request of the spirits for a human sacrifice must not, of course, be taken too literally. Looked at from the viewpoint of the spirits, every time a person dies from overfasting or during his fast, it is because the spirits desired his life. In human terms it simply signifies that an individual has attempted something which entails death. We are again, as on page 65, dealing with an enunciation of the Winnebago ethical creed. Here, however, it is enunciated by the deities. We know the son to be doomed. From the very beginning, however, the father has kept the center of the stage and he does so again by insisting that he become the sacrifice the spirits desire. We see him before he has made this unusual request, ostentatiously preparing only bad medicines from the body of the water spirit, although good ones were also at his disposal. When the son refuses to accept his offer the old man deliberately kills all of those most beloved in his village and actually forces the water spirit to recognize him as the stipulated human offering. Why, it may be asked, does he insist upon taking his son's place? Why, if he is to die, does not his son die also? That the death of the faster may include that of his father and all of his relatives, we saw at the conclusion of the "Traveller."

To explain, let me call attention to the opening of the tale. That an old man should stand awe-stricken before the prospect of a particularly sacred lake is quite natural; that he should ponder over the exceptional gifts possessed by the spirits presiding over such a place—that, too, is quite intelligible. Every Winnebago would both understand and sympathize with him. His regret that he cannot be young again is hardly a transgression against Winnebago ethics unless he draws unwarranted corollaries therefrom. But this is exactly what he does. In his enthusiasm he uses his son as a surrogate for himself, and here, of course, he sins most egregiously against a fundamental tenet. To obtain something no longer within his reach, he selfishly sacrifices his son and compels him to attempt the propitiation of one of the most powerful and dangerous of all deities, one who frequently inflicts death. Even if the father had been represented as wanting his son to fast at this particularly sacred lake because of the great love he bore him and of a natural excess of ambition for the boy he would, according to Winnebago notions, have· laid himself open to criticism. A loving and solicitous father is supposed to spur on his child to persistent effort in the attainment of gifts from the spirits but he is, at the same time, supposed to be extremely careful that the boy does not overstep the limits of discretion in his demands. No such excuse can be offered for the father in this instance. There is not the slightest trace of solicitude. It is he who plainly desires the powers the spirits can bestow.

The expected takes places and the life of the son is demanded. To judge from the insistence with which the narrator emphasizes the nature of the medicines the old man prepares, we must assume that as soon as his son told him of the demand of the spirits he realized the heinousness of his offense. It should be remembered that the old man is depicted as erring through too much piety, that he is not conscious of either his will-to-power or extreme selfishness. Once this is brought home to him, however, he makes up his mind to forestall fate as far as that is possible. He realizes that some one has to die and he resolves that he and not his innocent son shall be the victim. How is he, however, to force the hands of the deities? His method is as ruthless as it is thorough. He must so behave, commit such crimes, that the spirits will slay him.

This, then, is the obvious interpretation of the tale. The doom that befalls the old man is that which overtakes all those who, whatever be their motives, be they good or bad, sin against that sense of the proportion of things which the realities of life impose upon us. The father had fasted as a young boy; he had presumably obtained his share of the gifts of the spirits. He had no right to demand more, no matter how overpowering the situation. Had it been possible to limit the consequences of his act to himself, little would have been said. But that is exactly what life makes impossible. Here the practical consequence of his religious enthusiasm, if one were inclined to place the most lenient construction upon it, is death for someone else.

In actual life the Winnebago made definite applications of this viewpoint. Any person, for instance, could go on the warpath, despite the express prohibitions of the chief of the tribe, and any one who desired might accompany him. If the individual who thus led an unauthorized war party were killed, that was his own affair. It was merely interpreted as suicide, and that was regarded as unfair and wrong because it inflicted pain upon one's relatives. But if any of the men who accompanied him were killed, the leader was guilty of murder. In other words, you must not implicate others in your unwarranted acts. That is the practical statement of the problem. Doom is simply the symbolical restatement.

In our tale it is a dreadful punishment that follows a humanly intelligible transgression. What seems to us an excusable error brings about death, and in order to avoid one death, two additional crimes—murder and suicide—must be committed. The chain of events is inevitable and inexorable.

One point has still to be considered. Why is the

father transformed into a rock and why does the son tell him that when his time has come he will become the permanent companion of the water spirit of the sacred lake? The wish of the father is thus, after all, granted, and he has, in a way, fasted and obtained his recompense. But he does not obtain it in the anticipated way. Not life but death is to give him the happiness he craved. In the form of a rock, something that will last as long as the earth endures, he is to stand on the shores of the sacred lake and contemplate the majesty of the powers who control it. But why should he who has wrought so much destruction be granted even this boon? The answer seems to be because, after his manner, he aimed high. He erred from excess of enthusiasm. At least deities and the priests of the deities may be presumed to take this tolerant view of the case. Die he must, for he has sinned and wrought ruin. For his high purpose, however, he is to be rewarded and his death mitigated by a measure of reincarnation.

A similar theme recurs in the following tale and it is not at all infrequent in Winnebago mythology. It is entitled "The Faster" and runs as follows:

There was once a man who had an only child. One day he said, "My child, you must know that you are all alone in the world (i.e., without the protection of the spirits), with no one from whom to hope for anything. Only the spirits can help you." Thus he spoke to his child.

Then the son fasted. After he had been fasting for some time his father came to him and said, "My dear son, you have now been fasting for a very long period. Surely you have obtained some gift from the spirits. You had better stop now." "Father," answered the boy, "you are quite right but still I should like to continue. All that you have told me to fast for, all that I have now obtained. I have received the gift of killing an enemy at will; I have obtained the gift of old age. Indeed, the spirits came to me and took me to a doctor's lodge and there they brought me to a person who was dead and told me that I could restore him to life again. It was then they told me not to fast any longer. Yet in spite of their request I continued. Then the spirits from below came, from the creation lodge they came, and they bestowed all things upon me—victory in war, the ability to cure the sick, success in hunting, a long and complete life—all this they gave me. Indeed every spirit to whom Earthmaker had given power, each one bestowed something upon me. 'You have fasted enough,' they said. But, father, what I most desire is that I shall not die. That is why I do not want to stop. So let me continue. Indeed, only when I have obtained that gift shall I stop."

So the youth continued. The spirits came to him and said, "Young man, you have fasted enough. Earthmaker has bestowed upon you the gift of living to extreme old age, of obtaining everything you wish." "I am grateful," said the boy, "but what I desire is never to die." The spirits could not dissuade him. "Indeed, I shall never be satisfied until I obtain the gift of immortal life," continued the boy. He was unable to face the thought of death; he dreaded it very much.

In the council lodge of the spirits it was accordingly decided that he should die. So they looked down upon the place where the boy was fasting and there he lay, dead. Then the spirits spoke to the father and said, "All that we promised your son, you shall have. Do not think about this matter (i.e., your son's death) any more and bury him."

Then the father dug a grave and buried him. "I wonder how it all happened," he thought to himself. "They told me they were unable to dissuade him, and it was for that reason that they killed him; they told me not to think of the matter any more."

Sometime after, when the father went to the grave, he noticed a tree growing at its head. That was his son. Only a tree lives forever, and that is why the spirits transformed him into a tree. The father realized it and was happy. He lived contented and prosperous thereafter.

Now this is what the father himself reported and it is because of this (i.e., the fate of the youth) that young people are told not to fast for too long a period.

In this tale we have the principal features found in the two preceding ones occurring again. But we have no treacherous water spirit and no father spurring on his child to attempt the impossible or the hazardous merely to gratify a parent's insatiable taste for power. On the contrary, both spirits and parents warn and even beseech the youth to stop fasting. The spirits are particularly kind and compassionate. It is the faster himself who is here at fault. The others are definitely absolved from all blame. In what way, however, is this boy represented as transgressing? In desiring the one thing that man cannot have, immortality. The spirits are gentle because they realize that the hopeless plea of this child is a pardonable one. He does not want more power but he wants to possess the normal gifts of life forever. They pity him, but he must die just as inevitably as the faster in the "Traveller," as the father in the "Seer," because this youth, too, although in a different manner, has come into conflict with reality. Yet in his case, so excusable is the tragic reaching after the unattainable, the spirits grant the bewildered father as recompense for the pain they are inflicting upon him in destroying his son, the gifts they had bestowed upon the boy, and allow him to realize that his son has attained the only kind of immortality vouchsafed to man, reincarnation in an object whose age in comparison to man's is unlimited. But the young man, too, is rewarded by resurrection as a tree. Insensate as his request was, he did, in an inexperienced and groping manner, aim high, for to face the perils of long fasting and to persist in prayer through discouragement is to aim high and deserve reward.

That a definite lesson was to be taught by this tale would be perfectly apparent even if the narrator had not thought fit to add his little epilogue. The proof that the main object was to teach young fasters not to ask for the impossible is given by the fact that there was really a method they might have tried in order to dissuade the faster from his obsession. He could have been told that although he must die there was always an excellent chance of his becoming reincarnated. Reincarnation is a fundamental belief of the Winnebago and it is something that every Winnebago feels is obtainable in a number of ways, the principal one being that of joining the Medicine Dance. I can well imagine a Winnebago father holding out such a hope to a son who feared the thought of death. And it is, as a matter of fact, reincarnation that he is granted. There was not a word about it in the tale because a specific lesson was to be taught.

Thus all of our examples illustrate a specific conception of tragedy and doom. In the first, the faster and the father are destroyed because they have become enmeshed in a battle of the gods in which they had no concern; in the second, doom overtakes the father because he is seeking something he already possessed, and which, from the nature of the case is no longer possible for him, because he involves innocent people in the consequences of his overreaching; in the third instance, finally, doom follows inevitably from the fact that what is desired lies beyond human power. In all we find the cardinal tenet of Winnebago ethics enunciated, that death is the lot of all who sin against reality and the sense of proportion, and who involve others in their self-initiated transgression.

CHAPTER XII

MYSTICISM AND SYMBOLISM

A T a very early period of our contact with primitive peoples observers had already remarked on the strain of mysticism and symbolism found in their thought, their rituals, and their art. As we came to know them better these mystic and symbolic elements, far from decreasing in importance and significance, loomed even larger. To-day many investigators would probably insist that only when we have fully grasped the mystic and symbolic meanings inherent in most of the activities of primitive man can we hope to understand him. There is a very large element of truth in this contention, and it is certainly an arresting and fundamentally significant fact that whenever we obtain descriptions of their own culture from natives, symbolism and mysticism predominate. All this must be unhesitatingly granted. Yet it is a far cry from such an admission to the assumption that primitive man is inherently a mystic or that his thinking is not rational or logical like ours, but consists rather of a succession of symbols; or, if you wish, that his ostensible logical thinking is affected by all kinds of symbolic adhesions and references. Many theorists have made this assumption and have brought what must seem to many incontrovertible evidence for the correctness of their thesis.

Yet I, for one, feel rather definitely that there has been something of an overemphasis on this aspect of primitive thought for a variety of reasons. It is first of all easier to understand mysticism and symbolism than many other aspects of primitive culture. Secondly, they appeal to our imagination and have a tendency to evoke whatever mysticism and symbolism lies embedded in most of us. This is, indeed, one of the subtle dangers we must all guard against. However, I do not wish to stress this side of the question. In estimating the importance and the rôle of mysticism and symbolism we must bear in mind that it is misleading to emphasize unduly their presence in art and ritual. They are present in all art and ritual.

But leaving art and ritual aside I see no evidence for their dominating primitive life and thought to anything like the degree we are accustomed to believe. It is undoubtedly true that owing to the attitude assumed toward the nature of reality and personality, much of primitive man's thought seems eminently non-logical and mystical, but our analysis in Chapters XIII and XIV has shown that this is really an erroneous impression which disappears as soon as we become better acquainted with the facts in the case. It should likewise be remembered that a good deal of symbolism, at least that of primitive peoples, is stereotyped and often of a highly artificial and conscious nature. Take, for instance, the symbolical representation in literature of the four ages of man—a favorite subject in certain North American Indian tribes. Wherever among the Winnebago these ages are described, the same symbols are used; symbols that upon investigation turned out to be mere literary *clichés*. In other words the treatment is quite identical with that existing in such highly sophisticated and formal literatures as those of China and Japan.

To show how extremely sophisticated and conscious such symbolism and mysticism can become, let me quote a few examples from a ritual of the Winnebago which prides itself upon its twofold significance, a literal and a symbolical one. For example, where the literal meaning of the text has, "He bit the fish and light filled the gap made," the symbolical mystical meaning which has become stereotyped and is handed down from one generation to another is, "He imprinted daylight (life) upon the middle of the body." Or again, where the text reads, "He lay down on his back and pressed the stone to his breast and daylight (life) burst forth from his navel," this turns out to be but a stereotyped way, peculiar to this ceremony, of saying that "as the water was poured on the heated stone clouds of steam arose." "The tied hair of our grand-mother touches the turtle" merely signifies that the sprinkler has been placed on the water.

Of a much higher order is the mystical and quite secondary interpretation of an incident in one of the myths told in this ritual. Earthmaker, the Winnebago creator, is represented as taking a white cloud and a

blue cloud, combining them, and throwing the new substance, the nature of which is not specifically mentioned, toward the earth. As it floats downward it
pushes aside the bad clouds and is finally seized by an
otter, the last of Earthmaker's animal creations. The
mystical meaning of this passage runs as follows: By
rolling together the white and blue clouds Earthmaker
created the most important object in the ceremony, the
shell by whose means death and reincarnation are obtained. As this shell floats downward towards the
earth it dissipates all evil and is seized by that animal
who was of the least consequence and importance,
the otter. The otter was, in fact, the synonym in
Winnebago culture for stupidity and simplicity.
What is referred to here is the bag made of otter
skin used in the ceremony as a receptacle for the
sacred shell.

Now here we have an example of very profound
mysticism and yet it is, at least to-day, very definitely
a *cliché,* quite meaningless to the uninitiated and probably meaningless to a large number of the initiated.
It seems quite justifiable to assume that it was the
interpretation of a specifically gifted individual. And
this brings me to the point I wish particularly to mention, that having once shown the existence of a purely
secondary, conscious, and somewhat sophisticated type
of mysticism and symbolism among primitive peoples,
quite identical with that encountered among ourselves,
we have no right to assume that mysticism and symbolism play an inherently more dominant rôle among

the former than among us. I should not for a moment deny that mysticism and symbolism, particularly in its formal aspect, are more frequently utilized among them than among Western Europeans to-day. I doubt, however, whether they are more extensively used among primitive peoples than among the Chinese and Japanese, and yet those who really know the Chinese and Japanese would hesitate to characterize their thought as more specifically mystical and symbolical than our own.

Whether we shall ultimately, on the basis of authentic and critically controlled data, be able to prove that the prevailing impression—namely, that primitive peoples are in their thought more mystical or symbolical than ourselves—is right or not, I have surely furnished enough evidence to show that they have often elaborated their mysticism and symbolism in a highly conscious manner. To prove that point still further I shall devote the rest of this chapter to poems in which this symbolism and mysticism have attained a very high degree of literary excellence.

I

THE WATER OF KANE

A query, a question,
I put to you:
Where is the water of Kane?
At the Eastern Gate
Where the Sun comes in at Haehae;
There is the water of Kane.

A question I ask of you:
Where is the water of Kane?
Out there with the floating Sun,
Where cloud-forms rest on Ocean's breast,
Uplifting their forms at Nihoa,
This side the base of Lehua;
There is the water of Kane.

One question I put to you:
Where is the water of Kane?
Yonder on mountain peak,
On the ridges steep,
In the valleys deep,
Where the rivers sweep;
There is the water of Kane.

This question I ask of you:
Where, pray, is the water of Kane?
Yonder, at sea, on the ocean,
In the driving rain,
In the heavenly bow,
In the piled-up mist-wraith,
In the blood-red rainfall,
In the ghost-pale cloud-form;
There is the water of Kane.

One question I put to you:
Where, where is the water of Kane?
Up on high is the water of Kane,
In the heavenly blue,
In the black piled cloud,
In the black, black cloud,
In the black-mottled sacred cloud of the gods;
There is the water of Kane.

One question I ask of you:
Where flows the water of Kane?
Deep in the ground, in the gushing spring,
In the ducts of Kane and Loa,
A well-spring of water, to quaff,
A water of magic power—
The water of life!
Life! O give us this life!

Hawaii

II

I ran into the swamp confused,
There I heard the tadpoles singing.
I ran into the swamp confused,
Where the bark-clothed tadpoles sang.

In the west the dragonfly wanders,
Skimming the surfaces of the pools,
Touching only with his tail. He skims
With flapping and rustling wings.

Thence I ran as the darkness gathers,
Wearing cactus flowers in my hair.
Thence I ran as the darkness gathers,
In fluttering darkness to the singing-place.

Pima, Arizona

III

At the time of the white dawning,
At the time of the white dawning,
I arose and went away,
At Blue Nightfall I went away.

Pima, Arizona

IV

The evening glow yet lingers,
The evening glow yet lingers:
And I sit with my gourd rattle
Engaged in the sacred chant.
As I wave the eagle feathers
We hear the magic sounding.

The strong night is shaking me,
Just as once before he did
When in spirit I was taken
To the great magician's house.

Pima, Arizona

V

Pitiable harlot though I am,
My heart glows with the singing
While the evening yet is young.
My heart glows with the singing.

Pima, Arizona

VI

Now the swallow begins his singing;
Now the swallow begins his singing;
And the women who are with me,
The poor women commence to sing.

The swallows met in the standing cliff;
The swallows met in the standing cliff;
And the rainbows arched above me,
There the blue rainbow-arches met.

Pima, Arizona

VII

Down from the houses of magic,
Down from the houses of magic;
Blow the winds, and from my antlers
And my ears, they stronger gather.

Over there I ran trembling,
Over there I ran trembling,
For bows and arrows pursued me,
Many bows were on my trail.

Pima, Arizona

VIII

In the reddish glow of the nightfall,
In the reddish glow of the nightfall.
I return to my burrow
About which the flowers bloom.

With the four eagle feathers,
With the four eagle feathers,
I stir the air. When I turn
My magic power is crossed.

Pima, Arizona

IX

This my wish, my burning desire,
That in the season of slumber
Thy spirit my soul may inspire,
    A star-dweller,
    Heaven-guest,
    Soul-awakener,
Bird from covert calling,
Where forest champions stand.

There roamed I too with Laka,
Of Lea and Loa, a wilderness child;
On ridge, in forest boon companion she
To the heart that throbbed in me.
  O Laka, O Laka,
Hark to my call!
You approach, it is well;
You possess me, I am blessed!

Hawaii

X

A PRAYER TO KANE

Now, Kane, approach, illumine the altar;
Stoop, and enlighten mortals below;
Rejoice in the gifts I have brought.
Wreathed goddess fostered by Kapo—
Hail Kapo, of beauty resplendent!
Great Kapo, of sea and land,
The topmost stay and anchoring line.
Kapo sits in her darksome covert;
On the terrace, at Mo-o-he-lala,
Stands the god-tree of Ku, on Mauna-loa.
God Kaulana-ula twigs now mine ear,
His whispered suggestion to me is
This payment, sacrifice, offering,
Tribute of praise to thee, O Kapo divine.
Inspiring spirit in sleep, answer my call.
Behold, of *lehua* bloom of Kaana
The women are stringing enough
To enwreathe goddess Kapo;
Kapo, great queen of that island,
Of the high and the low.
The day of revealing shall see what it sees:
A seeing of facts, a sifting of rumors,

An insight won by the black sacred *awa*,
A vision like that of a god!
O Kapo, return!
Return and abide in your altar!
Make it fruitful!
Lo, here is the water,
The water of life!
Hail, now, to thee!

Hawaii

XI

The Chant of the Symbolic Colors

With what shall the little ones adorn their bodies, as they
tread the path of life? it has been said, in this house.
The crimson color of the God of Day who sitteth in the
heavens,
They shall make to be their sacred color, as they go forth
upon life's journey.
Verily, the god who reddens the heavens as he approaches,
They shall make to be their sacred color, as they go forth
upon life's journey.
When they adorn their bodies with the crimson hue shed
by that God of Day,
Then shall the little ones make themselves to be free from
all causes of death, as they go forth upon life's journey.

What shall the people use for a symbolic plume? they said
to one another, it has been said, in this house.
Verily, the God who always comes out at the beginning of
day,
Has at his right side
A beam of light that stands upright like a plume.
That beam of light shall the people make to be their sacred
plume.

When they make of that beam of light their sacred plume,
Then their sacred plume shall never droop for want of
strength as they go forth upon life's journey.

What shall they place as a pendant upon his breast? they
said to one another.
The shell of the mussel who sitteth upon the earth,
They shall place as a pendant upon his breast.
It is as the God of Day who in the heavens,
Close to their breast they shall verily press this god;
As a pendant upon his breast they shall place this god.
Then shall the little ones become free from all causes of
death, as they go forth upon life's journey.

Verily, at that time and place, it has been said, in this
house,
They said to one another: What shall the people place
upon his wrists?
It is a bond spoken of as the captive's bond,
That they shall place upon his wrists.
Verily, it is not a captive's bond,
That is spoken of,
But it is a soul
That they shall place upon his wrists.

Verily at that time and place, it has been said, in this house,
They said to one another: What is he upon whom a girdle
is to be placed?
Verily, it is not a captive that is spoken of,
It is a spirit upon whom they will place a girdle, they said,
it has been said, in this house.
Verily at that time and place, it has been said, in this house,
They said to one another: What is he upon whose feet these
moccasins are to be placed?

It is a captive
Upon whose feet these moccasins are to be placed.
Verily, it is not a captive that is spoken of,
It is a spirit
Upon whose feet these moccasins are to be placed, they
said, it has been said, in this house.

Osage, Oklahoma

XII

Priest's Prayer to Pupil About to Be Admitted to Instruction

By the occult powers of the dark, of the light, ages—
Such powers as thou, O Rongo-marae-roa (god of peace),
can exert.
Be fruitful, be plentiful, give the great and enduring power
to remove all evil—
The inherent original power, unto me, unto this one.

Be fruitful thy knowledge as also the love of it,
Be fruitful as the learned high priests of old,
Be fruitful thy memory, as the all-knowing gods,
Be fruitful of all things outside, as far as the thoughts may
extend,
Be fruitful of knowledge of the Sacred Heavens—
Of the Heavens where first arose the priests,
To the distant Heavens, to those divided from the upper-
most Heavens,

O Io-e.

Disclose thy way with the ancient and erudite,
The way of the Gods, O Io-the-origin-of-all-things!
Cause to descend without and beyond—
To descend within these pupils, these sons;
(That their memories may acquire the support of the gods)

The ancient learning, the occult learning,
      By thee, O Io-e.

Grow, grow, as young sprouts, shooting up like spreading
    leaves
The ardent desire towards thee, O Tane-the-life-giving!
Descend thy spirit into thy offspring, O Tane, O Rua-tau!
Inform (their minds with the spirit) of Tane-the-all-know-
    ing-of-Heaven,
With a matured memory, a god's memory, with thoughts
    of thy ascent.
(Hold all within) thy god-like memory,
Be fixed, hold fast, at the back of your strenuous desire—
Firmly affix to the inception of thought, thy ardent wishes,
To the ancient origin of thy offspring, O Pai! O Tane!

Enter deeply, enter to the very origins,
Into the very foundations of all knowledge,
      O Io-the-hidden-face!
Gather as in a great and lengthy net, in the inner recesses
    of the ears,
As also in the desire, and perseverance, of these thy off-
    spring, thy sons.
Descend on them thy memory, thy knowledge,
Rest within the heart, within the roots of origin;
      O Io-the-learned! O Io-the-determined!
      O Io-the-self-created!

                    Maori, New Zealand

XIII

    As my eyes
    Search
    The prairie
    I feel the summer in the spring.

                    Ojibwa

XIV

Yellow Butterflies

Yellow butterflies
Over the blossoming, virgin corn,
With pollen-spotted faces
Chase one another in brilliant throng.

Blue butterflies
Over the blossoming virgin beans
With pollen-painted faces
Chase one another in brilliant throng.

Over the blossoming corn,
Over the virgin corn
Wild bees hum;
Over the blossoming beans,
Over the virgin beans
Wild bees hum.

Over your field of growing corn,
All day shall hang the thundercloud,
Over your field of growing beans
All day shall come the rushing rain!

Hopi, Arizona

XV

The Land Is on Fire

A burst of smoke from the pit lifts to the skies;
Hawaii's beneath, birth-land of Keawe;
Malama's beach looms before Lohiau,
Where landed the chief from Kahiki,
From a voyage on the blue sea, the dark sea,
The foam-mottled sea of Kane,

What time curled waves of the king-whelming flood.
The sea upswells, invading the land—

Lo Kane, outstretched at his ease!
Smoke and flame o'ershadow the uplands,
Conflagration by Laka, the woman
Hopoe wreathed with flowers of *lehua,*
Stringing the pandanus fruit.

Screw-palms that clash in Pan-ewa—
Pan-ewa, whose groves of *lehua*
Are nourished by lava shag,
Lehua that bourgeons with flame.

Night, it is night
O'er Puna and Hilo!
Night from the smoke of my land!
For the people salvation!
But the land is on fire!

Hawaii

XVI

THE LAND IS PARCHED AND BURNING

The land is parched and burning,
The land is parched and burning;
Going and looking about me
A narrow strip of green I see

Yet I do not know surely,
Yet I do not know surely:
The harlot is here among us—
I go away toward the west.

The shadow of crooked mountain,
The curved and pointed shadow,
'Twas there that I heard the singing,
Heard the songs that harmed my heart.

The light glow of the evening,
The light glow of the evening
Comes, as the quails fly slowly,
And it settles on the young.

Pima, Arizona

XVII

THE BRIGHT DAWN APPEARS IN THE HEAVENS

The bright dawn appears in the heavens,
The bright dawn appears in the heavens;
And the paling pleiades grow dim,
The moon is lost in the rising sun.

With the women bluebird came running,
With the women bluebird came running.
All came carrying clouds on their heads
And these were seen shaking as they danced.

See there the gray spider magician,
See there the gray spider magician;
Who ties the sun while the moon rolls on.
Turn back, the green staff raising higher.

Pima, Arizona

XVIII

THE WILD GINGER PLANT

Its stem bends as its leaves shoot up,
Down to its root it bends and sways,
Bends and sways in diverse ways;
Its leaves are chafed and lose their stiffness:
On craggy Inas it is blown about,
On craggy Inas which is our home.
Blown about in the light breeze,

Blown about with the mist, blown about with the haze,
Blown about are its shoots,
Blown about in the haze of the mountain,
Blown about in the light breeze.
It nods and nods upon the mountains,
Mountains of Beching, mountains of Inas,
Mountains of Malau, mountains of Kuwi,
Mountains of Mantan, mountains of Lumu,
On every mountain which is our home.

Negrito, Malay Peninsula

XIX

FAREWELL TO OUR LAND

Introduction

Weep for the mountains, O Teivirau!
For friends left behind in the land.
Oh, those pleasant hills—
The long range of mountains at home.

Foundation

Lights are seen by Teivi' o'er the white-crested waves,
Intended for thy guidance.
Why venture so far out to sea?
The island is lessening in the distance.
Darkness o'erspreads the ocean.
The king is lost to sight in the waves!

First Offshoot

Weep for the well-known mountain tops,
Now hidden by the swelling waves;—
Though hidden they are covered with verdure,
Pouekakeariki is lost to view;
Stretching towards the east,

With a smooth summit and coconut tree.
Oh, those pleasant hills,
The long range of mountains at home!

Second Offshoot

How lofty those distant hills,
Lying piled one above another!
How vast are they!
Weep for the sight of Tongarei,
And its precipitous sides.
Oh, those pleasant hills on the west,
The long range of mountains at home!

Third Offshoot

Smoke is rising from the hills;
The mountain ranges are on fire!
The fierce heat is felt on the ocean;
The blaze is extending all around:
All Mangaia is on flames!
Oh, those pleasant hills on the south,
The long range of mountains at home!

Fourth Offshoot

Taa has gained the shore in the dark.
In the starless night he was preserved.
The "shark-god" was his protector,
And Kereteki too, to save him from
All monsters of the deep, and to bring him to shore.
Oh, the far-extending reef at our home!

Finale

Ai e ruaoo e! E rangai e!

Mangaia, Polynesia

PART TWO

THE HIGHER ASPECTS OF
PRIMITIVE THOUGHT

CHAPTER XIII

ANALYSIS OF REALITY AND THE EXTERNAL WORLD

IN the first part of this book we were primarily concerned with the general attitude of primitive man toward life and society. More particularly we were interested in his conception of the nature of man's relation to man, of his relation to the social world in which he lived and to the external world around him. We could only incidentally touch upon two preliminary problems, his analysis of the world and his analysis of human personality. Though we were able to show that he was able, when called upon, to formulate an ethical theory in fairly abstract terms, we have as yet had no occasion to broach the larger and more important question as to whether he ever speculated on the major problems of philosophy, and whether this speculation could justifiably be considered to spring from the same motives that presumably ours does, namely, an interest in knowledge and speculation for its own sake. This is what we shall attempt to do in part here, although we shall have to confine ourselves to only a few of the numerous questions that arise.

No notion of primitive man's concept of the external world, his analysis of himself, of the nature of the godhead, etc., is possible unless it be recognized that, as among us, there exist, roughly speaking, two general types of temperament: the man of action and the thinker, the type which lives fairly exclusively on what might be called a motor level and the type that demands explanations and derives pleasure from some form of speculative thinking. I would like to stress this point particularly although I am well aware that most ethnologists have always worked on this assumption, because there still exists a very marked tendency both among laymen and scholars in general to deny any such differentiation for primitive man. This denial has, indeed, received a classical expression in the famous work of the French philosopher Lévy-Bruhl entitled *Les Fonctions Mentales dans les Sociétés Inférieures*.

In this lucid and remarkable work M. Lévy-Bruhl contends that no primitive man can properly distinguish between subject and object, that the relation between them predicated by him does not constitute what we would call a logical relation, but rather one which can be best described by a term he has introduced into anthropological literature, *participation mystique*. Primitive man, according to Lévy-Bruhl, never in his thinking reaches the logical stage at all. His mentality is always *prelogical*. If this were true, then of course we should not expect to find the differentiation that I have predicated but we ought to find instead a type of man, or types of men who were almost exclusively men of action with logically undifferentiated thinking powers.

There is, however, no warrant for M. Lévy-Bruhl's contention. For its refutation the reader will not have to rely upon either my word or that of any other ethnologist or observer, but on the ample and incontrovertible evidence that primitive man can himself furnish and part of which will be found in the ensuing pages.

With this fundamental division into two contrasting types of temperament we must then begin. As among ourselves the man of action predominates overwhelmingly. But this predomination carries with it a far greater significance among primitive people than among us for the very simple reason that the population in any specific group is so small. Barring some of the African tribes and the ancient civilizations of Mexico, Central America, and Peru, it is and was exceedingly rare to have any tribe numbering 100,000. With the same type of distribution holding for them that holds for us, it would be ridiculous to expect a large percentage of thinkers. And to this we must add the well-known fact that neither the man of action nor the thinker has much understanding of and still less sympathy for the other, for which the reasons are perfectly transparent.

Let me, however, describe more accurately what I understand by these types. The man of action, broadly characterized, is oriented toward the object, interested primarily in practical results, and indifferent to the claims and stirrings of his inner self. He recognizes them but he dismisses them shortly, granting them no validity either in influencing his actions or in explaining them. The thinker, on the other hand, although he, too, is definitely desirous of practical results—and for cultural reasons this holds to a far more marked extent among primitive people than among us—is nevertheless impelled by his whole nature to spend a considerable time in analyzing his subjective states and attaches great importance both to their influence upon his actions and to the explanations he has developed.

The former is satisfied that the world exists and that things happen. Explanations are of secondary consequence. He is ready to accept the first one that comes to hand. At bottom it is a matter of utter indifference. He does, however, show a predilection for one type of explanation as opposed to another. He prefers an explanation in which the purely mechanical relation between a series of events is specifically stressed. His mental rhythm—if I may be permitted to use this term—is characterized by a demand for endless repetition of the same event or, at best, of events all of which are on the same general level. Change for him means essentially some abrupt transformation. Monotony holds no terrors for him. Among primitive people his mentality is indelibly written over the vast majority of myths and magical incantations. Indeed it is because of its great prominence in myths and incantations that many observers have, not altogether unjustly, regarded his mental rhythm as the characteristic feature of primitive culture.

Now the rhythm of the thinker is quite different. The postulation of a mechanical relation between events does not suffice. He insists on a description couched either in terms of a gradual progress and evolution from one to many and from simple to complex, or on the postulation of a cause and effect relation. In other words some type of coördination is imperatively demanded.

To illustrate the two types of rhythm I shall select portions of a number of myths, the first representing that of the man of action and the others that of the thinker. The first myth runs as follows:

A man once lived together with his younger brother and one day he said to him, "Younger brother, you need never fear anything for I am the only holy being in existence and I am very powerful here on earth."

Shortly after this all the spirits held a council to determine what was to be done with the one who had made this claim and it was decided that he was to be punished and that the water spirits were to mete out the punishment. The older brother, Holy-One, knew nothing about this.

One day his younger brother did not return home and Holy-One waited and waited but he did not appear. So he went in search of him. During his search he wept and wherever he stopped to weep *a great lake was formed* from his tears. Whenever he sobbed *the hills tumbled down and became valleys.*

In his search he came across the wolf. Said he to the wolf, "Little brother, do you happen to know anything about my brother who is lost?" The wolf answered, "Brother, I have heard nothing about him although I travel all over the earth." "Ah well, ah well," said Holy-One and started to walk away. Then the wolf said, "Holy-One, it is not my business to look after your brother." "Oh," said Holy-One, "that's it, is it?" and he raced after him. Holy-One soon overtook him, broke open his jaws with his bow and killed him, saying, "I suppose you too took part in the conspiracy against me." Then he hung him on a tree and walked on.

As he walked along he came across the fox and addressed him as follows: "Little brother, I feel that something has befallen my brother. Now you are a cunning fellow, perhaps you know something of his whereabouts." And the fox replied, "Brother, I go all over the earth but I have not heard anything about your brother." Then Holy-One started to walk away, but just then the fox said, "Holy-One, I am not supposed to be the guardian of your brother!" and ran away. "Ah, so that is it, is it?" said Holy-One. "I suppose you too are one of those who conspired against me." Then he ran after him and although the fox ran with all his speed he overtook him, broke his jaws open, and killed him. Then he hung his body on a tree.

Thus he went encountering different animals. The next one he met was the raven and he addressed him as follows: "Little brother, you are a cunning fellow. I feel that something has happened to my brother." "Brother," answered the raven, "I roam all over the earth and the heavens but yet I have not seen your brother." Then as Holy-One was

about to start the raven said, "Holy-One, I am not supposed
to look after your brother." "Ah," said Holy-One, "you
little rascal, I suppose even such as you were present at
the conspiracy against me," and he knocked him down
just as he was about to fly. He pulled open his jaws and
hung him on a tree.[1]

In this myth we have all the traits mentioned previously as distinctive of the psychic rhythm of the man
of action, the endless repetition of events of the same
general level, the same questions, the same answers,
the same procedure. The only idea of progress dealt
with is that of transformation; dry land becomes water
and hills become valleys. Compare this with the following origin myth of one of the Winnebago clans and
we immediately realize that we are in the presence of
an entirely different type of mentality:

In the beginning Earthmaker was sitting in space. When
he came to consciousness nothing was there anywhere. He
began to think of what he should do and finally he began to
cry and tears flowed from his eyes and fell below him.
After a while he looked below him and saw something bright.
The bright object below him represented his tears. As they ·
fell they formed the present waters. When the tears flowed
below they became the seas as they are now. Earthmaker
began to think again. He thought, "It is thus: If I wish
anything it will become as I wish, just as my tears have
become seas." Thus he thought. So he wished for light

---

[1] Paul Radin, unpublished manuscript.

and it became light. Then he thought: "It is as I thought, the things that I wished for have come into existence as I desired." Then again he thought and wished for the earth and this earth came into existence. Earthmaker looked at the earth and he liked it; but it was not quiet. It moved about as do the waters of the sea. Then he made the trees and he liked them but they did not make the earth quiet. Then he made some grass but it likewise did not cause the earth to become quiet. Then he made rocks and stones but still the earth was not quiet. It was however almost quiet. Then he made the four directions and the four winds. At the four corners of the earth he placed them as great and powerful people, to act as island-weights. Yet still the earth was not quiet. Then he made four large beings and threw them down toward the earth and they pierced through the earth with their heads eastward. They were snakes. Then the earth became very still and quiet. Then he looked at the earth and he liked it.

Then again he thought of how it was that things came into being just as he desired. Then for the first time he began to talk and he said, "As things are just as I wish them I shall make a being in my own likeness." So he took a piece of clay and made it like himself. Then he talked to what he had created but it did not answer. He looked at it and saw that it had no mind or thought. So he made a mind for it. Again he talked to it but it did not answer. So he looked at it again and saw that it had no tongue. Then he made it a tongue. Then he spoke to it but still it did not answer. He looked at it and saw that it had no soul. So he made it a soul. Then he talked to it again and it very nearly said something, but it could not make itself intelligible. So Earthmaker breathed into its mouth and then talked to it and it answered.[2]

Now this is obviously the expression of a temperament craving for a logical coördination and integration of events. The creation of the earth is pictured as a physical accident. Once in existence, however, the deity infers that it came into being through his thought and thereupon he creates everything else. Explanation and progress there must be and the explanation must be in terms of a gradual progression. In the case of the shaping of our present world it is in terms of the evolution from motion to rest, from instability to stability and fixity; in the case of the development of human consciousness it is in terms of a specific endowment of newly created man first with thought, then with the mechanism for speech, with the soul, and finally with intelligence.

How very far the thinker among primitive people can push this urge toward analysis and synthesis is reflected in the following remarkable poem of the Maori. It is an account of the creation of life:

Seeking, earnestly seeking in the gloom. Searching—yes on the coast line—on the bounds of night and day; looking into night. Night had conceived the seed of night. The heart, the foundation of night, had stood forth self-existing even in the gloom. It grows in gloom—the sap and succu-

[2] Paul Radin, 37th *Report of the Bureau of American Ethnology,* p. 212.

lent parts, the life pulsating, and the cup of life. The shadows screen the faintest ray of light. The procreative power, the ecstasy of life first known, and joy of issuing forth from silence into sound. Thus the progeny of the Great-Extending filled the heaven's expanse; the chorus of life rose and swelled into ecstasy, then rested in bliss of calm and quiet.[3]

I must even at the risk of overstressing my point give an explanation of what represents, to all intents and purposes, a compromise between the thinker's and the man of action's temperament, but a compromise that is exceedingly frequent, selecting for this purpose the creation legend of the Maidu:

When this world was filled with water, Earthmaker floated upon it, kept floating about. Nowhere in the world could he see even a tiny bit of earth. No persons of any kind flew about. He went about in this world, the world itself being invisible, transparent like the sky.

He was troubled. "I wonder how, I wonder where, I wonder in what place, in what country, we shall find a world!" he said. "You are a very strong man, to be thinking of this world," said Coyote. "I am guessing in what direction the world is, then to that distant land let us float!" said Earthmaker.

In this world they kept floating along, hungry, having nothing to eat. "You will die of hunger," said Coyote. Then he thought. "No, I cannot think of anything," he

---

[3] J. C. Anderson, *Maori Life in Aotea,* p. 150.

said. "Well," said Earthmaker, "the world is large, a great world. If somewhere I find a tiny world, I can fix it up."

Then he sang, "Where, little world, art thou?" It is said he sang, kept singing, sang all the time. "Enough!" he said, and stopped singing. "Well, I don't know many songs," he said. Then Coyote sang again, kept singing, asking for the world, singing, "Where, O world, art thou?" He sang, kept singing, then "Enough," he said, "I am tired. You try again."

So Earthmaker sang. "Where are you, my great mountains?" he said. "You try also," he said. Coyote tried, kept singing, "My foggy mountains, where one goes about," he said. "Well, we shall see nothing at all. I guess there never was a world anywhere," said he. "I think if we find a little world, I can fix it very well," said Earthmaker.

As they floated along, they saw something like a bird's nest. "Well, that is very small," said Earthmaker. "It is small. If it were larger, I could fix it. But it is too small. I wonder how I can stretch it a little!" "What is the best way? How shall I make it larger?" So saying, he prepared it.

When all (the ropes) were stretched, he said, "Well, sing, you who were the finder of this earth, this mud! 'In the long, long ago, Robin-Man made the world, stuck earth together, making this world.'" Then Robin sang and his world-making song sounded sweet. After the ropes were all stretched, he kept singing; then, after a time, he ceased.

Then Earthmaker spoke to Coyote also. "Do you sing too," he said. So he sang, singing, "My world, where one travels by the valley edge; my world of many foggy mountains; my world, where one goes zigzagging hither and thither, range after range," he said. "I sing of the country I shall travel in. In such a world I shall wander."

Then Earthmaker sang—sang of the world he had made, kept singing, until by and by he ceased. "Now," he said, "it would be well if the world were a little larger. Let us stretch it!"—"Stop!" said Coyote. "I speak wisely. This world ought to be painted with something, so that it may look pretty. What do ye two think?"

Then Robin-Man said, "I am one who knows nothing. Ye two are clever men, making the world, talking it over; if ye find anything evil, ye will make it good." "Very well," said Coyote, "I shall paint it with blood. There shall be blood in the world; and people shall be born there having blood. There shall be birds born who shall have blood. Everything shall have blood that is to be created in this world. And in another place, making it red, there shall be red rocks. It will be as if blood were mixed up with the world, and thus the world will be beautiful," he said. "What do you think about it?" "Your words are good," he said, "I know nothing." So Robin-Man went off. As he went he said, "I shall be a person who travels only in this way," and he flew away.[4]

The same contrast in viewpoint is visible in the domain of religious beliefs. There we find the thought of the man of action concrete and unintegrated, that of the thinker coördinated, unified, and at times ab-

---

[4] Roland B. Dixon, *Maidu Texts* (American Ethnological Society), IV, pp. 4 *ff.*

stract. Thus among the Winnebago the sun is regarded by the man of action as composed of a number
of separate entities—the disk, the heat, the rays, the
corona; for the thinker these are all aspects of one and
the same thing. Similarly in the same tribe the clan
ancestors were regarded by the man of action as either
animals or as vague spirit-animals who had become
transformed into human beings at one time, whereas
the thinker postulated a generalized spirit-animal to
whom the Winnebago are related through the intermediation of animals sent by them. Among the Dakota Indians the contrast is pushed much farther.
What the ordinary man regards as eight distinct deities, the priest and thinker takes to be aspects of one
and the same deity.

If consequently we wish adequately to understand
primitive man's concept of the external world we must
bear in mind carefully the existence of these two
temperaments, for the external world will be described
differently depending upon the person from whom our
information has been obtained. And these differences
are fundamental for they concern the concept of the
actual nature of the external world, its form, configuration, appearance, its origin, the proofs of its existence,
and its relation to us. Throughout these pages I shall
therefore, as far as the evidence permits, try to keep
the testimony of these two contrasting temperaments
distinct. Let us first examine the viewpoint of the
man of action.

In one sense it is quite erroneous to speak of the

concept of the external world of the man of action if
we mean to imply thereby that it is ever made the object of his conscious thought. Strictly speaking he
has none. In the main he unhesitatingly accepts the
form which the thinker has given to ideas. This holds
more particularly for all those questions connected with
the shape, configuration, and origin of the world around
him. The man of action follows the lead of the
thinker or at least repeats somewhat mechanically what
the thinker has to say on these matters because his
interests are centered not upon the analysis of reality
but upon the *orientation of reality* and the proofs for
its existence. Much of the indefiniteness, the vagueness, and the inconsistency in his characterization of
the phenomenal world, can be safely ascribed to this
type of interest on his part. Among the Winnebago
the sun is represented either by rays of light, a disk,
or as some vague anthropomorphic being; the thunderbird as an eagle, a mythical bird, or as a bald-headed
man wearing a circlet of cedar leaves. Similarly among
the Ewe of West Africa the various spirits grouped
under the generic name of *tro* are vaguely described as
invisible but yet as having hands and feet resembling
human beings, etc. Their shape is continually changing. In the Banks' Islands, again, the natives told
Bishop Codrington that the spirits called *vui,* live,
think, have more intelligence than man, have no form
to be seen and have no soul.

When we try to discover what are the connotations
for the man of action, of such simple things as a tree,

a mountain, a lake, etc., similar difficulties immediately arise. The first positive fact that emerges when we attempt to make such an inquiry is that an object is *not thought of as the sum of all the sense data connected with it.* A mountain is not thought of as a unified whole. It is neither static nor is it a series of inherently connected impressions. It is a continually changing entity from which one is repeatedly subtracting and to which one is repeatedly adding. In the case of the idea of a tree this lack of unification is of course even more marked. To talk of a tree being the same when it is constantly undergoing transformations is based on an assumption which the man of action simply does not make. We may, in fact, even go farther and claim that he does not in the least see the absolute necessity, for instance, of assuming that an acorn contains all the potentialities of an oak, or that the shape and appearance of some specific object, even granted that it retains this shape and appearance more or less permanently, is inevitably and indubitably its ultimate form. He conceives the possibility of imagining it having an entirely different appearance on the following day.

As far as we can judge, therefore, for the man of action in a primitive community, the external world is dynamic and ever changing. So much his experience tells him. He refuses to state categorically or to assume even provisionally that it is permanent merely because his past and his present experience have shown it to be so. Since he sees the same objects changing in appearance day after day he regards this as definitely depriving them of immutability and permanence. Now this is really tantamount to saying that all the attributes of an object are not outside of the perceiver, that the object cannot be adequately defined in terms of sense data alone. However, as soon as an object is regarded as a dynamic entity, then analysis and definition become both difficult and unsatisfactory. Thinking is under such circumstances well-nigh impossible for most people. To think at all logically, no matter how concretistic the thought may be, there must be some static point. Where, now, are we to look for this point? The man of action answers, *in its effect*. Then an object becomes completely separated, even though it be only for a short time, from all other objective elements as well as from the perceiving self. A deity, for example, *is* his effect, an object *is* essentially its relation to man. Reality, in other words, is pragmatic. That the above analysis is not an imaginary one of my own the following examples will prove: "The god of whom I speak is dead," said a Maori witness in a native land court of New Zealand. The court replied, "Gods do not die." "You are mistaken," continued the witness, "Gods do die unless there are *tohungas* (priests) to keep them alive." [5] And in one of the Maori myths one deity is represented as addressing another deity in the following fashion: "When men no longer believe in us, we are dead." A Fiji Islander told an investigator that "a thing has *mana* when it

---

[5] J. Gudgeon, *Journal of the Polynesian Society*, XV, pp. 27 ff.

works; it has not *mana* when it doesn't work." In Eddystone Island it was said of a certain native that he was a spirit, a deity, when he said, "Go, for you will catch fish," and he caught fish. Then he possessed *mana*. But if he was not successful then he had no *mana*. Perhaps the most convincing proof is given by the example quoted on page 30.

What functions, therefore, is true and what functions exists. Yet, what are we to understand by functioning, by a happening? I feel certain that our man of action would not deny that events take place between two objects outside of him and which in no way affect him, but it is a matter that hardly interests him. An event means essentially something that transpires between an object and himself. We have therefore to ask ourselves, how can he recognize an event?

Now we are accustomed to derive all our proof for the existence of a thing from the evidence of our senses. The cultured man of Western Europe is, in the main, as we all know, visual-minded. That some inward feeling or stirring, some sudden and vague sensation or intuition, might be taken as real proof for the existence of an event would not occur to him. Not that any one to-day seriously denies the reality of such inward experiences. We all know that certain religions take the presence of an inward response as proving the existence of God and of specific dogmas. But no one of us, as far as I am aware, would seriously contend that an inward experience—the presence of an inward thrill —could establish the reality of the whole cultural background. Yet this is precisely what does happen in primitive culture, for the man of action. Why, so he would contend, should something affect him in this way, if it were not true—an argument well known, of course, among us. This is to him as much of a real proof as anything happening outside of him.

It can, therefore, be said that primitive man feels that reality is given to him in a threefold fashion. He is born into it; it is proved by external effects; and it is proved by internal effects. He is thus literally living in a blaze of reality. This is more particularly true of the man of action. An aura envelops every object in the external world due to the projection of this inward thrill upon it. It is difficult for one brought up in the scientific externalism of the natural sciences of the nineteenth century to visualize or appreciate this heightened atmosphere in which primitive man works. Perhaps the best he can do is to follow a philosopher like Lévy-Bruhl, and develop a theory of prelogical mentality and mystic participation. Yet both of these conceptions are, I feel, far from the mark. Primitive man in no sense merges himself with the object. He distinguishes subject and object quite definitely. In fact the man of action spends a good part of his time in attempting to coerce the object. What he says is simply this: not all the reality of an object resides in our external perception of it. There is an internal side and there are also effects, constraints, from sub-happens must happen and in happening proves itself to ject to object and from object to subject. Whatever be a reality; not the only reality necessarily, but the only one with which the man of action has any immediate concern.

After this long and rather difficult analysis of the nature of reality and the external world, as understood by the man of action, and one which is never well formulated because it is that of the man of action, let us turn to the analysis made by the thinker, remembering always that he shares many of the basic views of the man of action.

The first point to be emphasized is that the stresses are all different. From the man of action's viewpoint, a fact has no symbolic or static value. He predicates no unity beyond that of the certainty of continuous change and transformation. For him a double distortion is involved in investing the transitory and ceaselessly changing object with a symbolic, idealistic, or static significance; first, because we then remove it farther from reality; and second, because in thus separating the perceiving self from the object, we really render both of them meaningless. Now it goes without saying that in order to think systematically facts must have some degree of symbolic meaning; they must be static and there must be a fairly clear-cut distinction between the ego and the external object. Every thinker must, in other words, study the subject and the object as though they were isolated units.

The thinker, like the man of action, accepts both the ego and the external world—the phenomenal as well as the social—as to a very marked extent self-conditioned. But he is not interested merely in the fact that the world exists and that it has a definite effect upon him; he is impelled by his whole nature, by the innate orientation of his mind, to try to discover the reason why there is an effect, what is the nature of the relation between the ego and the world, and what part exactly the perceiving self plays therein. Like all philosophers, he is interested in the subject as such, the object as such, and the relations between them. In the external world, as within himself, he is aware of movement and the shifting forms of things. He is as much impressed by this as is the man of action. But the world must first be static and objects must first take on a permanent or, at least, a stable form before one can deal with them systematically. Both these tasks he therefore sets out to achieve. The attempts of these primitive thinkers are embodied in numerous creation myths, examples of which are given on pages 354ff. There we see that the task is always the same—an original, moving, shapeless or undifferentiated world must be brought to rest and given stable form. This unstable and undifferentiated primal condition is remarkably well formulated in the cosmological myths of the Polynesians. Let me mention but one of variant versions of the Maori creation myth. There, for example, we find described six æons of darkness:

1. Te Po-tamaku (the age smoothed off).
2. Te Po-kakarauri (the age of extreme darkness).

3. Te Po-aoao-nui (the age of great dawn).
4. Te Po-uriuri (the age of deep black darkness).
5. Te Po-kerikeri (the age of darkness).
6. Te Po-tiwhatiwha (the age of gloom).[6]

And surely the following is a perfect description of instability:

Because Rangi-nui overlaid and completely covered Papa-tua-nuku, the growth of all things could not mature, nor could anything bear fruit; they were in an unstable condition, floating about the world of darkness. And this was their appearance: some were crawling after the manner of lizards, some were upright with the arms held up, some were lying with the knees partly drawn up, some lying on their sides, some were lying stretched out at full length, some on their backs, some were stooping, some with their heads bent down, some with their legs drawn up, some embracing, some kicking out with legs and arms, some kneeling, some standing, some inhaling deep breaths, some with exhausted breath, some crawling, some walking, some feeling about in the dark, some arising, some gazing, some sitting still, and in many other attitudes—they were all within the embrace of Rangi-nui and Papa.[7]

But having made the world static and given objects a form is not enough. This form must be made reasonably permanent. This problem likewise our primitive

[6] S. Percy Smith, "The Lore of the Whare-Wananga," *Memoirs of the Polynesian Society*, III, pp. 99-100.

[7] *Ibid.*, pp. 117-118.

philosophers attacked. I shall illustrate the nature of their attempts at solution by examples taken from two tribes, the Winnebago and the Maori.

According to the Winnebago no organic objects had any permanent form originally. They were all a sort of *tertium quid,* neutral beings, that could at will transform themselves into human beings or spirit-animals. At one particular period in the history of the world these neutral beings decided to use all this unlimited power of transformation in order to change themselves definitely into either animals or human beings. That accordingly happened and since then animals have remained animals and human beings human beings, except that there are a few human beings who still possess the power of transforming themselves, for short periods of time, into animals.

The Maori solution is quite different. The capacity for unlimited transformation credited to objects among the Winnebago was an unknown concept to the Maori, but they in their turn raised an entirely different problem. All things, they insisted, contain within themselves elements of both good and evil and it is essential to have some control over them lest in their mutual reactions they nullify each other. Good and evil are here thought of in the most general way, in the sense of predicating for each thing inherent proper and positive qualities. In order to achieve this control, certain supernatural beings called guardians were appointed. They were to watch over everything, prevent quarrels and all interferences, and confine each thing to its own proper activities. There were eleven of such guardians whose functions may be described as follows:

1. Those who controlled the place where the souls of the dead congregated.
2. Those who controlled the suspension of the heavenly bodies, the leading stars of the various realms, and the stars of the Milky Way.
3. Those whose duty it was to maintain the arrangement of all ocean currents and other things connected with the sea.
4. Those who arranged and controlled the movements of the winds, of the snow, of rain, of the clouds, of mists, lightning, and thunder, lest they contend against each other or turn on the Earth Mother and work evil in this world.
5. Those whose duty it was to control the ravages of disease, sickness, etc.
6. Those who were to regulate the seasons of summer and winter, lest either be prolonged so as to cause continual summer or continual winter.
7. Those who were appointed to control the violent contentions of certain deities.
8. Those who were appointed to be the preservers of all occult knowledge pertaining to the realms of heaven and earth, etc.
9. Those who were appointed to preserve unity and peace among themselves, to confine each to the proper duties assigned to him, etc.

10. Those who were appointed to preserve the welfare of all things pertaining to Punihoniho-o-tau, lest trees, herbage, vegetation, lose their vitality, their fruitfulness and deteriorate and decay, or become infertile or incapable of assimilating nourishment, or seedless; lest fish, insects, etc., become infertile.

11. Those who were appointed to protect the powers of tapu in respect to places where religious ceremonies were performed, etc.; to protect and cherish all occult arts, declining, arranging, or supporting the attitude, acts, and *position* of all things as planned.[8]

There exist, however, many things that manifestly do not have permanence of form and do look different at different times. Philosophers have always given the same answer to this problem and predicated a unity behind these changing aspects and forms. Primitive philosophers are at one with their European and Asiatic brothers here. Among the Winnebago, according to some individuals, the clan animal is a spirit whom you never see except in his manifestations as a real animal, or some object he has bestowed upon you, or some stirring within you, etc. Among the Dakota the priests taught that one can never see the real sky but merely one aspect of him, the blue heavens. Similarly they claimed that we never see the real earth and rock but only their *tonwanpi,* i.e. (as nearly as one can translate the word), their divine

---

[8] Elsdon Best, "Maori Religion and Mythology," 10th *Bulletin of the Dominion Museum* (New Zealand), I, pp. 65-66.

semblance. Among the Maori we find the same philosophy. Many of the deities cannot really be seen. All we see of them is their *aria,* i.e., their reflections. What enables us to see a stone and what gives it shape is not the physical stone but the soul of the stone. The well-known authority on the Maoris, Elsdon E. Best, tells the following remarkable story: "A missionary speaking to an old man remarked, 'Your religion is false; it teaches that all things possess a soul.' The Maori answered, 'Were a thing not possessed of the *wairua* of an *atua,* then that thing could not possess form,' " i.e., it could not have form unless it possessed the soul of a god. The further discussion of this unifying abstract principle must be relegated to the chapter on monotheism, pages 342 *ff.*

The thinker, we have thus seen, is forced in the interests of his analysis to differentiate sharply between the subject and the object, and their respective relation to each other. Just as the man of action is primarily interested in the object, so is the thinker in the subject. The clashing of the two views is brought out most beautifully in connection with one of the most famous aspects of primitive religion, the belief in *mana* or magical power. Here, too, I think we can find an admirable example of how the thinker's formulation is more or less mechanically accepted by the others and how its failure to merge with the man of action's attitude leads to endless contradiction and confusion.

Every discussion of *mana* must necessarily go back to the famous definition of Codrington: *"Mana* is a force altogether distinct from physical power which acts in all kinds of ways for good and evil and which it is of the greatest advantage to possess and control . . . (and which) shows itself in physical force or in any kind of power or excellence which a man possesses."[9] This has been the generally accepted view since Codrington's time. Now quite apart from the fact, as some investigators have already pointed out, that Codrington's actual material contradicts such an interpretation, it must be borne in mind that this definition of Codrington is not one given to him by a native. It represents, on the contrary, his own interpretation of a number of facts. He was a very keen thinker and he is here giving us a thinker's attitude. I believe it is also the thinker's attitude among the Melanesians, although we have no definite proof of this.

The thinker's viewpoint on *mana* comes out clearly among the Dakota and the Maori. A Dakota priest told Mr. James Walker the following: "All the gods have *ton*. *Ton* is the power to do supernatural things." [10] This the native expressly states is the priest's interpretation. "When the people say *ton*," he continued, "they mean *something that comes from a living thing,* such as the birth of anything or the discharge from a wound or a sore or the growth from a seed." Here, therefore, the two views are neatly con-

---

[9] *The Melanesians,* pp. 118-119.
[10] "The Sun Dance of the Oglala Division of the Dakota," *Anthropological Papers of the American Museum of Natural History,* XVI, Part II, pp. 152 *ff.*

trasted. But what is the essence of the priest's, the thinker's view? Here, likewise, the Dakota material comes to our aid. According to one of the priests, anything that acquires *ton is wakan* because it is the power of the spirit or the quality that has been put into it. "Every object in the world has a spirit and that spirit is *wakan.*" But where does *wakan* come from? "*Wakan* comes from the *wakan* beings. These *wakan* beings are greater than mankind in the same way that mankind is greater than animals. They are never born and they never die." [11]

This same concept of the divine in objects and in man we find also among the Maori. It will be discussed in greater detail in another part of the book. All I wish to point out here is that according to the Maori every sentient being—and therein he includes the whole phenomenal world—possesses a *toiora,* i.e. "the soul of God, of Io." This it is that gives him power and prestige.

To bring this very cursory discussion of *mana* to a close, I think we are amply justified in saying that the two interpretations of *mana* which we seem to find cutting across each other everywhere, represent respectively the view of the thinker and of the man of action. To the thinker it is the generalized essence of a deity residing in an object or in man, and to the man of action it is *that which works, has activity, is an effect.*

The clash of the two temperaments which we see manifesting themselves so clearly in the *mana* concept

---

[11] *Ibid.,* pp. 153-154.

is even more pronounced when we attempt to study the theories postulated as to the interrelationship of the external world and man. Two entirely different ideas of the nature of this relation and of the reaction of the one upon the other have been developed. These will be touched upon in the following chapters. But before we can really properly understand or appreciate these ideas, it is essential to obtain some notion of the concept of the ego, of the perceiving self, as held by the thinker.

CHAPTER XIV

THE NATURE OF THE EGO AND OF HUMAN PERSONALITY

IT may be confidently assumed that just as there are differences between the man of action and the thinker in his attitude toward the external world and his concept of reality, so there must be a marked contrast between their respective ideas concerning the nature of the Ego and of human personality. In the present condition of our sources it is impossible, except in the most general way, to keep the two apart consistently. I think we are on fairly safe ground, however, in assuming that none of the very remarkable formulations with which we will specifically deal in this chapter —those of the Maori of New Zealand, the Oglala Sioux, and the Batak of Sumatra—are the work of the man of action or that such a man, if questioned, would be able to give us an account even remotely as unified and consistent as these in question. Many of the ideas centering around personality and human relations and involving magic are obviously shared by the man of action and the thinker. But the thinker gives them a specific orientation and a definite formulation which is then inconsistently adopted by the man of action. This seems to me to be clearly illustrated by many of the "theories" of disease, of death, of the soul, of the nature of human attraction, etc., current among all tribes. In general it may be claimed that the thinker employs the vast mass of folkloristic and magical beliefs clustering around the Ego and personality, to develop a more or less definite system of psychotherapy. Let me give a number of examples to make clear what I mean by this very important function of the thinker, a function that shows itself in connection with many aspects of primitive culture but which is perhaps best seen here.

Among the Maori a charm is recited over the corpse prior to burial in order to dispatch the soul to spirit land and to prevent it from remaining in the world to annoy and frighten the living. Practices of this nature are to be found among all peoples. What interests us, in this particular case, however, are the actual words of the charm. These run as follows: "Farewell, O my child! Do not grieve; do not weep; do not love; do not yearn for your parent left by you in the world. Go ye for ever. Farewell for ever."[1]

Here what in origin was a mere magical incantation to assure the definite and complete separation of the dead from the living has been invested with a psychical side. In other words, the mere physical separation that presumably was attained by the simple recitation of a charm did not satisfy every one. A psychical separation had likewise to be provided, and this we may

---

[1] Elsdon Best, "Spiritual and Mental Concepts of the Maori," *Dominion Museum Monograph No. 2* (New Zealand), p. 12.

infer was the work of the thinker. This psychothera-
peutic side to magic has been overlooked by most students of ethnology and yet it could be easily demonstrated that not to recognize it means a failure to understand certain fundamental aspects of the primitive
psyche. Another example, also taken from the Maori,
brings out even more strikingly what I have in mind.

Among the Maori divorce consists of two parts, the
external ritual, a kind of legal pronouncement that the
two people concerned are no longer man and wife, and
a second part which has as its object the obliteration
of the sympathy and affection that once bound these
two together. As the Maori priest told Mr. Best, our
informant, "The priest effaced the affections—that is,
he cleansed or washed away the semblance of such;
he abolished it."[2]

But to return to our main problem: how does primitive man regard the Ego? It may at once be said that
one thing he has never done: he has never fallen into
the error of thinking of it as a unified whole or of
regarding it as static. For him it has always been a
dynamic entity, possessed of so many constituents that
even the thinker has been unable to fuse them into one
unit. If what we have said about the unusual knowledge and intuition of character possessed by primitive
people is true, then we might have assumed, even in the
absence of available data, that he would attempt fairly
elaborate analyses of the Ego. Fortunately we have
the facts and from their study it is quite clear that

---

[2] *Ibid.*, p. 21.

the Maori and the Dakota—to select only those for whom our material is exceptionally good—look upon the Ego as composed of two parts, a body which is relatively unimportant, and an unsubstantial element made up, in its turn, of three constituents. Some such general formula will, I think, turn out to hold true for all primitive peoples.

In the descriptions of primitive man's analysis of the Ego which I shall now attempt, certain difficulties confront us. Few ethnologists have ever attempted to obtain from a native any systematized account of their own theory. It has, in fact, been generally contended that they have none. As a result our material consists of isolated statements on different aspects of the Ego and we are perforce compelled to weld them into a consistent or inconsistent whole—as the case may be —in order to see their complete bearings. This, unfortunately, cannot be helped. I have tried, however, to adhere rigorously to the facts and to let the native speak for himself wherever that is possible.

The procedure I shall follow is a very simple one: I shall analyze the concept of the Ego and of personality of three tribes—the Maori, the Oglala Sioux, and the Batak, and regard them as fairly representative of that of all primitive peoples.

The Maori analysis is very complex and unusually profound. According to them man and every sentient thing, that is, every thing conceived of as living, consists of an eternal element, an Ego which disappears after death, a ghost shadow, and a body. The eternal element is, as we have already mentioned, the soul of God in man. It is called *toiora*. Some notion of what is understood by this term is given by an incident in the myth of Hine, the Earth-formed Maid. In this myth, when she is about to acquire mortal life, we find the sentence, "At that juncture Hine brought herself to the world of life and also attained mortal life with the *toiora* of the enduring world."[3]

The Ego proper consists of three things: the dynamic element, the life-essence or personality, and the physiological element. The first is named *mauri* and appears in two forms, an immaterial and a material. The material *mauri* is the active life principle itself whereas the immaterial *mauri* is its symbol. The material *mauri* might be practically any object. Mr. Best tells us that in the north of New Zealand a tree was sometimes planted at the birth of a child and this tree was then regarded as the child's material *mauri*.

The same division into immaterial and material held for the life-essence, the *hau*, and apparently also for the third constituent of the Ego, the physiological aspect, called *manawa ora*. This was translated as breath, and breath of life, the first connoting more the spiritual and the second the purely physical breath of life.

In the ghost shadow, the *wairua*, we are dealing with the soul strictly speaking. It is partially visible but does not properly possess a material form until it appears in the underworld. *Wairua* is the ingredient

---

[3] *Ibid.*, pp. 10-11.

which mediates us to the external world; we would be lifeless and would decay without it. We might possess the life-principle and form but we could not be seen. In the same way it is the *wairua* that enables us to give form to things, to actually accomplish them. A Maori remarked to Best, "My *wairua* is very intent on this work that it may be well done."[4] It is well to remember this, to realize that it is not simply with our senses that we see and touch and think. "Be of good cheer," a woman was told, "although we are afar off, yet our *wairua* are ever with you." And it is in the same strain that an old Maori wrote to Best, "We have long been parted and may not meet again in the world of life. We can no longer see each other with our eyes, only our *wairua* see each other, as also our friendship."

Although the *wairua* could not be destroyed, a person could be killed through his *wairua*. It was easily affected by magical spells. It was the *wairua* that was affected when a man found himself afflicted with fear of coming evil, with a dread of impending danger, or if he polluted his *tapu*.

The *wairua* is thus the integrating mechanism within us and it is exceedingly suggestive that it should be viewed as nonaggressive.

The fundamental distinction between immaterial and material is also illustrated by the Maori philosopher's interpretation of the body. It is viewed from two aspects: first, as an integrated whole, the resting place of the *toiora, wairua, mauri* and *manawa ora* with all

---

[4] *Ibid.,* pp. 8 *ff.*

that this implies; and second, as composed of distinct organs, the bowels, the heart, the stomach, the liver, etc. Looked upon as a material entity it may have an immaterial form and regarded as an immaterial entity it may possess a material form. In other words it possessed as an integrated unit both form and substance. The first the Maori called *ahua* and the second *aria*. Best gives as examples of the latter two greetings addressed to him, "Greeting to you, the *ahua* of your grandchild Marewa" and "Greeting to you, the *ahua* of the men of yore." As an example of the contrast in meaning, Best quotes a Maori as follows: "I saw clearly his bodily form (*ahua*); it is not the case that I saw him distinctly (*aria*)."[5] In the one case we are dealing with the material, in the other with the immaterial representation.

We now come to the specifically organic aspect of the body. The Maori had a very good knowledge of internal anatomy. Like most primitive people, however, they did not associate the organs of the body with physiological but rather with psychical functions. The viscera were the seat of thought, of the mind, and of conscience; the heart, of feelings, desires, and inclinations; and the stomach, of feelings, memory, etc. In other words the traits that we associate with personality are all regarded as located in definite organs.

Such is the picture the Maori draw of the Ego. Its most salient feature is the insistence upon multiple personality and its extension into the past and future.

---

[5] *Ibid.*, pp. 16-20.

Although no attempt has been made here to fuse these various constituents into one organic whole, this does not mean that all are not necessary before there is a true Ego which can function. What it does signify, however, is that these various elements can become dissociated temporarily from the body and enter into relation with the dissociated elements of other individuals. The nature of the impingement of individual upon individual and of the individual upon the external world is thus utterly different from anything that a Western European can possibly imagine. The medley of combinations and permutations it would permit is quite bewildering. What prevents anarchy is that all these constituents, independent as they are, nevertheless fall into a definite configuration within each man's Ego. The error the Maori make lies, of course, in their concretization of ideas. Yet as an attempted solution of the problem of substance and form it should rank very high. To have recognized in man the physiological, the vital essence and the functioning of these two in a temporal body, and to have split up the body itself into form, substance, and "resting place," represents an unusual achievement. The recognition of multiple personality, which happens to be in consonance with the very latest results of psychological and psychiatric research is, on the other hand, not due to any conscious thought, intuitive or otherwise, but is the direct consequence of primitive man's unconquerable and unsentimental realism and his refusal to assume fictitious and artificial unities.

Many of the salient traits of the Maori analysis of personality are to be found in the next system to be discussed, that of the Oglala Dakota, although the emphasis is naturally enough quite different. As among the Maori there are two external elements, the divine in man and the soul that begins its existence after death, and last a mortal soul. In formulating their analysis, however, the Oglala proceeded from another angle. Their interest was not so much centered upon characterizing the various constituents, the diverse souls that went into the making of the Ego, as in determining the relation of these souls to the various aspects of personality. It is from this point of view that I shall present the facts. The important elements of the Ego, according to the Dakota, are courage and fortitude, general disposition, the power to influence others and of forewarning oneself of good and evil, unusual actions, and finally negative elements such as jealousy, maliciousness, etc.

Courage and fortitude come from the *sicun*. The *sicun* is given a man by Wakan Tanka, the supreme spirit, at birth. A *sicun* is the *ton* (divine essence) of a deity. Perhaps I had better quote Mr. James Walker's description:

The *sicun* is an immaterial God whose substance is never visible. It is the potency of mankind and the emitted potency of the Gods. Considered relative to mankind it is many, but apart from mankind it is one. *Skan* (the supreme deity) imparts a *sicun* to each of mankind at birth. It remains with the person until death when it returns whence it came. Its functions are to enable the possessor to do those things which the beasts cannot do and to give courage and fortitude. It may be pleased or displeased with its possessor and may be operative or inoperative according to its pleasure. It may be invoked by ceremony or prayer, but it cannot be imparted to any other person or thing. Most of the Gods can emit their potencies and when so emitted their potencies become *sicunpi*. Such a *sicun* can be imparted to material things by a proper ceremony correctly performed by a shaman.[6]

The general disposition of a man comes from the *nagi*. The *nagi*, like the *sicun*, is immaterial and is bestowed upon man by the supreme deity at birth. Its substance, however, is visible at will and can communicate with mankind either directly or through a shaman. The *nagi* stays with a man until he dies.

The power to influence others, to forewarn of good and evil, to cause vitality, comes from the *niya*. It is immaterial but its substance is visible whenever it so wills. It, too, is imparted by the Supreme Deity to man but it does not reside in the body as do the *sicun* and the *nagi* but abides with it like a shadow. Upon death it goes to the supreme deity to testify regarding the conduct of the Ego to which it belonged. When it leaves the body, this means death.

---

[6] "The Sun Dance of the Oglala Division of the Dakota," *Anthropological Papers of the American Museum of Natural History*, XVI, Part II, p. 87. See also pp. 78-94 and 132-161.

It is the *niya* that causes life, i.e., life from the physiological side, although just as among the Maori there is strictly speaking nothing in life that is purely physiological. A native described it as follows: "A man's *ni* is his life. It is the same as his breath and that which gives him his strength. It is the *ni* which keeps the inside of a man clean. If the *ni* is weak he cannot perform this office and if it goes away the man dies. *Niya* is the ghost or spirit which is given to a man at birth and which causes the *ni*. The Lakota have a ceremony which they call the *inipi* (sweat bath). The idea of the Lakota is that the *inipi* makes man's spirit strong so that it may cleanse all within the body, and so that the *ni* may drive from his body all that makes him tired or that causes him to have evil thoughts."[7]

Certain peculiar actions, such as a man behaving in a non-human way and acting, for instance, as though he possessed a bear nature, are caused by the *nagiya*. This is one of the most difficult things in Dakota philosophy to understand properly. The *nagiya* is apparently some immaterial essence whose substance may appear in any form it chooses. It is never imparted to man by the supreme deity but it is bestowed by the supreme deity upon every material object save man, at its beginning. It may possess any other thing. For instance, the *nagiya* of a wolf may possess a tree and then the tree will have the nature of a wolf. It is in this connection that it affects man, for the *nagiya*

---

[7] *Ibid.*, p. 156.

of any animal may possess a man and then he will act in a manner suggestive of that animal.

Jealousy, maliciousness, etc., are not conceived of as caused by any soul or entity residing within but are regarded as due to discarnate *sicun*. If the *nagi* after death is adjudged unworthy to go on the spirit trail it becomes a wandering *sicun*. Such a *sicun* can communicate with mankind but its communications are uncertain and not to be relied upon. It is a *sicun* of this type that causes jealousy, etc.

The fate of the three cardinal constituents of the Ego is extremely suggestive. The *sicun* goes to the deity to which it belongs, for it is but the divine essence temporarily implanted in man; the *nagi* goes to spirit land and lives there, and the *niya* apparently disappears into the universe.

The body itself is merely an envelope which, after death, rots and becomes nothing.

The marked difference between the Maori and the Dakota conception is that the latter throws infinitely more of the responsibility for our actions upon the gods. We might therefore have expected that most of the expressions of the Ego would be regarded as predetermined. But this is not true except for two things, the power to influence others and the instincts. Apart from this there is complete free will and personal responsibility, just as their ethical system clearly implies.

Among the Dakota we pointed out that a considerable degree of responsibility for one's actions was theoretically thrown upon the gods. In the next theory of the Ego to be discussed, that of the Batak of the East Indian Archipelago, this responsibility of the gods becomes complete, leading to a peculiar kind of dualism in each Ego and, theoretically at least, to a rigid fatalism.

According to the Batak the Ego consists of the body, of the Ego consciousness (*roha*), the ghost (*begu*), and the soul (*tondi*).[8] In the *tondi* we have the divine in man but in a sense different from what we have found to be the case among the Maori and the Dakota. The *tondi* is divine only because it is bestowed by the deities. It does not apparently partake of the divine itself. The *tondi* of man is an individualized piece of the soul-substance existing in the universe and of which everything partakes. The *tondi* is, so to speak, a man within a man and with its own will and desires which do not always correspond to those of the Ego, i.e., the *roha*. Yet it is the *tondi* that represents the true and fundamental part of every man's consciousness because it is regarded as having of its own free will selected its fate from among a large number of others before its incarnation in some particular person. The *tondi* alone is held responsible if it has not chosen a good fate.

Man is thus prejudged. This would imply that according to the Batak man has within him two voices, the true, essential and predetermined (the *tondi*), and the ephemeral (the *roha*). Although it is the latter

---

[8] J. Warneck, *Die Religion der Batak*, pp. 8-24.

which does the actual thinking, feeling, desiring, etc., it is the *tondi* that is responsible for our corporeal and our psychical well-being; and though the fate of each *tondi* has been predetermined, no one knows it except by his experience in life.

The *tondi* is supposed to reside in all the parts of the human body but in addition it manifests itself in numerous other ways. First of all it becomes materialized in the human shadow; second, in a man's name; third, in the splendor that shines in the face of a happy man; and fourth, in the personal power he exercises over others. Indeed, as might have been expected, some native thinkers have found it necessary to break with this unity in the idea of one *tondi* and have postulated seven, although little seems to be known about them.

How distinct from man the *tondi* is felt to be, in spite of its pervading the body, is shown by the worship accorded to it. We are in fact, notwithstanding certain inconsistencies, dealing with a concept identical with that of the Dakota *sicun* and of the "Guardian Spirit" so common in North America.

Perhaps the following quotation will do more than any discussion toward enabling us to understand both the nature of the *tondi* and the rôle it plays in the life of the Batak:

There once lived a great prince beloved by all on account of his power and wealth. But he had no children. So one day he prayed to God, "O Grandfather Mula Djadji, you

have given my brother seven children, give me at least one!"
Shortly after his wife became pregnant and in due time a
son was born to her. But when this child came into the
world it was found to be but half of a human being; it had
but one eye, one ear, one arm, one foot. For this reason it
was called the "one-sided." As the child grew up it naturally waxed more and more indignant at its hideous appearance and finally it decided to go to Mula Djadji himself
and complain directly against the fate that had been allotted
him. After many difficulties the boy arrived in the presence
of God and to him he complained directly, "Grandfather,
why did you make me so completely different in appearance
from all other people? Give me at least a shape like theirs."
Then God answered him, "You must not find fault with
me in this matter. I would like to bestow upon all people
a nice shape, for that would redound to my credit. But is
it my fault if a man's *tondi* refuses to accept the lot I had
predestined for him? To prove to you that I am telling
you the truth, follow me to the sixth heaven and there you
will be able to convince yourself that you have no cause
for complaint against me." Thereupon God showed the boy
the mould of his father's and mother's fate and explained
to him how beautiful had been the lot that he had destined
for him too. "When you were born I showed you the fate
that I had arranged for you, that would be yours on earth,
but your *tondi* refused it saying it was too heavy for you.
I told your *tondi* thereupon to select something that would
fit you but it insisted that everything I showed it was un-
suitable and too heavy, and told me to split the mould in
two. 'Good, I will do that for you,' and it was done. You

can see for yourself what the original mould was like. You see how it is the mould of a complete man. When I split it, of course, only half a man developed, for only that which a man selects for himself comes to fruition."

God, however, had pity on the poor half-man and spoke to him. "Good, I will cancel your fate and again give you a chance to select your destiny." The cripple immediately set himself to the task of selection. He weighed all the moulds but everything was too heavy. Finally God asked him which he had chosen and the man answered, "I have tried them all but they are too heavy. O let me not die! Give me my old mould back again for only that one can I carry!" "Well and good," said God, "but do not complain again. I allow all people to choose the good, but if they refuse, then they must suffer the consequences." [9]

Of the Ego proper from our point of view, the *roha,* very little is said except that it thinks, feels, etc. It is apparently regarded as of no consequence except when it comes into conflict with the *tondi.* With regard to the significance of the ghost (*begu*) there seem to be two contradictory theories. According to one the *begu* is the *tondi* after death; according to the other the *begu* constitutes all that is left of a man's personality after the *tondi* has left him. The *begu* is thus not a separate entity to the living man as is the *wairua* of the Maori or the *nagi* of the Dakota. It is only potentially in him. After death, however, it attains an importance and significance a thousandfold greater than that of

---

[9] *Ibid.,* pp. 50-51.

the *wairua* or *nagi*. It becomes associated with the dead, with ancestors, with all that is evil.

In other words the cause of evil is sought outside of man although conceived of as emanating from something that lies within him. This part of man's personality is thus completely projected outside of himself and it is perhaps in consequence of this complete projection upon the outside world, of evil and of misfortune, that the Batak live in an atmosphere apparently pervaded by terror. This is not true among either the Maori or the Dakota.

Now what are the implications of such analyses of the Ego as these just described? It is clearly manifest that the dynamic principle is here fundamental. The static principle is definitely only the temporary shell, the body, doomed to early extinction and decay. Also, there is the inability to express the psychical in terms of the body; the psychical must be projected upon the external world. The Ego, in other words, cannot contain within itself both subject and object, although the object is definitely conditioned by and exists within the perceiving self. Thus we have an Ego consisting of subject-object, with the object only intelligible in terms of the external world and of other Egos. This does not in any sense, of course, interfere with the essential dualism of primitive thought but it does imply a tie between the Ego and the phenomenal world foreign to that which we assume. And this connection is very important, for it takes the form of an attraction, a compulsion. Nature cannot resist man,

man cannot resist nature. A purely mechanistic conception of life is thus unthinkable. The parts of the body, the physiological functions of the organs, like the material form taken by objects in nature, are mere symbols, *simulacra*, for the essential psychical-spiritual entity that lies behind them.

CHAPTER XV

SPECULATION FOR ITS OWN SAKE

THE preceding chapters must have convinced even the most obdurate skeptic that some individuals in every primitive group are capable of something much higher than mere phantasy-thinking. But even these converts, I am inclined to believe, would shrink from admitting my next contention, that there exist certain individuals in each group who enjoy thinking for its own sake, that, in fact, a good deal of discussion takes place between the leaders of the different ceremonies—and it is these priests who are almost invariably the thinkers—on questions which are of a purely speculative nature. It may seem trivial to us, for instance, whether the rock and the earth are to be regarded as married or not. Among the Dakota Indians, however, it is a question upon which a good deal of discussion has taken place and which looms as an important problem of theology.

Now to obtain the requisite information on this aspect of speculation we must go to the thinker and philosopher when he is philosophizing, and that is not easy to do under the very best of circumstances. First of all there are extremely few philosophers in any primitive group and second, these have more important things to do most of the time than to philosophize. The moment, however, a kind fate directs us to the philosopher of the group we discover evidence of a considerable degree of directed thought. For our purposes it is immaterial whether some of this speculation is connected with recent European influence or not since all I am desirous of proving is that a few individuals in every community indulge in speculation and enjoy it. Some of the examples I shall quote are definitely connected with recent Christian influence, but these are particularly instructive because the questions they develop are often quite new to Christian theology.

As it is obviously impossible to do more than touch on so vast a subject in the space I wish to devote to it here, I shall arbitrarily select a number of the more important abstract questions upon which first-hand information is available. Some of the problems of a speculative nature such as the theory of the soul and of human personality, the nature of the external world, etc., have already been discussed, others connected with the creation of the world and monotheism are to be reserved for a subsequent chapter. I shall therefore confine myself here primarily to examples which I believe to be specifically representative of speculation for its own sake and to illustrations of religious-philosophical systematization.

Let me begin with the Oglala Dakota who seem to exhibit an unusual *penchant* for abstract thinking. Our authority, Mr. James Walker, quotes the following interesting discourse on the nature and significance of the circle:

The Oglala believe the circle to be sacred because the great spirit caused everything in nature to be round except stone. Stone is the implement of destruction. The sun and the sky, the earth and the moon, are round like a shield, though the sky is deep like a bowl. Everything that breathes is round like the body of a man. Everything that grows from the ground is round like the stem of a plant. Since the great spirit has caused everything to be round mankind should look upon the circle as sacred, for it is the symbol of all things in nature except stone. It is also the symbol of the circle that marks the edge of the world and therefore of the four winds that travel there. Consequently it is also the symbol of the year. The day, the night, and the moon go in a circle above the sky. Therefore the circle is a symbol of these divisions of time and hence the symbol of all time.

For these reasons the Oglala make their *tipis* circular, their camp-circle circular, and sit in a circle in all ceremonies. The circle is also the symbol of the *tipi* and of shelter. If one makes a circle for an ornament and it is not divided in any way, it should be understood as the symbol of the world and of time.[1]

Manifestly this is speculation for its own sake. It is obviously the attempt of some speculative mind

---

[1] "The Sun Dance of the Oglala Division of the Dakota," *Anthropological Papers of the American Museum of Natural History*, XVI, Part II, p. 160.

to explain the tremendous religious significance the circle has among the Oglala. Many—the vast majority —are content to accept the circle, or to feel satisfied with the religious thrill it arouses in them. This man was not. He shows this same philosophical tendency in his disquisition on the number four, the sacred number of his tribe and, for that matter, of the vast majority of tribes of North America. The ordinary man has no interest whatsoever in explaining why everything must be done four times. It is for them simply a fact. This particular individual, however, was interested. Here is his speculation on the number four:

In former times the Lakota grouped all their activities by fours. This was because they recognized four directions: the west, the north, the east, and the south; four divisions of time: the day, the night, the moon, and the year; four parts in everything that grows from the ground: the roots, the stem, the leaves, and the fruit; four kinds of things that breathe: those that crawl, those that fly, those that walk on four legs, and those that walk on two legs; four things above the world: the sun, the moon, the sky, and the stars; four kinds of gods: the great, the associates of the great, the gods below them and the spiritkind; four periods of human life: babyhood, childhood, adulthood, and old age; and finally, mankind has four fingers on each hand, four toes on each foot and the thumbs and the great toes taken together form four. Since the great spirit caused everything to be in fours, mankind should do everything possible in fours.[2]

---

[2] *Ibid.*, p. 159.

Another Oglala philosopher gave Mr. Walker an exceedingly interesting account of the invocation used by a shaman which ran as follows:

Before a shaman can perform a ceremony in which mysterious beings or things have a part, he should fill and light a pipe and say:

"Friend of Wakinyan, I pass the pipe to you first. Circling I pass to you who dwell with the father. Circling pass to beginning day. Circling pass to the beautiful one. Circling I complete the four quarters and the time. I pass the pipe to the father with the sky. I smoke with the great spirit. Let us have a blue day."

The pipe is used because the smoke from the pipe, smoked in communion, has the potency of the feminine god who mediates between godkind and mankind, and propitiates the godkind. When a shaman offers the pipe to a god, the god smokes it and is propitiated. In this invocation, when the shaman has filled and lighted the pipe, he should point the mouth toward the west and say, "Friend of Wakinyan, I pass the pipe to you first." Thus he offers the pipe to the west wind, for the west wind dwells in the lodge of Wakinyan and is his friend. The pipe should be offered to the west wind first, because the birthright of precedence of the oldest was taken from the first born, the north wind, and given to the second born, the west wind, and the gods are very jealous of the order of their precedence.

When he has made this offering the shaman should move the pipe toward the right hand, the mouthpiece pointing toward the horizon, until it points toward the north. Then he should say, "Circling, I pass to you who dwells with the grandfather." Thus he offers the pipe to the north wind, for because of an offense against the feminine god, the great spirit condemned the north wind to dwell forever with his grandfather, who is *Wazi,* the wizard. Then the shaman should move the pipe in the same manner, until the mouthpiece points toward the east and say, "Circling, pass to beginning day." This is an offering to the east wind, for his lodge is where the day begins and he may be addressed as the "beginning day." Then the shaman should move the pipe in the same manner until the mouthpiece points toward the south, and say, "Circling, pass to the beautiful one." This is an offering to the south wind, for the "beautiful one" is the feminine god who is the companion of the south wind and dwells in his lodge, which is under the sun at midday. It pleases the south wind to be addressed through his companion rather than directly.

The four winds are the *akicita* or messengers of the gods and in all ceremonies they have precedence over all other gods and for this reason should be the first addressed.

When the offering has been made to the south wind the shaman should move the pipe in the same manner until the mouthpiece again points toward the west, and say, "Circling, I complete the four quarters and the time." He should do this because the four winds are the four quarters of the circle and mankind knows not where they may be or whence they may come and the pipe should be offered directly toward them. The four quarters embrace all that are in the world and all that are in the sky. Therefore, by circling the pipe, the offering is made to all the gods. The circle is the symbol of time, for the daytime, the night time, and the moon time are circles above the world, and the year time is a circle around the border of the world. Therefore the lighted pipe moved in a complete circle is an offering to all the times.[3]

In conclusion let me add a few more examples of speculation from the same tribe collected by another observer. Some of them may contain indications of Christian influence but this is really more apparent than actual.

All living creatures and all plants derive their life from the sun. If it were not for the sun, there would be darkness and nothing could grow—the earth would be without life. Yet the sun must have the help of the earth. If the sun alone were to act upon animals and plants, the heat would be so great that they would die, but there are clouds that bring rain, and the action of the sun and earth together supply the moisture that is needed for life. The roots of a plant go down, and the deeper they go the more moisture they find. This is according to the laws of nature and is one of the evidences of the wisdom of Wakan tanka. Plants are sent by Wakan tanka and come from the ground at his command, the part to be affected by the sun and rain appearing above the ground and the roots pressing downward to find the moisture which is supplied for them. Animals and plants are taught by Wakan tanka what they are to do. Wakan tanka teaches the birds to make nests,

---

[3] *Ibid.*, p. 160.

yet the nests of all birds are not alike. Wakan tanka gives them merely the outline. Some make better nests than others. In the same way some animals are satisfied with very rough dwellings, while others make attractive places in which to live. Some animals also take better care of their young than others. The forest is the home of many birds and other animals, and the water is the home of fish and reptiles. All birds, even those of the same species, are not alike, and it is the same with animals and with human beings. The reason Wakan tanka does not make two birds, or animals, or human beings exactly alike is because each is placed here by Wakan tanka to be an independent individuality and to rely on itself. Some animals are made to live in the ground. The stones and the minerals are placed in the ground by Wakan tanka, some stones being more exposed than others. When a medicine man says that he talks with the sacred stones, it is because of all the substance in the ground these are the ones which most often appear in dreams and are able to communicate with men.

All animals have not the same disposition. The horse, dog, bear, and buffalo all have their own characteristics. This is also true of the fowls of the air, the living creatures in the water, and even the insects; they all have their own ways. Thus a man may enjoy the singing of all the birds and yet have a preference for the melodies of certain *kinds* of birds. Or he may like all animals and yet have a favorite among them.

From my boyhood I have observed leaves, trees, and grass, and I have never found two alike. They may have a general likeness, but on examination I have found that they differ slightly. Plants are of different families, each being adapted to growth in a certain locality. It is the same with animals; they are widely scattered, and yet each will be found in the environment to which it is best adapted. It is the same with human beings; there is some place which is best adapted to each. The seeds of the plants are blown about by the wind until they reach the place where they will grow best—where the action of the sun and the presence of moisture are most favorable to them, and there they take root and grow. All living creatures and all plants are a benefit to something. Certain animals fulfill their purpose by definite acts. The crows, buzzards, and flies are somewhat similar in their use, and even the snakes have a purpose in being. In the early days the animals probably roamed over a very wide country until they found their proper place. An animal depends a great deal on the natural conditions around it. If the buffalo were here today, I think they would be different from the buffalo of the old days because all the natural conditions have changed. They would not find the same food, nor the same surroundings. We see the change in our ponies. In the old days they could stand great hardship and travel long distances without water. They lived on certain kinds of food and drank pure water. Now our horses require a mixture of food; they have less endurance and must have constant care. It is the same with the Indians; they have less freedom and they fall an easy prey to disease. In the old days they were rugged and healthy, drinking pure water and eating the meat of the buffalo, which had a wide range, not being shut up like cattle of the present day. The water of the Missouri River is not pure, as it used to be, and many of the creeks are no longer good for us to drink.

A man ought to desire that which is genuine instead of that which is artificial. Long ago there was no such thing as a mixture of earths to make paint. There were only three colors of native earth paint—red, white, and black. These could be obtained only in certain places. When other colors were desired, the Indians mixed the juices of plants, but it was found that these mixed colors faded and it could always be told when the red was genuine—the red made of burned clay.

All classes of people know that when human power fails they must look to a higher power for the fulfillment of their desires. There are many ways in which the request for help from this higher power can be made. This depends on the person. Some like to be quiet, and others want to do everything in public. Some like to go alone, away from the crowd, to meditate upon many things. In order to secure a fulfillment of his desire a man must qualify himself to make his request. Lack of preparation would mean failure to secure a response to his petition. Therefore when a man makes up his mind to ask a favor of Wakan tanka he makes due preparation. It is not fitting that a man should suddenly go out and make a request of Wakan tanka. When a man shuts his eyes, he sees a great deal. He then enters his own mind, and things become clear to him, but objects passing before his eyes would distract him. For that reason a dreamer makes known his request through what he sees when his eyes are closed. It has long been his intention to make his request of Wakan tanka, and he resolves to seek seclusion on the top of a butte or other high place. When at last he goes there he closes his eyes, and his mind is upon Wakan tanka and his work. The man who does this usually has in mind some animal which he would like for protection and help. No man can succeed in life alone, and he cannot get the help he wants from men; therefore he seeks help through some bird or animal which Wakan tanka sends for his assistance. Many animals have ways from which a man can learn a great deal, even from the fact that horses are restless before a storm.

When I was 10 years of age I looked at the land and the rivers, the sky above, and the animals around me and could not fail to realize that they were made by some great power. I was so anxious to understand this power that I questioned the trees and the bushes. It seemed as though the flowers were staring at me, and I wanted to ask them "Who made you?" I looked at the moss-covered stones; some of them seemed to have the features of a man, but they could not answer me. Then I had a dream, and in my dream one of these small round stones appeared to me and told me that the maker of all was Wakan tanka, and that in order to honor him I must honor his works in nature. The stone said that by my search I had shown myself worthy of supernatural help. It said that if I were curing a sick person I might ask its assistance, and that all the forces of nature would help me work a cure.

It is significant that certain stones are not found buried in the earth, but are on the top of high buttes. They are round, like the sun and moon, and we know that all things which are round are related to each other. Things which are alike in their nature grow to look like each other, and these stones have lain there a long time, looking at the sun. Many pebbles and stones have been shaped in the current of a stream, but these stones were found far from the water and have been exposed only to the sun and the wind. The earth contains many thousand such stones hidden beneath its surface. The thunderbird is said to be related to these stones, and when a man or an animal is to be punished, the thunderbird strikes the person, and if it were possible to follow the course of the lightning, one of these stones would be found embedded in the earth. Some believe that these stones descend with the lightning, but I believe they are on the ground and are projected downward by the bolt. In all my life I have been faithful to the sacred stones. I have lived according to their requirements, and they have helped me in all my troubles. I have tried to qualify myself as well as possible to handle these sacred stones, yet I know that I am not worthy to speak to Wakan tanka. I make my request of the stones and they are my intercessors.

Ever since I have known the old Indians and their customs, I have seen that in any great undertaking it is not enough for a man to depend simply upon himself. Most people place their dependence on the medicine men, who understand this life and all its surroundings and are able to predict what will come to pass. They have the right to make these predictions. If as we sit here we should hear a voice speaking from above, it would be because we had the right to hear what others could not hear, or we might see what others had not the right to see because they were not properly qualified. Such are some of the rights and privileges of the medicine men, and those who desire to know mysterious things must seek their aid.

I have noticed in my life that all men have a liking for some special animal, or plant, or spot of earth. If men would pay more attention to these preferences and seek what is best to do in order to make themselves worthy of that toward which they are so attracted, they might have dreams which would purify their lives. Let a man decide upon his favorite animal and make a study of it, learning its ways. Let him learn to understand its sounds and motions. The animals want to communicate with man, but Wakan tanka does not intend they shall do so directly—man must do the greater part in securing an understanding.[4]

I pass now to an entirely different region, to the Ewe of West Africa. The German missionary Johann Spieth has published a number of so-called "Discourses on God" which show the same interest in speculation as those quoted from the Oglala. "We can never attain a knowledge such as God's," states the first of these discourses. "You saw me bring back a calabash and you now see me working on it. I have scraped it and in this fashion made a drinking vessel for myself. The seed that lay within it was exceedingly small, but I placed this seed in the ground and, as you now see, it

---

[4] Francis Densmore, *Bulletin 61 of the Bureau of American Ethnology*, pp. 122, 172-173; 184; 208.

has become a useful utensil. I (man) cannot do that; but the wisdom with which God made it, that, too, I do not understand. The child must not say to its father, 'I surpass you.' " [5]

But it is the third of the discourses that is most interesting. It deals with the world and God.

"When night or day approach do we know what is going to happen to us on either occasion? But whether we are in a stream or whether it is night, we are everywhere still in the world. That is why we say that God is the world. Everything in the world is the creation of God: the fish in the water, men, good and evil, God has sent them all. The world is stronger than everything else and that is why we say that the world is God. You only know what you can know to-day, not that which is to take place in the future. God alone knows what will take place to-morrow. Mankind will never be able to comprehend God completely and that is why we say the world is God. No one can know everything that happens in the world. If you go to one town you can learn what takes place in that town but you will not know what is taking place in another town." [6]

As another example of this kind of speculative interest let me give the account of the various inferences by which a Winnebago informant identified himself successively with God, with his soul, and with his thought: "I prayed to Earthmaker (God). And as

---

[5] *Die Ewe Staemme*, pp. 327-328.
[6] *Ibid.*, pp. 834-836.

I prayed I was aware of something above me and there he was! That which is called the soul, that is it, that is what one calls Earthmaker. Now this is what I felt and saw. All of us sitting together there, we had all together one spirit and I was their spirit or soul. I did not have to speak to them and get an answer to know what had been their thoughts. Then I thought of a certain place far away and immediately I was there; I was my thought. I would not need any more food for was I not my spirit? Nor would I have any more use of my body. My corporeal affairs are over." [7]

The remarkable thing about the passage I have just quoted is its absolute originality. There is nothing in Winnebago theology to justify the identification of their supreme deity, Earthmaker, with the soul nor, as far as I am aware, is there any warrant for it in Christian theology. The quasi-pantheism developed in the sentences following whereby all the worshipers present were regarded as having one soul which was then identified with this man's soul, that, too, is quite unique in Winnebago speculation. The belief in fore-knowledge and in thought-reading existed but never before had any speculative mind drawn the inference that because thought in the moment apparently enabled you to be in a certain place far distant, therefore logically you must be your thought.

To the same individual we owe a most interesting

[7] *Crashing Thunder: the Autobiography of an American Indian,* edited by Paul Radin, pp. 190-192.

disquisition on the Trinity. In a recent new religion to which many Winnebago became converted the Christian belief in the Trinity plays a minor rôle. Most of the members of the new sect give a lip service to this dogma and then pay no more attention to it. Our philosopher, however, could not refrain from explaining and elaborating upon it. In fact he discovered what I feel confident is an absolutely new proof of the Trinity. Apparently the problem that exercised his mind was, very properly, how the Deity could be one and three at the same time. The customary Christian demonstrations of the Trinity he did not know and he would unquestionably neither have understood nor accepted them if he had known them, for nothing ever convinced this individual except some inward warrant or some definite concrete evidence. In this case it was concrete evidence that he obtained. He found the proof in an English word found in the Gospel of St. Matthew, in a passage that has played an enormous part in the history of Christianity, the famous nineteenth verse of the sixteenth chapter of St. Matthew. There the word *key* is found and it is this word that led him to his extraordinary interpretation. But let me quote the passage in full for it is deeply interesting:

My body told us how this new religion of ours was an affair of God's and that even if one knew only one portion of it, one could still partake of God's religion.

Thus did my body speak. God, the Son of God, and His Holiness (the Holy Ghost), these are the three ways of saying it. Even if you knew. only one of these three, it means all. Every one here has the means of opening the road to God. It is given to you. With your belief only can you open this door to God. You cannot open it with knowledge alone.

"How many letters are there to the key, i. e., the road to God?" "Three." "What are they?" There were many educated people present but none of them said anything. "The first letter must be a *K*, so that if a person said *K*, that would be the whole of it. But let me look in the book (the Bible) and see what that means," said the body. Then the body took the Bible and began to turn the leaves. The body did not know where it (the passage sought) was itself, for it was not learned in books. Finally in Matthew, in chapter 16, it stopped. In that chapter this *K* is mentioned for it says, "Peter did not give himself up." For a long time he could not give up his own knowledge. There in that passage you will find the word *key*.[8]

In other words the word *key* fulfills the conditions, for the first letter *k* is pronounced like the whole word *key*. Here certainly we have true subtlety and a praiseworthy philosophical and theological striving.

---

[8] *Ibid.,* p. 200.

CHAPTER XVI

THE SYSTEMATIZATION OF IDEAS

FROM speculative discussion for its own sake we shall now turn to the more usual subjects of philosophical interest, the systematization of the various ideas concerning the origin of the world, and the nature of things. Some of the concepts underlying these attempts at systematization have already been discussed before, others such as those embodied in the creation myths of various tribes we must postpone to the chapter on monotheism. In this chapter we will limit ourselves exclusively to the definite philosophical implications found in certain cosmological myths and related material, and still further circumscribe our inquiry by discussing only Polynesian data. I do not feel that any objection can legitimately be advanced against thus limiting ourselves to a very restricted ethnological province, for in a tentative work like the present, our object must be to demonstrate the existence, among peoples customarily regarded as primitive, of certain intellectual tendencies and accomplishments. The question of their universality, while important, can for the time being be relegated to the background.

The Polynesians have long been known for their

unusually elaborate cosmological chants. In these chants, many of them possessing a beauty of thought and expression that can be still felt in the translation, a complete cosmogony is outlined containing not only an account of the origin of the world and the earth but what is to all appearances a fairly definite theory of the origin of consciousness. I say this advisedly for I can find no other interpretation for the first five lines of the following Maori chant. The story of creation is divided into four large periods, each one showing within itself a secondary and progressive evolution. The first period, which as I said contains a theory of the development of consciousness, is as follows:

> From the conception the increase,
> From the increase the swelling,
> From the swelling the thought,
> From the thought the remembrance,
> From the remembrance, the desire.[1]

It is only after the development of physical and psychical differentiation and of personal consciousness —so we must interpret these lines—that an external world can be apprehended. This is the first period. It is with this external world, or better with what is outside of the perceiving self, that the second period is concerned. One is naturally inquisitive about the transition between the two periods and here our unknown Maori philosopher is both stimulating and sug-

---

[1] Richard Taylor, *Te Ika A Maui*.

gestive. He does not apparently regard the external world as having been created from, or as responding to, what he has predicated as the last stage of the first period, namely, desire; but he assumes that the second period was created by the *word*. Is it too far-fetched to see herein an attempt to obviate the necessity of ascribing the existence of the external world to thought or will, by the predication of a mediating principle, the *word;* that is, by what represents the first articulate and external expression of thought, remembrance, and desire? I do not think so. To people more qualified than myself, however, do I leave the task of interpreting the following lines, which give the account of the second cosmic period. The problem of the origin of matter is here most skillfully dodged—or shall I say delayed—in the most approved manner of the early evolutionists:

> The word became fruitful;
> It dwelt with the feeble glimmering;
> It brought forth night:
> The great night, the long night,
> The lowest night, the loftiest night,
> The thick night to be felt,
> The night to be touched, the night unseen.
> The night following on,
> The night ending in death.[2]

Here we have evolutionism *in excelsis*. The absolute consistency and inevitableness of this thinking—call it intuitive or definitely rational as you wish—is simply

---

[2] *Journal of the Polynesian Society*, XVI, p. 113.

appalling. From desire came the word. But this first
phase of articulateness creates nothing. It merely
dwells with the feeble glimmering. Is this feeble
glimmering to be construed as the dawn between non-
consciousness and consciousness? Our Maori philosopher leaves this unresolved. Then follows the description of the absoluteness of night, perfect in its
kind; the night that can be touched but is yet unseen,
the lowest yet the highest, the night that follows on,
but ends in death. Yet this night has one distinctive
quality which philosophically is fundamental—it can
be apprehended, and thus becomes quite different from
that night which the Maori describe as existing when,
unborn, they dwelt within the womb of their mother,
the earth.

The third period represents the genealogical history
of matter. It is strictly parallel to the account given
in the first period of the origin of consciousness.

> From the nothing the begetting,
> From the nothing the increase,
> From the nothing the abundance,
> The power of increasing, the living breath;
> It dwelt with the empty space,
> It produced the atmosphere which is above us.

As compared with the first period there is a flaw in
the evolutionary account. Nothing leads to begetting,
increase, abundance and the power of increasing, the
living breath. Apparently our ancient philosophic
friend, after having delayed the vexatious problem of

how something could have arisen out of nothing, throws all logic and caution to the winds and hurdles over the question. Let us not throw stones; he has some illustrious successors.

The fourth period is philosophically not so interesting. Light is about to appear and with it our problems become dissipated.

The atmosphere which floats above the earth,
The great firmament above us, the spread-out space
dwelt with the early dawn,
Then the moon sprang forth;
The atmosphere above dwelt with the glowing sky.
Forthwith was produced the sun;
They were thrown up above as the chief eyes of heaven;
Then the heavens became light,
The early dawn, the early day,
The midday. The blaze of day from the sky.

Where such remarkable chants are developed one naturally expects that the philosophy in one version may be better or worse than in another. I wish to quote one such version which logically is better, although the Maori philosopher simplified his problem and instead of positing the question of mind and matter, frankly assumed both from the very beginning. He still further simplified the problem of the origin of the mind by assuming a divine mind, the deity Io. Although everything superficially comes into existence as the *fiat* of Io, this version contains in reality a profounder understanding of development than did our first:

Io dwelt within the breathing-space of immensity.
The universe was in darkness, with water everywhere.
There was no glimmer of dawn, no clearness, no light.
And he began by saying these words,
That he might cease remaining inactive.
"Darkness, become a light-possessing darkness."
(He) then repeated these selfsame words in this manner,
That he might cease remaining inactive.
"Light, become a darkness-possessing light."
And again an intense darkness supervened.
Then a third time he spake saying:
"Let there be darkness above,
Let there be one darkness below (alternate),
Let there be darkness unto Tupua,
Let there be darkness unto Tawhito,
A dominion of light,
A bright light."
And now a great light prevailed.
(Io) then looked to the waters which compassed him
   about and spoke a fourth time saying,
"Ye waters of Tai-kama, be ye separate,
Heaven be formed." Then the sky became suspended.
"Bring forth, thou Tupua-hono-nuku."
And at once the moving earth lay stretched abroad.[3]

Even at the risk of wearying the reader I cannot
refrain from giving one more chant, a Tahitian creation hymn, in its entirety. Much of its content is
contained in the two chants already quoted but this
third chant has some new features, new subtleties, and
bears the impress of a different type of temperament
and personality:

---

[3] *Journal of the Polynesian Society*, XVI, p. 113.

He abides—Taaroa by name—
In the immensity of space.
There was no earth, there was no heaven,
There was no sea, there was no mankind;
Taaroa calls on high;
He changed himself fully.
Taaroa is the root;
The rocks (or foundations);
Taaroa is the sands;
Taaroa stretches out the branches (is wide-spreading).
Taaroa is the light;
Taaroa is within.
Taaroa is below;
Taaroa is enduring;
Taaroa is wise;
He created the land of Hawaii;
Hawaii great and sacred,
As a *cruse* (or shell) for Taaroa.
The earth is dancing (moving).
O foundations, O rocks,
O sands! Here, here.
Brought hither, press together the earth,
Press, press again!
Stretch out the seven heavens, let ignorance cease.
Create the heavens, let darkness cease.
Let anxiety cease within.
It is the time of the speaker.
Fill up (complete) the foundations.
Fill up the rocks,
Fill up the sands.[4]

Finally let me quote a theory of the origin of night which developed among the Hawaiians and which is directly opposed to the notions expounded in the first

---

[4] J. Fornander, *The Polynesian Race*, I, pp. 221 *ff*.

two Maori chants. As far as I can make out, in this account heat and light preceded night, and night came into being at midwinter when the light of the sun was "subdued." Its evolution is extremely interesting—slime, earth, deepest darkness, night. Whether the mysticism here is more apparent than real, I have no means of telling. The chant follows:

> At the time that turned the heat of the earth,
> At the time when the heavens turned and changed,
> At the time when the light of the sun was subdued
> To cause light to break forth,
> At the time of the night of winter,
> Then began the slime which established the earth,
> The source of deepest darkness;
> Of the depth of the darkness, of the depth of the darkness,
> Of the darkness of the sun, in the depth of night;
>> It is night:
>> Thus was night born.[5]

All this evolution is admirably summed up in the preamble to a well-known Maori lament:

> For thee, O *whai,* my love is ever great.
> From germ of life sprang thought,
> And god's own medium came:
> Then bird and bloom; and life in space
> Produced the worlds of night—
> The worlds where bowing knee
> And form in abject crouching lost,
> Are lost—for ever lost.
> And never now return ye

---

[5] *Journal of the Polynesian Society,* IX, pp. 39 *ff.*

From those worlds of gloom.
'Twas nothing that begot
The nothing unpossessed
And nothing without charm.

'Twas Rangi who with Atu-tahi
Brought forth the moon.
And Rangi Wero-wero took
And, yet unseen, the sun produced.
He, silent, skimmed the space above,
And then burst forth the glowing eye of heaven
To give thee light, O man!
To wage thy war on fellow-man.

Turn and look this way.
On Tara-rua's distant peak now
Shines the light of coming day—
The dawn of eating-man and feats of war.[6]

All the speculations so far quoted have been couched in fairly abstract terms. But there was another kind of cosmological speculation not uncommon among the Polynesians where the ideas were drawn primarily from the domain of plant life. Thus among the Maori we have the following periods:

1. *Te Pu* (origin, source, root, base, foundation).
2. *Te More* (tap-root; figuratively, cause).
3. *Te Weu* (rootlet, fibers).
4. *Te Aka* (long, thin roots; stem of climbing plant).
5. *Te Rea* (growth).
6. *Te Wao-nui* (primeval forest).

---

[6] John White, *The Ancient History of the Maori*, I, pp. 7-8.

Here the plant analogies stop and we find

7. *Te Kune* (pregnancy, conception, form acquired).
8. *Te Whe* (sound, as of creaking of tree branches).
9. *Te Kore* (non-existence).
10. *Te Po* (night).

From night then came the Sky-father and the Earth-mother; from them, in turn, the god Tane and from him finally man.[7]

We have in our discussion of the Polynesian material so far been carried only to the period of the creation of the sky and the earth. Naturally speculation did not stop there. The same feeling for an evolutionary systematization which we saw evinced for the development of the cosmos is shown for the period subsequent to the appearance of the sky and earth and for the origin of man himself. The order of creation among the Maori ran as follows:

1. The waters of ocean that are in the world, these were all created by the waters; and then grew out of them the land, the earth, which on maturity was taken to wife by the Sky-father.
2. Next were created the trees of all kinds, to clothe the skin of the earth which had heretofore been naked.
3. Next were created the minor vegetation growing each after its own kind.
4. Next were created the reptiles and insects of every kind.

---

[7] *Journal of the Polynesian Society*, III, p. 158.

5. Next were created the animals, dogs of every species.
6. Next were created the birds of different kinds to dwell on the plains and in the woods of the earth and on lady-ocean also.
7. Next were created the moon, the sun, and all the stars. When this had been accomplished, the "world of light" became permanent.
8. Next and finally were created the first woman and her daughter, from whom sprang mankind.[8]

The Maori informant added the following characteristic note: "Each one of these, from the very first down to the creation of man, mentioned each in his own period, growing up in its own time, increasing in its own period, living in its own period, endowed after its own manner and time. Each had its own time of conception or sprouting. We now understand that this was the nature of all things, that each thing has its female counterpart through which it conceives."

For the origin of man the Maori developed a type of speculation whose counterpart I have yet to find. Now as a rule, in creation myths, the creation of man is comparatively simple. He is generally created directly by the deity either out of nothing, out of a portion of the deity, or out of the cosmic material that already exists. Here nothing of the kind occurs. From the very beginning it is assumed that man can arise only in the proper biological manner, from a female. The

---

[8] S. Percy Smith, "The Lore of the Whare-Wananga," *Memoirs of the Polynesian Society*, III, pp. 135-137.

problem that then confronts the gods is to discover
the appropriate female. This is not so easy to determine, because the Maori gods were sharp logicians in
whom Anatole France would have taken keen delight.
They argued that their own kind must be excluded,
for from gods only gods can be born. They soon
realized that the type of female required would have to
be created *de novo* and they proceeded to create her,
after having first agreed that the mammalian method
of reproduction was to be followed, that of reptiles
and birds having been examined and found wanting.
The myth follows:

Then Tane and his elder brother asked one another, "By
what means shall we raise up descendants to ourselves in
the world of light?" Their elder brother said, "Let us seek
a female that may take on our likeness and raise up offspring for us in the world of light." Some suggested they
should fetch some of the female Apas (divine messengers) of
the twelve heavens. But the older brother replied, "If we
fetch our females from there, then all our descendants will
be gods like ourselves. Rather let us take of the earth,
that it may be said they are the descendants of the earth."
Hereupon it was agreed to search for such a female.

The family of gods now dispersed by two and two to
search for the female. Every place was sought out but
not one single thing was found suitable to take on the
functions of a female similar to the female Apas of the
conjoint heavens. All assembled again—none had found
anything.

It was then decided by the gods to ascertain or no whether the female was to be found in any of the living beings that had been appointed to dwell in the world (i. e., the animals, insects, etc.). For all females of living things conceive. An examination of the offspring was made. Some were found partly appropriate, some not. The reptiles have their particular issue in the form of eggs; they were not found suitable on examination and so were discarded. It was considered better that something which produced after its own kind or bodily shape should be adopted—and hence offspring by eggs was assigned to birds. It was now obvious that the kind of female required from which the *iho-tangata* (the form or likeness and attributes of man) could be born, was not to be found.

So the gods all assembled again to declare their various ideas. And then spoke Ro-iho, Ro-ake, and Hae-puru to Tane. "O Tane, what is it ye are seeking?" Tane replied, "We are searching the way to the female." The three then said, "Try the earth at Kura-waka and commence your operations there for in that place is the female in a state of virginity and potentiality; she is sacred for she contains the likeness of man."

The gods then went off to seek the earth at Kura-waka. Here they formed a body in the likeness of a woman and completed the arrangements of the head, the arms, the bust, the legs, the back, and the front; and then the bones. Here ended the work of the elder brethren. Then followed the arrangements of the flesh, the muscles, the blood, and the fat. On the completion of these parts the breath of life was assigned to Tane to place in the nostrils, the mouth, and the ears. That was done. Then for the first time the breath of man came forth—the eyelids opened, the pupils saw, and the hot breath of the mouth burst forth, the nose sneezed. After this the body was taken to the altar at Muritakina where all the proceedings were voided (i. e., where all evil influence of earthly origin was removed and the first woman became a fitting recipient of the germ of life).

The parts were at first all made separately in different places but afterwards gathered and joined together and on completion, it was said to be a human body. It was Io and one of his messengers who implanted the thoughts and the living spirit.[9]

The creation myth of the Maori is so remarkable in many ways and shows in its elaboration and sequence so clearly the hand of the thinker and the systematizer, that in spite of its length it merits quotation in full:

INTRODUCTION

The Rangi-nui, Great Sky, which stands above, felt a desire towards Papa-tua-nuku, the Earth, whose belly was turned up towards him; he desired her as a wife. So Rangi came down to Papa. In that period the amount of light was nil; absolute and complete darkness prevailed; there was no sun, no moon, no stars, no clouds, no light, no mist— no ripples stirred the surface of ocean; no breath of air, a complete and absolute stillness.

And so Rangi-nui dwelt with Papa-tua-nuku as his wife;

---

[9] *Ibid.,* pp. 138-141.

and then he set plants to cover the nakedness of Papa; for her armpits, her head, and the body; and after that, the smaller trees to clothe them both, for the body of the earth was naked. Subsequently he placed the upstanding trees of the forest, and now Papa felt a great warmth which was all-embracing. After this were placed the insects of all kinds, the ancestors of *tuatara,* the great lizard, appropriate to the recesses of the smaller vegetation, the clumps of smaller trees, and the great forests whose heads reach the skies. Then the crabs, the larger species of univalves, the bivalves, the *ngakihi,* the mussel, the haliotis, and similar things which have shells, were assigned to their places to animate the earth and the waters thereof.

CREATION OF THE GODS

After the last of all these things had been planted by Rangi-nui and Papa, they then created their proper offspring, i. e., the gods; the eyes were made first, and then the "house" to hold them, i. e., the head. After the head, the bust and body and the bones of the legs, according to their growth (shapes).[10]

THE AGES OF DARKNESS; OF CHAOS

It was after this manner that they dwelt in the ages of darkness, within the space included in the embrace of their parents. It was very long that condition of affairs existed; until at last a faint glimmering of light, a scintillation like the light of a star was seen, or like the will-o'-the-wisp at

---

[10] The nature of the existence of the gods was such as has been explained (cf. pp. 249 *f.*).

night. And now commenced a desire on the part of the family of gods to go forth from between their parents to follow the faint appearance of light. Some of the gods consented, some did not; and thus it became a matter of strife between them. Tane, Tupai, and others said, "Let us seek a means by which we may go forth." The matter was then assented to. Now Uru-te-ngangana, the eldest of the family, had been persuaded by Whiro-te-tipua's arguments against going forth, and hence they remained until the last.

THE GODS GO FORTH TO THE WORLD OF LIGHT

Now, at a certain time after, Ue-poto went to bathe and wash away the clammy feeling arising through the warmth of their dwelling-place (within the embrace of their parents). He was carried outside away on the current of his mother's urine and found himself outside in a gentle cooling breeze which was sweet-scented in the nostrils of Ue-poto. He thought this is the best place, here outside. So he called out under the sides of his parents: "O Sirs! Come outside, for this is a pleasant place for us."

When the menstruous time of their mother Earth came, then Tane came forth. This was in the seventh Po, or age of their desire to search for the "way of the female" in order to go forth. On reaching the outside world they then saw that it was indeed a pleasant place for them to dwell. There was, however, a drawback; for the different kinds of the cold of heaven (or space) there spread out their intense cold. Hence did Rangi and Papa closely embrace to exclude the cold from their offspring and hence also originated the "goose-flesh" and trembling through cold. These are the enemies that afflicted the family of their father. In consequence of this they sheltered under the sides of their mother, where they found warmth which they named shelter-by-the-side, which name has come down to us and is applied to a warm and pleasant place where no winds blow.

After this when the ninth and tenth ages had come, Uru-te-ngangana and others came forth—they formed the second party; and then Whiro-te-tipua and his friends were urged to come forth. He did so in anger and afflicted some of the other gods with baldness on the top of the head and the same on the forehead, the eyelashes, and the eyebrows. Great indeed was the wrath of Whiro at Tane because of his inducing them to come forth from the shelter of their parents to be "bitten" by the cold of space—that was the cause of his anger.

The Separation of Heaven and Earth

Some time after the foregoing events Tane said, "Let us now separate our parents that Rangi and Papa may occupy different places." Whiro would not consent to this proposition and there was much strife in consequence. But Tane-nui-a-rangi became more urgent; and then Tangaroa, Tu-mata-uenga, and Tawhiri-matea finally agreed. And now Rangi-nui was propped up into the position he now holds. In the propping up by Tane with the four props, one was placed at the head, one on each side, and one at the legs, making the four that separated Rangi from Papa. But as the props were lifted and Rangi was still suspended in space, one at the legs and one at the head slipped. Tane called out to Paia, "O Pai!" Paia replied, "Here am I."

Tane said, "Raise him up above." In this uplifting and raising in order that Rangi-nui might float above, he did not quite rise to the position required, because the arms of both Rangi and Papa grasped one another and held fast. Then Tane called out to Tu-mata-kaka and Tu-mata-uenga telling them to get an axe to cut the arms of their parents. Tu-mata-kaka cried out, "O Tane, where is the source of axes to be found?" Tane said, "Fetch one from the pillow of our elder brother, Uru-te-ngangana, to cut them with. Fetch a handle from Tua-matua who will put a keen edge on the axe and fasten it to a handle." The two axes named Te-Ahwio-rangi and Te Whiro-nui were then fetched, and then the arms of Rangi-nui and Papa-tua-nuku were severed and they were completely separated. At that time Paia cut off from the neck of Rangi-nui the *ahi-tapu* or sacred fire, which he subsequently used to make fire with, using his *karakia* (incantation) in doing so.

Now when Rangi-nui had been properly placed in position as is now to be seen, the blood from the arms dripped down on to Papa and hence is the red oxide of iron and the blue phosphate of iron, that his descendants in this world use in painting. And hence also is the red appearance that inflames the skies at sunrise or sunset—that is the blood of Rangi's arms.

Now at this time the family of gods proceeded to arrange the knowledge of things celestial and terrestrial of Rangi-nui; that is, to direct matters so that they might be able to adopt a course leading to their benefit. But they were not able to accomplish it, for they were confused about the direction of earthly things—they could not manage it.

The Separation of the Dwellings of the Gods

They now decided to have separate dwelling places. Whiro-te-tipua, Uru-te-ngangana, and their immediate friends dwelt in Tu-te-aniwaniwa (Where-stands-the-rainbow)—that was their house, and the place where they lived.

Tane, Paia, and others dwelt in Huaki-pouri with their friends.

Thus it was that the family dwelt separately; an envious heart was the reason and the following were the causes of this ill feeling:

1. On account of the persistence of Tane that they should go forth from the embrace of their parents.

2. The "biting" of the cold of space, the cold of the waters, the extreme cold and the excessive cold.

3. The persistence of Tane, Tupai, and their faction that their parents Rangi and Papa should be separated.

4. The "evil heart" of Tane, Tupai, and others in deciding to cut off the arms of their parents with the two axes.

5. The presumption of Tane and his faction in undertaking these works. If it had been the seniors of the family, Whiro would have consented.

6. The conceit of Tane in declaring that he could ascend the sacred winds of a conjoint heavens that stand above. Rather should Whiro himself have accomplished the journey to the highest heaven.

The Sanctification of Tane

Now at this time, Io-matua, the Supreme God, said unto Rua-matua and Rehua, two of the guardians of the heavenly treasures, "Go ye down to the earth and on Maunga-nui, the great mountain, command Tane and Tupai to ascend to ye up the mountain. You will there purify them and baptize them in the 'waters of Rongo' on that mountain, and then return." These were the sons of the family.

So these two messengers descended to the summit of Maunga-nui and commanded Tane and Tupai to climb up to them. The two gods did so and on reaching Rua-tau and Rehua they were taken to the "waters of Rongo" and baptized. Thus were they purified; and now for the first time did Tane receive his full name of Tane-nui-a-rangi, the Great Tane of the heavens, whilst Tupai received that of Tupai-a-tau. After this the two messengers ascended to the uppermost heavens to Io-the-hidden-faced and Tane and Tupai returned to their dwelling-place at Huaki-pouri.

7. This was the seventh cause of Whiro-te-tipua's ill feeling; the sanctification, and the baptism of those new names for Tane and Tupai.

After these events Io-the-origin-of-all-things said to his two messengers, "Go! Ask of the family of Rangi-nui which single one of them will be able to ascend the Ascending Clouds of the heavens to Tikitiki-o-rangi, the uppermost heavens, to meet me at Matangi-reia (the sun's path in the heavens, the home of Io). Then these two descended to Tu-te-aniwaniwa (one of the separate houses in which the gods dwelt after coming forth from the parental embrace) and laid their mission before Uru-te-ngangana and Whiro and their faction.

Whiro informed them that he could climb up by the winds of heaven and bring back the *wananga* (all knowledge, etc.). Rua-tau asked, "By what way wilt thou climb, O Whiro?" The latter answered, "By the Taepatanga (where the sky hangs down) of the heavens will I ascend." "You will not succeed for the winds of the conjoint heavens are difficult to overcome."

The two gods then went to Whare-kura (another of the houses of the gods) and Rua-tau asked, "Which of you is able to ascend the conjoint heavens to Io-the-origin-of-all-things?" Rongo-marae-roa and his faction replied that Tane-nui-a-rangi could accomplish it. The two messengers then went to Huaki-pouri (Tane's house) and asked them, "Which of you will be able to climb by the winds of the conjoint heavens to Io-the-origin- of-all-things, at Matangi-reia in its beauty and expanse?" Tane replied to this, "I can do it!" Then said Rua-tau, "By which way will you ascend?" Tane replied, "I will ascend by the Ara-tiatia, the Toi-hua-rewa (two names for the ascent) of the family of my elder brother, the god of winds, who dwells above in the third heaven." Rau-tau and Pawa then said, "Enough! Ascend to Pumotomoto (entrance to) Tikitiki-o-rangi (highest heaven), to Tawhiri-rangi (guard-house of) Te Toi-o-nga-rangi-tuhaha (summit of all the heavens)." After that Rua-tau and Aitu-pawa returned.

Hearing of this Whiro said unto his elder brethren, "I intend to go and fetch the *wananga* (knowledge) at the Summit of the heavens." Uru-te-ngangana and others said, "Leave our younger brother to fetch it—he who has ascended Maunga-nui and Maunga-roa and been consecrated to the Three Currents of Death." Whiro was very wroth at this and said, "Who, indeed, has said that he, a younger son, will ascend above through all the heavens?"

THE FIRST TEMPLE IS BUILT ON EARTH

Tane-nui-a-rangi now urged his brethren saying, "Tama-kaka, Tupai-a-tau, etc., let us all go to Rangi-tamaku (the eleventh heaven from the summit) and obtain the design of Whare-kura and build a similar one here on earth; in which to deposit the *tahu* (i.e., the origin, the very commencement of all knowledge) of the *wananga* of the heavens." Tawhire-matea consented to this. When they reached Rangi-tamaku, they carefully copied the design of the temple.

TANE ASCENDS TO THE UPPERMOST HEAVEN

After the events described above, the ascent of Tane to the Uppermost Heaven was considered by the Gods. Whiro-te-tipua was most urgent that he should go on before; so he proceeded by way of the Taepatanga (edge of the sky) of the heavens to climb up above. Whiro had proceeded on his way for a long distance when Tane told his elder brethren that they ought to start. So they went aided by the family of Para-wera-nui (a mighty southerly tempest) who carried them along. That family is as follows: the black whirlwind, the ascending whirlwind, the great windy whirlwind, the whirlwind ascending to heaven. These then were the families of Tawhiri-matea who carried Tane to the entrance of the guardhouse to the uppermost heaven. His companions accompanied Tane to the third heaven to Kautu and Tapuhi-kura who were the spirits whose duty it was to take Tane to the entrance into the third heaven where Tane was purified by Kautu and Tapuhikura. (Some of his companions) returned from here to Earth whilst (others) carried Tane to the heaven below the summit.

In the meantime Whiro had ascended to the two lowest heavens where he learnt that Tane had passed on before him; he followed to the tenth heaven in descent but did not overtake him. Here his son-in-law said to him, "Go back! You cannot succeed for that man Tane has been consecrated above on Maunga-nui by Rua-tau and Rehua." At this Whiro was very distressed and wrathy; he ordered the Tini-o-Poto to follow in pursuit of Tane. They are the mosquito, the ant, the centipede, prionoplus, daddy-long-legs, the great parrot, the hawk, the sparrow-hawk, the bat, and the owl. This was the war party of Whiro which he sent to follow Tane, to peck and draw his blood—to kill him. The war party went on and ascended the horizon of the first-heaven-below-the-summit; and there attacked Tane. But they could not approach near him—they were whirled away by the great gales. They could not get near him.

Tane now reached the guardhouse of the uppermost heaven and there entered the house where were Rua-tau and many other of the guardian-gods of the supreme god, Io. Two of his companions returned from here to the first-heaven-below-the-summit to await Tane's return.

And, also, the war party of Whiro returned to the third heaven to await Tane on his return.

TANE RECEIVES NEW NAMES

Now when Tane entered the guardhouse he had arrived at the summit-of-the-heaven. He was then taken by Rua-tau to the waters of Rongo and there again purified and the following additional names were given him: Great-Tane-of-the-heaven, Tane-the-parent-of-mankind, Tane-who-brought-knowledge-from-heaven, Tane-the-salvation, etc.

These are the names then given him; but the first one he had already received from Rua-tau when he was sanctified on Mount Maunga-nui.

TANE AND IO

After the above occurrence, Tane was conducted into Matangi-reia, the house of Io, the sun's path in the heavens, where Io was awaiting him. On his arrival Io asked him:

"By whom are we?"

"By the Sky-father and the Earth-mother is thy child, O Io-the-father!"

"Who is thy companion?"

"My elder brother, Whiro-te-tipua. He went by way of the Taepatanga of the heavens to ascend."

"Thy elder brother will not succeed; the winds of the conjoint heavens blow too strongly." Io added, "What is thy reason for ascending here?"

"The sacred contents of the 'baskets' pertaining to the Sky-father and Earth-mother to obtain; hence have I ascended up to thee, O Io!"

Io then said, "Let us go to the Rauroha" (the space outside Io's dwelling). When they got there then for the first time was seen how numerous were the male guardian-gods and the female guardian-gods staying there. Tane was again purified in Rauroha and after this had been accomplished they entered the temple treasure house. It was here that the guardian-gods gave into Tane's charge the three baskets and the two sacred stones. They were "god-stones" (i.e., endowed with miraculous powers).

THE THREE BASKETS AND TWO STONES

These are the names of the three baskets and two stones:

1. The *kete-uruuru-matua*, of peace, of all goodness, of love.

2. The *kete-uruuru-rangi*, of all prayers, incantations, ritual, used by mankind.

3. The *kete-uruuru-tau*, of the wars of mankind, agriculture, tree or woodwork, stonework, earthwork—of all things that tend to well-being, life, of whatsoever kind.

(Te Matorohanga held that the original teaching of this branch was derived from the first created thoughts, which were good alone; it was afterwards that evil thoughts came into being. The Creator first gave man eyes in order to distinguish good from evil and then the heart, to hold such knowledge.)

1. *Te Whata-kura*, i.e., foam-of-the-ocean.

2. *Te Whatu-kura*, i.e., white-sea-mist.

These stones are both white in color, like sea-foam, that is, they were white according to description handed down; they are stones that may indicate either good or evil according to man's desire. They are sacred stones and are used at the termination of the session of teaching, that is, the pupils are placed thereon when the classes break up. After the proper ritual of *karakia,* the stones are touched by the mouths of the pupils and then the classes break up for the season.

TANE RETURNS TO EARTH

Now after three baskets of the *wananga* (knowledge) and the two stones had been acquired, the guardian-gods escorted Tane and his properties to the next lower heaven. Tane and his companions descended until they reached the fourth-heaven-from-the-summit where they were attacked by the war party of Whiro-te-tipua.

As soon as the war party was discovered it was assaulted by the company of Tane. The war party of Whiro was defeated at Te Rangi-haupapa and the following brought down to earth as prisoners: the hawk, the sparrow-hawk, the crane, the great parrot, the night parrot, the bat, the owl, and the parrokeet.

The grandchildren of the hawk were taken prisoners. They are: the mosquito, the little sandfly, the sandfly, the ant, the wingless locust, the butterfly, the blowfly, and the grasshopper.

And now the face of the sky above flashed forth in brilliant red. Hence did Tupai, etc., know that the *wananga* had been acquired by Tane-matua. Great was the joy and the rejoicing of the family of gods, even including those at the dwelling place of Whiro. But Whiro alone was not glad; he was continuously angry and jealous on account of the exceeding *mana* (prestige) that had accrued to Tane-matua. And now Uru-ao and Tupai took their trumpets and sounded a fanfare. They were named the Arch-of-heaven and Trumpet-sounding-in-heaven. The whole of the family of gods heard the trumpet blasts and knew thereby that Tane-matua had succeeded in his quest.

When the party arrived at the first temple built on earth, and after the purification ceremony, they entered the temple and there suspended the three *wananga* at the back of the temple, where also the two stones were deposited. Whiro demanded that the baskets and stones should be delivered up to him. Tane said to him, "Where are others to be found if we agree to that? It is sufficient that you have some of our elder brethren with you; the baskets must be left with these members of our elder and younger brethren." Whiro was very angry at this and returned to his home with two of the stones.

THE GUARDIAN-GODS ARE APPOINTED

Now, at this period the attention of Tane-matua and his elder and younger brethren was turned to the separation of the guardian-gods to their different spheres of action in their separate places, by twos and threes, to each plane of the earth, the heavens and even the ocean. Thus was the work directed and the valuable contents of the three baskets were distributed.

THE WARS OF THE GODS

At this time the hatred and jealousy of Whiro and his faction became permanent, (finally) leading to actual war. Whiro was defeated (in a series of twenty-one battles) and that was the reason he descended to Raro-henga. Hence is that fatal descent of his named the-eternal-fall.

THE OVERTURNING OF MOTHER-EARTH

Before Tane ascended to the summit-of-the-heaven and after the Sky-father and Earth-mother had been separated, the face of their mother had been overturned so that she faced Raro-henga. The youngest child of these parents was at that time a child at the breast. They left this child as a comfort to their mother. Now hence are the earthquakes and volcanic phenomena that constantly war against us in every age.

The reason why the gods overturned the Earth to face downwards to Raro-henga was because she continually lamented for the Sky-father and because the Sky-father constantly lamented over her; that is, this was the nature of their lamenting, she continuously closed the avenues of light by means of clouds and mists whilst the Sky-father constantly obscured things by his tears, both day and night; that is, the rain was constant, never ceasing, as was the snow, the black frost, the driving snow. The family of gods were perishing with the rain and the snow, and hence did they overturn their mother to face downwards to Raro-henga. After this their condition was much ameliorated. But they still dwelt in a faint light like the moonlight of this earth, because neither stars, the moon, nor the sun had been placed in position.

The name given by Rua-tau, a messenger of Io, to this world was this: He said to the Sky-father and the Earth-mother, "Let your offspring go forth and dwell. Leave them to move about on you two." He added, "Do not continue to enclose them between your bodies. Let them go forth

to the great-wide-open-space and therein move about."
Hence we learn the name given by Rua-tau to this world,
the-great-spread-out-space-of-Rua-tau. It was Hine-titama
that gave the commonly used name (of the world), the-
enduring-light. It was thus that her relative Te Kuwata-
wata spoke to her, saying, "O Lady! Return hence!
Here ceases the world of light. Beyond me is darkness-
ever-present." Hine-titama replied to him, "Let me remain
there that I may catch the living spirit of my descendants
(mankind) in the world-of-everlasting-light." [11]

From this consistent evolutionism and preoccupation
with problems of origin, which the thinkers among the
Polynesians have carried to its highest point among so-
called primitive people but which the thinkers in all
groups shared with them, we will now turn to the
attempts made to develop some systematized theory
of the nature of things. That speculation on the nature of reality and of the external world existed we
have given adequate proof in a former chapter. We
saw there that both among the Maori and the Oglala
Dakota, thinkers had begun to wrestle with some of
the eternal problems of philosophy; what it is we per-
ceive when we see an object; what it is that bestows
form upon an object; and finally, what it is that gives
the gods reality. But the answers given to these questions might all conceivably be interpreted as isolated
intuitions, valuable and instructive, it is true, but not

---

[11] S. Percy Smith, *op. cit.*, pp. 119 *ff.* For the order of creation
see pp. 301 *ff.* of the present book.

definitely proving that the problems involved had been objectively visualized. The skeptically inclined layman has the right to demand a fairly elaborate and systematized body of thought before allowing himself to be convinced. Fortunately that is to be found among the Maori. Among the latter there are, in fact, different schools of thought. The knowledge imparted to the priests was, for instance, definitely classified. There were two branches called respectively the *upper-jaw* and the *lower-jaw*. The first branch contained everything pertaining to the gods, the heavens, the origin of things, the creation of man, the science of astronomy, the record of time, etc., and the second dealt with the history of the people, their genealogies, migrations, terrestrial things, etc. According to the Maori scribe from whom our best knowledge of this subject has been obtained, no one universal system of teaching was taught, but each Maori tribe had its own priests, its own places of instruction, and its own methods. The teaching was often diverted from the true doctrine, this man insists, by the self-conceit of the priests who inculcated it. The scribe himself admits the possibility of deviation and divergence of opinion, although he postulates vaguely one correct system. "The omissions in my teaching," he says, "the innovations, variations, interruptions, or divergence from the main argument or true story, they (certain sages present) will be able to supply." Yet this "true story" was more in the nature of a devout wish than an actual fact, for he himself adds: "My wish was, had Te Ura consented, that there should have been only one house of teaching for all of us together. In that case there would have been no trouble, for one of us would have laid down the main line of teaching, whilst two would have listened in case of divergence and one would have supplemented or, in the case of 'the solution of continuity,' the other would have caused the discourse to flow again and become reaffixed to the root of the subject, or supply any omissions." [12]

Here we have a clear-cut recognition of the pursuit of knowledge for its own sake. It differs only in degree from that search for knowledge for its own sake that characterizes the philosophic systems of our own thinkers. One fundamental difference it has, which is certainly to be reckoned to its merit: It is not divorced from life, from the immediate interests of the present, in the same degree that most philosophies since Plato have been. This connection with the world of ordinary experience is shown in a multitude of ways, perhaps nowhere so well as in the somewhat ironical fact that a fairly abstract discourse on the nature of things is prefaced by a hymn to knowledge that has come to be a magical incantation. This hymn must be recited without a break to take breath, otherwise its efficacy is destroyed. Herein it is possibly not so different from the preamble to later philosophies. But let me quote this apostrophe to divine knowledge:

---

[12] *Ibid.*, pp. 84-85.

Cause to descend, outside, beyond,
Cause to enter into these offspring, these sons,
The ancient prized knowledge, the esoteric learning, O Io!

Be received, be possessed, be it affixed,
This esoteric knowledge; be firm in thy thoughts, nor deviate,
From the powerful, the ancient, the god-like knowledge,
Be fixed in thy root and origin; affixed thy constant attention,
Firm be thy inspiration, thy ardent desire,
Within the roots and rootlets of thy thoughts.
May it grow, the fullness of this knowledge—
This ancient knowledge, this original learning,
And be like thine, O Io-omnierudite!
Let ardent desire direct from thee, O Io-all-knowing! Be his.
May thy inspiration grow equal to thine, O Rua-tau-e!
And to that of Tane and of Paia-who-acquired-all-knowledge,
And to Tangaroa (god of ocean) and Tawhiri-matea (god of strong winds)
In the beating and the trembling of the heart.
Hold firm forever, with desire towards the ways of Tu (god of war).
May he draw forth the abundant knowledge.
And entwine in his desires, the ways of Rongo (god of peace).
Let them combine with matured inspiration.
Be effective, the sanctifying meal of Tu-horo-mata,
And full advantage be taken of the teaching, by these sons,
For they are thy offspring, that desire thee, O Io-the-all-father! [13]

---

[13] *Ibid.*, p. 95.

Can a finer hymn to knowledge in all its fullness and in all its implications possibly be penned? For what does it say? Let thy knowledge be like Io-the-omnierudite, thy inspiration like Ruatau, the guardian of the heavenly treasures, thy foresight like that of Tane, the Polynesian Prometheus, the trembling of thy heart like that of the god of the ocean and of the wind; may thy desire for the god of war give thee knowledge for the ways of the god of peace, and may these combine with matured inspiration! Nothing is here omitted.

The extreme richness of the Maori data is such that it is at times very difficult to escape the temptation of going into bypaths. The hymn to knowledge given above is, as I have said, merely a preamble to a discourse on the nature of matter. The theory of matter there expounded is essentially a philosophy of relativity, and is definitely nonegocentric. Matter consists of four fundamental ingredients—earth, water, fire, and air. Each one of these elements as such, however, has neither life nor form. Air is the complement of all things or, as the Maori scribe says, "that which continues or holds the life of all things." But although none of these four primordial ingredients exist except when they are combined, each one then not only possesses individuality but this individuality in each case is *sui generis*. This essential uniqueness is extended to everything, in fact, in the world. We cannot, therefore, predicate anything about the nature of the "life" of water from what we know about "fire," or say anything about plants from what we know about animals. This universe of nonrelated monads is given unity by the postulation of a cosmic deity, Io. Io is not only the creator of all things but, while it is apparently implied that he has no longer the power to draw back to himself certain aspects that belong to the external world, he has retained to himself three things—the spirit, the life, and the form. Everything is gathered in his presence; proceeds from him. There is nothing outside or beyond him—life, death, divinity. Obedience to his commands is life; disobedience, death. Indeed death is defined as *something which does not proceed from Io.* By death here we must, however, understand nothingness, i.e., what is not capable of having spirit, life, or form, and therefore not capable of being apprehended by us. Death, in the sense of its proceeding from Io, on the other hand, simply means the preordained termination which Io has given to all things that exist. One great and all-embracing ethical postulate flows from this conception of Io, known under the epithet of he-in-whose-presence-all-things-are-combined. Since everything emanates from him, since he appoints each thing to its proper place, then everything must have a function by which it fulfills itself. And this we do indeed find. "Each thing has its own function," our discourse says, "even the smallest particle, such as grains of dust or pebbles."

Because of its significance and inaccessibility I shall quote the whole discourse:

Now let it be clearly understood about the-great-sun, the sun, and the waxing moon and their younger brethren the stars. All of these are worlds with their earth, waters, rocks, trees, mountains, open places, and plains. On this earth the ocean and the rivers made the plains and open places which we see. It was the gods Mataaho and Whakaru-au-moko that changed the surface of the earth and caused the present ill condition of the plains and rivers.

This is to be clearly understood: All things have their being through water and fire. If there were soil alone, the land would be dead without water and fire; water without land and fire would be dead; fire without water and land would be dead. Hence, these three things combined give life to the land, and to each other, and to all things that grow and live and have their own forms, whether trees, rocks, birds, reptiles, fish, animals, or men. It is these three things that give life to them all. It is the same with the sun, the moon, and the stars; they are worlds; earth, water, and fire give them their form; and the same actuate all things.

Now, the air is the complement of all things, whether of the earth or the heavens, the sun, the moon, or the stars. It is this that continues, or holds, the life of all things—hence are there four in all. If there were the earth, the ocean, fire, or air alone, nothing would exist, nor have shape, or growth—nothing would have life. Hence be ye clear it is through the *earth, water, fire,* and *air* combined that all things have form and life.

It is the same with Rangi-tu-haha (the whole of the heavens), including the Toi-o-nga-rangi (the uppermost

heaven, the abode of Io), each has its own form of everything within them; with its own form of life suited to each.
The earth has its own form of life, as has the water, fire,
trees, rocks; all plants of every description have their own
particular form of life. The air, the moon, the sun, the
stars, have their own form of life; everything, also, that has
been mentioned above has its spirit (*wairus*, spirit, soul)
of its own, similar to its self.

Io-te-wananga (Io-the-omnierudite) of the heavens is the
origin of all things. These are the things that Io-mata-ngaro
(Io-the-unseen-face) retained to himself; the spirit and the
life and the form; it is by these that all things have form
according to their kind.

You must also be clear on this point: There is nothing
made by the god Io that has not an end; everything has a
termination, whether it be a draught, burning by fire, injury
by water, by the wind, excepting always those forms that the
god himself decreed should have an end in this world, or
other worlds.

All things were subservient to Io-the-great-one, and hence
the truth of the names of Io:

Io-the-great-god-over-all, Io-the-enduring (or everlasting),
Io-the-all-parent, Io-of-all-knowledge, Io-the-origin-of-all-
things (the one true god), Io-the-immutable, Io-the-summit-
of-heaven, Io-the-god-of-one-command, Io-the-hidden-face,
Io-only-seen-in-a-flash-of-light, Io-presiding-in-all-heavens,
Io-the-exalted-of-heaven, Io-the-parentless (self created),
Io-the-life-giving, Io-who-renders-not-to-man-that-which-he-
withholds. . . .

Now, it is clear that all things, the worlds and their belongings, all gods of mankind, his own gods, all are gathered in his presence (i.e., proceed from him). There is nothing outside or beyond him; with him is the power of life, of death, of godship. Everything that proceeds from other than Io and his commands, death is the collector of those. If all his commands are obeyed and fulfilled by everyone, safety and well-being result therefrom.

Now, it is obvious that all things of life and death are combined in the presence of (or are due to) Io-the-hidden-face; there is nothing outside or beyond him. All godships are in him and he appoints them their places; the gods of the dead and the gods of the living. All things are named (i.e., created) by the god of the worlds, in the heavens, the planes and the water, each has its own function. Even the smallest atom, such as grains of dust, or pebbles, has its place—to hold the boundaries of the ocean or the waters.[14]

[14] *Ibid.*, pp. 105-107.

CHAPTER XVII

THE NATURE OF GOD

SO elaborate a philosophy as that recorded in Chapter XVI we find nowhere else among present primitive peoples, although I feel quite confident that comparable ones are to be found in Africa and in parts of North America. The data in our possession to-day, where they at all deal with attempts at unification of knowledge, are strictly confined to the realm of religion. Theological systems are not uncommon. I shall discuss only two of them in any detail, that of the Oglala Dakota and that of the Bavili of West Africa. Among the Oglala this systematization is definitely and consciously confined to the priests and is clothed in a ceremonial language known only to them. The following are among the doctrines they inculcate:

The great mysterious, Wakan Tanka, is one although he has four individualities—the chief god, the great spirit, the creator, and the executive.

The chief god is composed of four individuals but they are to be considered as one. They are the sun, the moon, the buffalo, and the spirit.

The great spirit also consists of four individuals to be considered as one—the sky, the wind, the bear, and the ghost.

The creator-god also consists of four individuals to be considered as one—the earth, the feminine, the four winds, and the spirit-like.

Finally we have the executive god. He, too, has four individuals who are as one—the rock, the winged, the whirlwind, and the potency.[1]

But Wakan Tanka can also be separated in another manner into benevolent and malevolent gods. The benevolent gods are of two kinds, the gods and the gods' kindred. The gods in their turn can be further subdivided into the superior gods and the associate gods. The gods' kindred in their turn are subdivided into the subordinate gods and the god-like. Each of these four classes consists of four individuals. The individuals of the superior gods are the sun, who is the chief of the gods; the sky who is the great spirit, the earth who is the all-mother, and the rock who is the all-father. The individuals of the associate gods are the moon, the associate of the sun; the wind, the associate of the sky; the feminine, the associate of the earth; and the winged god, the associate of the rock. The individuals of the subordinate gods are the buffalo god, the bear god, the four winds, and the whirlwind. The individuals of the god-like are the spirit, the ghost, the spirit-like, and imparted supernatural potency.

All these individualities of the great mysterious have

---

[1] James Walker, "The Sun Dance of the Oglala Division of the Dakota," *Anthropological Papers of the American Museum of Natural History*, XVI, Part II, pp. 72-92.

the following properties: with the exception of the four
winds they had no beginning though some existed before the others and some bear the relation of parent
and offspring to one another. No person can understand this contradiction for it is *akan*, a mystery. All
these individualities, it is contended, will likewise have
no end.

That a godhead with sixteen aspects, each one of
which is a different individual, is a conscious priestly
construction, needs no demonstration. The various
persons in the Wakan Tanka are, for the most part,
simply the deities of the tribe still worshiped by the
lay population and the majority of the priests. The
task of unification must, in fact, have been extremely
difficult and it is therefore not to be wondered at if
some of the statements made about the more important
deities such as the sun, the sky, the rock, and the four
winds contain a few inconsistencies. The sun, for instance, is described as a "material god's and ranks first
among the superior gods though the other three were
before him. He may be addressed as the great one,
the revered one, or our father. His domain is the
spirit-world and the regions under the world. The sky
gave him his power and can withhold it, but he is more
powerful than the sky.[2] Now if we compare this
description with the following one about the sky, contradictions emerge immediately: "The sky is an immaterial god whose substance is never visible. His
titles given by the people are *taku skan-skan* and

---

[2] *Ibid.,* p. 81.

nagi tanka or the great spirit, and those given by the priests are *skan* and *to*, blue. The concept expressed by the term *taku skan-skan* is that which gives motion to anything that moves. That expressed by the shamans by the word *skan* is a vague concept of force or energy and by the word *to* is the immaterial blue of the sky which symbolizes the presence of the great spirit. His domain is all above the world, beginning at the ground. He is the source of all power and motion and is the patron of directions and trails and of encampment. He imparts to each of mankind at birth a spirit, a ghost, and a *sicun* and at the death of each of mankind he hears the testimony of the ghost and adjudges the spirit. He may sit in judgment on other gods. His word is unalterable except by himself. He alone can undo that which is done. His people are the stars and the feminine is his daughter." [3]

The problem becomes still more complicated when we are told that the rock, although ranking fourth among the superior gods, existed first of all, that he is addressed as the all-father and considered the ancestor of all things and of all the gods. Although he is associated with the all-mother, the earth, they are not related as husband and wife nor has either a child by the other. The rock, however, has children. In one case the other parent is the winged god and in the other the water spirit. A few words about the four winds are also necessary in this connection. They are regarded as one god with four aspects, each one pos-

---

[3] *Ibid.*, pp. 81-82.

sessing definite individuality and appearing as a god; he (the four winds) is immaterial and his substance is never visible. In ceremonies he, the four winds, has precedence over all the gods except *wohpe*, the feminine.

What is significant in all these inconsistencies and contradictions is the manner in which the priests harmonized them by predicating, as in the case of a god like the four winds, that he may be one yet have four appearances or, as in the case of Wakan Tanka, that he may be one and have sixteen appearances, and that this double nature is intelligible to the shamans, but *akan* and therefore incomprehensible to the layman.

To reënforce what I have said I shall quote part of a disquisition on Wakan Tanka dictated by an Oglala priest to Mr. Walker:

The shaman addresses Wakan Tanka as *tobtob kin.* This is part of the secret language of the shamans. *Tobtob kin* are four times four gods, while *tob kin* is only the four winds. The four times four are the sun, the sky, the earth, the rock, the moon, the wind, the feminine, the winged god, the buffalo god, the bear god, the four winds, the whirlwind, the spirit, the ghost, the spirit-like, and the imparted supernatural potency.

Wakan Tanka is like sixteen different persons; but each person is *kan.* Therefore they are all only the same as one. All the god persons have *ton.* *Ton* is the power to do supernatural things. Half of the good gods are *ton ton* (have physical properties) and half are *ton ton sni* (have no physical properties). Half of those who are *ton ton* are *ton ton yan* (visible) and half of those who are *ton ton sni* are *ton ton yan sni* (invisible). All the other gods are visible or invisible as they choose to be. All the evil gods are visible or invisible as they choose to be. The invisible gods never appear in a vision to anyone except a shaman. Except for the sun dance the ceremonies for the visible and the invisible gods differ. The sun dance is a ceremony the same as if the sun were both visible and invisible.[4]

Let us now proceed to another tribe.

Among the Bavilis, R. E. Dennett [5] found existing alongside of the fetishism of the people at large a definitely monistic viewpoint resulting apparently from the same tendency toward unification which we have just pointed out among the Oglala Dakota. Nzambi, the supreme god of the Bavili, is regarded by some as an abstract entity from which proceed three elements designated by Dennett as the maternal or passive principle, the paternal or active principle and *fu*, properly speaking, habit or sequence.[6] The name *Nzambi* itself means literally *imbi*, personal essence and *zia* or *za*, of the fours or four. The fours are the groups, each of four powers called *bacici baci*, i.e., the sacred

---

[4] *Ibid.*, p. 153.

[5] *At the Back of the Black Man's Mind*, Chaps. X and XVI. Dennett's manner of presentation is unfortunately unduly obscure. His contentions seem, however, to be borne out by the facts.

[6] *Ibid.*, p. 165. Dennett adds, "We may perhaps express it in one word by evolution, understanding thereby rather the process by which the individual is produced rather than the life history of a species. In another sense it may almost be said to be the individual himself."

symbols. Each group is composed of (1) a cause; (2) a male part; (3) a female part; (4) an effect. *Nzambi* itself may be said to have four parts, viz., *Nzambi,* the abstract idea, the cause; *Nzambi Mpungu,* god almighty, the father god who dwells in the heavens and is the guardian of the fire; *Nzambi ci,* god the essence, god on earth, the great princess, the mother of all animals; and *kici,* the mysterious inherent quality in things that causes the Bavili to fear and respect.

The unification and mysticism encountered here are obviously quite different from that of the Oglala and are far more closely allied to the abstractions and the different appellations given to the supreme deity, Io, of the Maori (see pages 321 *ff.*).

The last example, that from the Batak, is of a far simpler nature, representing a unification possibly in its first stages. There we find four distinct and individualized deities, also known under a collective name, *Asiasi.* Whenever *Asiasi* is prayed to he is never thought of as a separate deity but always as the sum of the other four. *Asiasi* can thus be said to have four aspects or, to be more accurate, to consist of four individuals.[7]

From our examination of the philosophic and religious systems we can now turn to the primitive thinker's attempts at defining the nature and attributes of god. In part this has been discussed before. I am taking it up here as a separate topic because I wish to

---

[7] J. Warneck, *Die Religion der Batak,* p. 28.

show that in some instances these attempts took the form of a series of postulates or elaborate epithets. For illustration I shall select a very interesting discourse about God from the Batak, epithets applied to Io, the supreme deity among the Maori, and those applied to Leza, the supreme deity among the Ba-ila of Rhodesia.

The Batak discourse about God states very succinctly the complete religio-ethical system of these people. To them he is essentially the final judge and arbiter to whom everything is possible and who determines our destiny. The discourse contains eighteen postulates:

1. Earth-betel, planted in the market-place;
   May God aid us, may he increase our knowledge.
2. Where *situngguk* exists, there also plants are to be found.
3. Two follows one in counting.
   There are long things and short things
   Just as God created them in this world.
4. God is an adequate judge.
5. To supply the needy, to take from the overabundant,
   All that lies within God's power.
6. Plants grow in rows.
   If God aids
   Then a dewdrop may be converted into food.
7. The felled tree still stands, held upright by creepers.
   God stands and looks down upon conquered man.
8. What God has done, man may not alter.

9. Take not devious paths;
   God is the master of riches.
10. May God aid; may he give craftiness.
11. May our worship of God make the slender stout.
12. Even though it be little that we eat,
    God aid us that we fatten thereon.
13. However great be your desire to cheat me,
    God, our grandfather, is there to exercise compassion.
14. With rice iron is bought.
    The word of the master, may the *tondi* recollect it.
15. If God helps, the old will become rejuvenated.
16. If God blesses, then barren soil will become fertile.
17. God is sanctified.
    He takes care of all our *tondi*.
18. God has so arranged it
    That there be people whom we must honor.[8]

The epithets applied to the supreme deity of the Maori are, as we might have expected, of an entirely different order. They are concerned exclusively with trying to define his transcendent power and describe his attributes:

Io. The core of all gods; none excel him.

Io-nui. He is greater than all other gods.

Io-roa. His life is everlasting; he knows not death.

Io-the-parent. He is the parent of the heavens and of their different realms, of the worlds, of clouds, of insects, of birds, of rats, of fish, of moons, of stars, of lightning, of winds, of waters, of trees, of all plant life, of the land, the

---

[8] *Ibid.*

sea and the streams, as also of all other things. There is no single thing that does not come under his control. He is the parent of all things—of man and of the lesser gods under him. He is truly the parent of all.

Io-the-parentless. He has no parents; no mother, no elder or younger brothers or sisters. He is nothing but himself.

Io-taketake. This denotes the permanence of himself and all his acts, his thoughts, and his governments. All are enduring, are firm, complete, and immovable.

Io-te-pukenga. He is the source of all thought, reflection, memories, of all things planned by him to possess form, growth, life, thought, strength. There is nothing outside his jurisdiction; all things are his and with him alone rests the matter of possession or non-possession.

Io-te-wanaga. He is the source of all knowledge whether pertaining to life or to death, to evil or to good, to dissensions or to lack of such, to peace making or to failure to make peace. Nought is there outside his influence.

Io-the-crown-of-heaven. He is the god of the uppermost of all the heavens. There is no heaven beyond that one which is known to him.

Io-the-large- (many-) eyed. No place is hidden from his eyes and thoughts, whether in the heavens or the various realms, the worlds, the waters or the depths of the beds of the rivers, or the clouds. All things are gathered together in his eyes.

Io-the-hidden-face or the-unseen-face. He is unseen by all things in the heavens, in the world, and various divisions of the heavens or worlds. No matter what it be he is not seen. Only when he intends to be seen can he be

seen by any being. He is unseen by all beings of the
heavens, of the divisions of the worlds, of the waters, of
the clouds, of vegetation, insects, supernatural beings; only
when he wills that they see him can they do so.

Io-mataaho. His appearance as he moves about is as
that of radiant light only; he is not clearly seen by any
being of the heavens, of the worlds or divisions thereof.

Io-te-whiwhia. This denotes that nothing can possess
anything of its own volition; by his intention only can it
possess aught or not so possess it, no matter who or what it
be—persons or supernatural beings, heavens or the divisions
of such, moons or suns, stars or waters, wind or rain.

Io-urutapu. He is more *tapu* than all other gods, than
all other things of the heavens, of the realms or divisions
of space, of the sun, of the moon, of the stars and depths.[9]

The last of the series of epithets to be mentioned is
that applied to the supreme deity of the Ba-ila. The
philosophy they suggest is in its constructive aspect
altogether on a much lower plane than that of the
Oglala and the Maori. It shows a very marked tendency, however, toward pessimism, doubt, and critique.
Finally, it is fairly definitely egocentric or, at best,
earth-centric. Epithets applied to him can be divided
into three classes, the first consisting of the generic
epithets in common use; second, those called by the
natives the *praise-names;* and third, a small group of
miscellaneous names, all showing the limits to the

---

[9] Elsdon Best, "Maori Religion and Mythology," 10th *Bulletin of
the Dominion Museum* (New Zealand), pp. 89-90.

deity's power.[10] Let us begin with the first. There are four:

1. He who besets anyone or persecutes with unremitting attentions.
2. He who stirs up to do good or bad by repeated solicitation.
3. He who trades on a person's good name; he who asks things which he has no title to ask for.
4. He who is changeable in speech.

The first of these is the most common name applied to him. Taken in conjunction with the others it seems to indicate that for the Ba-ila, God has become identified with the impulse that prompts us to our actions, good or bad. He is the great reality which constrains us. We have neither to expect much nor little from him but merely accept him as patiently as we can. In a Ba-ila story which I have already quoted, an old woman who has spent all her life seeking for Leza in order that she might complain to him is answered by the old men to whom she pours out her story, "In what do you differ from others? The Besetting-One sits on the back of every one of us and we cannot shake him off!"

To offset these four generic epithets we have a large series of "praise-names" in which Leza's attributes of creator, controller, and determiner are extolled. Thus he is the creator, the molder, the constructor, the

---

[10] E. W. Smith and A. M. Dale, *The Ila-Speaking Peoples of Northern Rhodesia*, II, pp. 197 *ff*.

everlasting and omnipresent, he-from-whom-all-things-come, the guardian, the giver, he-who-gives-and-causes-to-rot, the flooder, the rain-giver, the water-giver, he-of-the-suns, deliverer-of-those-in-trouble, he-who-cuts-down-and-destroys, he-who-takes-away-till-there-is-only-one-left, the leader.

Finally we have a number of critical names, where rebellion breaks out into open flame:

1. Dissolver of ant heaps but the *maumbuswa* ant heaps are too much for him.
2. He can fill up all the great pits of various kinds but the little foot print of the Oribi he cannot fill.
3. The giver who gives also what cannot be eaten.

Never surely was a more mordant and utterly destructive criticism passed upon a god.

CHAPTER XVIII

IN the preceding chapter we passed through the whole gamut of attitudes toward God, from the philosophic reverence of the Maori to the trenchant criticism of the Ba-ila. We have still to discuss one other aspect and one that is so significant that I shall devote a whole chapter to it, namely, monotheism and monotheistic tendencies.

To most men monotheism is intimately bound up with the Hebrew Scriptures and with those religions manifestly built upon its foundation—Judaism, Christianity, and Mohammedanism. Because of the definite association with these three great historic faiths of the last three thousand years, and of the integral part it plays in those civilizations which, rightly or wrongly, we regard in many ways as representing the highest cultural expressions to which mankind has hitherto attained, monotheism has come to have a very specific meaning and has been given a special evaluation.

To the average man it signifies the belief in an uncreated, supreme deity, wholly beneficent, omnipotent, omniscient, and omnipresent; it demands the complete exclusion of all other gods. The world in its most minute details is regarded as his work, as having been created out of nothing in response to his wish. To presuppose the existence of anything prior to him is to deny his most salient attribute. He it is who intervenes in the affairs of man and any assumption that he can act through the intermediation of other deities is idolatry by implication, even though he has expressly given these deities their forms, their attributes, and their powers. It is never pure monotheism.

It is perhaps only natural that with so sharp and clear-cut a definition of the deity there should have arisen the feeling that such a monotheism represents the highest attainable type of religious expression. Nations without it, however high their contributions to the world's progress in other directions may be, are looked upon unconsciously as inferior. Yet it would be unfair to state that it was merely this vague and unconscious estimate that lay at the basis of man's evaluation of the significance of monotheism. A cursory glance at the history of religious thought of the so-called primitive peoples or at the religious evolution of civilized nations before the advent of Christianity— the Jews alone excepted—did seem to indicate the existence of a number of distinct phases through which religion had progressively passed. The earliest stage, it seemed, was to be found among primitive peoples. There we find a religion characterized by a faith in innumerable, often indefinite, spirits, a belief in the general animation of nature—animism, in short. All the great historical religions show, it is now generally admitted, definite indications of having passed through such a period.

This seemed to be followed by a second and much later stage in which the worship of definite mainly anthropomorphic deities prevailed; the polytheism of the ancient Egyptians, Babylonians, Greeks, and Romans.

It is the prevalent view to-day that where animism or polytheism prevails monotheism is excluded, and where monotheism prevails animism and polytheism are in the main absent; that as we pass from animism to polytheism, from dualism to monotheism, we are proceeding from a belief in a multiplicity of spirits devoid of special attributes to a belief first in two deities and then to a belief in a single god—a god endowed with the highest ethical attributes. The evolution of religion thus manifests, it would seem, a definite tendency toward an integration of our mental and emotional life, a tendency toward the development of an exalted and positive ethical ideal. Both, it can be claimed, imply progress, one in the realm of the intellect and the other in that of morality. It is not astonishing, therefore, that even to many nonreligious individuals pure monotheism should consequently connote the highest form of religious experience. And yet it is perhaps not amiss to point out that in a development such as that just outlined we are basing our evolution on factors that, in large measure, are essentially nonreligious.

Be this as it may, certainty no one would seriously deny that it is the intellectual and ethical estimate of

pure monotheism that has colored the attitude of most
people toward nonmonotheistic and nonethical faiths,
and no fact could perhaps have demonstrated this so
clearly as the reception accorded to the famous book
written by that most courageous thinker, Andrew Lang.
In 1898, he published *The Making of Religion,* in
which he claimed that the evolutionary school in ethnology was hopelessly wrong in one of its fundamental
assumptions, namely, that belief in a supreme deity
did not now and never had existed among so-called
primitive tribes. He contended that ethnologists, misled by certain preconceptions, had misinterpreted those
indications pointing in such a direction, crediting to
Christian influences those definite instances where the
facts could not possibly be denied.

It might have been surmised that such a theory
would have been hailed with delight by the layman.
Yet this was not the case. The layman indeed seemed
to feel a certain resentment at having mere "savages"
anticipate a supposedly exalted religious faith. That
the professional ethnologist and ethnological theorist
should have scouted the idea is natural enough, considering the ascendency of the evolutionary theory at
the time. To have admitted among primitive peoples
the existence of monotheism in any form would have
been equivalent to abandoning their whole doctrine of
evolutionary stages. And this they were not prepared
to do nor did the facts at the time definitely warrant it.
No one, for instance, would have contended that the
vast majority of the members of those tribes, among

whom the belief in a supreme deity had been found, shared this belief except perhaps in the vaguest degree, and it seemed apparent that even the few to whom it was in appearance an active faith found no difficulty in worshiping other deities as well. It might, in fact, have been said that actual worship was the precise thing the supreme deity did not receive. So attenuated and functionless a concept, known to a selected few in each community, could assuredly, the critics insisted, be best explained as due to Christian influence.

Twenty-five years have elapsed since Lang wrote his book and his intuitive insight has been abundantly corroborated. The ethnologists were quite wrong. Accurate data obtained by trained specialists have replaced his rather vague examples. That many primitive peoples have a belief in a supreme creator no one to-day seriously denies. For the notion, however, as held by Lang, that it represents a degeneration from a higher and purer faith, there is not the slightest justification; nor is there any adequate reason for believing that the specific forms which it has assumed, the "contaminations" to which it has been subjected, or the inconsistencies in which it has been involved, have ever been different.

It was one of Lang's great merits that he recognized some of the salient features of this belief in a supreme deity of the aborigines. Such a deity had no cults; prayers were only infrequently directed to him and he rarely intervened directly in the affairs of mankind. As we shall see, these statements are only partially true and, at best, hold for only the first of the two general groups into which creative deities can be divided. The second group embraces those where the supreme deity is represented as only partially a creator, and where he has become fused with mythological heroes—with the sun or the moon, with animals, or with anthropomorphic and, occasionally, indefinite spirits. The main character with which he became most frequently amalgamated was one who is the dominant actor in the mythologies of practically all primitive peoples. He is known in ethnological literature as the Transformer, Culture-hero, Trickster. The first term owes its origin to the fact that it is his rôle to transform the world into its present shape and to bestow upon mankind all the various elements of culture. We thus have two concepts: the supreme deity, creator of all things, beneficent and ethical, unapproachable directly and taking but little interest in the world after he has created it; and the Transformer, the establisher of the present order of things, utterly nonethical, only incidentally and inconsistently beneficent, approachable, and directly intervening in a very human way in the affairs of the world.

These two figures represent two contrasting and antithetic modes of thought, two completely opposed temperaments continually in conflict. All that has been called contamination and degeneration is but the projection of the image of the Transformer upon that of a supreme creator and vice versa. Indeed, it is only thus that certain inconsistencies in the portrayal of either can be understood. If, as we shall see, it is true that the Transformer has introduced certain human-heroic, occasionally but extremely rarely, even gross features, into the otherwise elevated concept of the supreme deity, it is equally true that wherever the belief in a supreme deity has prevailed he has in large measure been purged of his nonmoral character and become invested with many of the attributes of a purposive and benevolent creator. It will be best to give a number of concrete examples, however; first, of a creator who in varying degrees partakes of the attributes of a transformer and culture-hero; and second, of a creator quite freed from such accretions.

Among the Crow Indians of Montana the Sun is the supreme deity, but he has in the minds of many become so definitely merged with the Transformer, in this particular instance the Coyote, that the two cannot be kept apart. "Long ago," so the myth runs, "there was no earth, only water. The only creatures in the world were the ducks and Old Man (Sun, Coyote). He came down to meet the ducks and said to them, 'My brothers, there is earth below us. It is not good for us to be alone.'" He thereupon makes them dive and one of them reappears with some mud in its webbed feet. Out of this he creates the earth and when he has made it he exclaims, "Now that we have made the earth there are others who wish to be animate." Immediately a wolf is heard howling in the east. In this manner everything in the world is created.

Not a very exalted type of creator, one will justly

exclaim. But he is a creator none the less in two essential respects: first, in that practically nothing exists until he creates it; and second, in that all his creative acts are the results of his expressed will and that they are beneficent. Let me point out one other fact—the new ethical reëvaluation of the Sun-Coyote. In the cycle connected with him as a Transformer he possesses hardly one redeeming feature. He is obscene, a fool, a coward, and utterly lacking in self-control. Yet the moment he becomes associated with the creative deity all this disappears.[1]

Let us take another example. Among the Thompson River Indians of British Columbia the concept of a creator is still vague, but the creator himself is definitely dissociated from the Coyote. "Having finished his work on earth and having put all things to rights, the time came that the Coyote should meet the Old Man. When he met him he did not know that he was the 'Great Chief' or 'Mystery,' because he did not appear to be different from any other old man. The Coyote thought, 'This old man does not know who I am. I will astonish him. He knows nothing of my great powers.' After saluting each other the Old Man derided the Coyote as a person possessed of small powers: the latter consequently felt annoyed and began to boast of the many wonders he had performed. 'If you are he (Coyote) and so powerful as you say, re-

---

[1] Robert H. Lowie, "Myths and Traditions of the Crow Indians," *Anthropological Papers of the American Museum of Natural History,* XXV, Part I, pp. 14 *ff*.

move that river and make it run yonder.' This the
Coyote did. 'Bring it back.' The Coyote did so.
'Place that high mountain on the plain.' The Coyote
did so. 'Replace it where it was'; but this the Coyote
could not do because the Old Man, being the superior
in magic of the two, willed otherwise. The Old Man
then asked Coyote why he could not replace it and the
latter answered, 'I don't know. I suppose you are
greater than I in magic, and make my efforts fruitless.' The Old Man then made the mountain go back
to its place."

After declaring himself as the Great Chief, the Old
Man addresses Coyote as follows: "Now you have
been a long time on earth; and since the world, mostly
through your instrumentality, has been put right, you
have nothing more to do. Soon I am going to leave
the earth. You will not return again until I myself
do so. You shall then accompany me and bring back
the dead to the land of the living." [2]

Often enough we are told very little about the creation of the world itself and we first meet the creator
in a fully formed world of his own. His task then
becomes that of creating the present universe. This is
the case, for instance, with an interesting figure of the
Wintun Indians of Northern California, called Olelbis,
"he who dwells on high." "The first that we know of
Olelbis," the natives claim, "is that he was in Olepanti.
Whether he lived in another place is not known, but

---

[2] James Teit, *Traditions of the Thompson River Indians of British
Columbia*, p. 48.

in the beginning he was in Olepanti, the highest place. He was there before there was any one here on earth and two old women always with him." What interests us in Olelbis is that, although presumably only a creator of the universe in a very partial sense and although he subsequently creates the world in which we live, human beings, etc., and behaves very much as a normal culture-hero, he possesses no traces whatsoever of the attributes generally associated with such an individual. He is a highly ethical, beneficent deity concerned only with the welfare of mankind.[3]

If we turn to the famous "Supreme Beings" of the Australian aborigines the picture again changes. They are generally, though not always, complete creators, but it is their culture-hero and transformer aspects that dominate. They are, for instance, married and have children. Yet in spite of all this they differ from the Transformer in one important respect, in being highly ethical and beneficent.[4]

Strictly speaking, the example to which I shall now turn does not belong to the above type at all. But as the supreme deity in this case has been affected by the dominant faith of the people, namely, ancestor-worship, it seems best to include it here. I refer to the very marked monotheism of the Amazulus of South Africa as described by Bishop Callaway. "Unkulunkulu," so

---

[3] Jeremiah Curtin, *Creation Myths of Primitive America*, pp. 3 *ff*.

[4] For an excellent discussion of the conditions found in aboriginal Australia, see the well-known work of W. Schmidt, *Der Ursprung der Gottesidee*.

their creation-account runs, "is no longer known (i.e., no memory of him exists). It is he who was the first being; he broke off in the beginning (i.e., sprang from something). We do not know his wife and the ancients do not tell us that he had a wife. Unkulunkulu gave men the spirits of the dead; he gave them doctors for treating disease, and diviners. The old men say Unkulunkulu is (i.e., was a reality); he made the first men, the ancients of long ago."

There are a number of suggestive features about this Unkulunkulu. The name itself means the "old-old one" and his other designations imply priority and potential source of existence. But what is his relation to mankind? There the versions differ, some regarding him as having created men, others as having begotten them. It is likewise quite difficult to decide often whether he is regarded as the direct ancestor of man or as a true creator. What has happened seems clear. The Amazulus are ancestor-worshipers, worship the spirits of the departed, and this has influenced their conception of the supreme being to the extent of transforming him into the mythical ancestor of his race. Something of the irresponsible Transformer still clings to him at times as the following story indicates. He sends a chameleon to say, "Let not men die," but the chameleon lingers along the road and he then dispatches a lizard to say, "Let men die." Thus it is that death came into the world. But such traits are unimportant. When, indeed, it is recalled that the spirit of the deceased ancestor is predominantly evil and has to be propitiated, the fact that the partial transformation of Unkulunkulu into an ancestor has in no way affected his ethical and benevolent activities lends additional corroboration to the well-nigh universal moral nature of the supreme being among primitive peoples. Whatever else may happen his ethical nature apparently can in no way be contaminated.[5]

As we pointed out previously, all these creators have some of the features of the Transformer, and yet it seems obvious that they cannot be explained as gradual developments from the latter. They are manifestly quite independent and if consequently we find a supreme deity with the attributes of a culture-hero, this is to be regarded as secondary, as an accretion which I cannot help feeling represents an attempt to bring him nearer to man. It failed, we may surmise, because of the strength of other religious currents and because of the absence of a cult in his honor.

In the second class of supreme deities, that group where we find only a faint admixture of the attributes of the Transformer, all doubt as to the deity's creative rôle and complete lack of intimate relation with mankind is removed. Intermediate divinities carry out his commands and it is to them that man must pray. These two new factors have led to a strengthening of his former traits. His character becomes correspondingly ennobled and to his ethical attributes are added omnipotence and omniscience. Yet as he becomes further removed from men, though reverence and awe

---

[5] Bishop Callaway, *The Religious System of the Amazulu*, pp. 1 ff.

may increase, he becomes of less interest to the ordinary individual, for the latter is naturally concerned only with those deities associated with his daily needs, i.e., with the minor gods. The supreme being thus develops into what has been admirably described as an otiose deity, one resting on his laurels after the creation of the world and leaving it entirely to its own devices.

Such an otiose deity is found, for instance, among the Wichita of Texas. "In the times of the beginning there was no sun, no stars nor anything else as it is now. Time passed on. Man-never-known-on-earth was the only man that existed, and he it was who created all things. When the earth was created it was composed of land and water, but they were not yet separated. The land was floating on the water and darkness was everywhere. After the earth was formed, Man-never-known-on-earth made a woman whose name was Bright-shining-woman. After the man and woman were made they dreamed that things were made for them and when they awoke they had the things of which they had dreamed. Thus they received everything they needed. Still they were in darkness not knowing what was better than darkness."

Here we have most emphatically an otiose deity. Apart from the creation of the earth and man he bestows, so to speak, only the potentiality of things. It is this first man who causes the sun and moon to appear and who creates day and night, but only in obedience to an impulse, be it remembered, which

Man-never-known-on-earth has implanted within him. "The man that creates things is about to improve our condition," he is informed later on. "Villages shall spring up and more people will exist, and you will have power to teach the people how to do things before unknown to them." Throughout the story of creation this divine impulse is expressed by a voice directing the activities of the hero.[6]

At times fortunately the creation is described at greater length. Thus among the Uitoto of Colombia, South America, we find the following poetic account: "In the beginning there was nothing but mere appearance, nothing really existed. It was a phantasm, an illusion that our father touched; something mysterious it was that he grasped. Nothing existed. Through the agency of a dream our father, He-who-is-appearance-only, Nainema, pressed the phantasm to his breast and then was sunk in thought.

"Not even a tree existed that might have supported this phantasm and only through his breath did Nainema hold this illusion attached to the thread of a dream. He tried to discover what was at the bottom of it, but he found nothing. 'I have attached that which was non-existent,' he said. There was nothing.

"Then our father tried again and investigated the bottom of this something and his fingers sought the empty phantasm. He tied the emptiness to the dream-thread and pressed the magical glue-substance upon it.

---

[6] George A. Dorsey, *The Mythology of the Wichita*, pp. 25 ff.

Thus by means of his dream did he hold it like the fluff of raw cotton.

"He seized the bottom of the phantasm and stamped upon it repeatedly, allowing himself finally to rest upon the earth of which he had dreamt.

"The earth-phantasm was now his. Then he spat out saliva repeatedly so that the forests might arise. He lay upon the earth and set the covering of heaven above it. He drew from the earth the blue and white heavens and placed them above." [7]

The creation of all the various animals and plants then follows. We hear no more of him thereafter.

What are we to make of this wonderful bit of imagery? Surely there can be little doubt but that it represents an attempt to solve the riddle of creation by postulating something that existed before the beginning, and our primitive philosopher and theologian has quite logically assumed that the appearance of things preceded their actual existence. In the evolution of reality, according to him, three stages may be said to exist: nothing, the appearance of reality, reality. It is an admirable solution of the much vexed question of how a creator can create something out of nothing. There are other solutions conceivable and one of them is found among these very people; namely, the creation of the world out of the one thing that existed, the body of the creator himself.

But the speculation of the Uitoto monotheist has

---

[7] Karl T. Preuss, "Die hoechste Gottheit bei den Kulturarmen Voelkern," *Psychologische Forschung,* II, p. 182.

gone much farther than this. In one myth we are told that "when in the beginning of things nothing existed, our father created words and gave us these words from the Juka tree. Nofugeri and our ancestors brought these words to the earth. After he had brought these words to the earth in consequence of a dream, our ancestors gave us the words that our father had created." [8]

In another instance the formulation is even more specific: "In the beginning the word gave origin to our father."

These are, of course, all interpretations of the religious man. The nonreligious man, the realist, has had comparatively little influence upon the figure of the creator except in one important respect, namely, in the strenuous efforts he has made to equate him with the ancestor of man, for the Uitoto are ancestor-worshipers. But even he never went to the point of representing these ancestors as directly begotten of the creator as we saw the Amazulu in part do.

Not far from the above-mentioned tribe we find the Kagaba, among whom we encounter a female supreme deity and a profession of faith that should satisfy even the most exacting monotheist.

"The mother of our songs, the mother of all our seed, bore us in the beginning of things and she is the mother of all types of men, the mother of all nations. She is the mother of the thunder, the mother of the

---

[8] Karl T. Preuss, *Religion und Mythologie der Uitoto*, I, pp. 165-168.

streams, the mother of trees and of all things. She is the mother of the world and of the older brothers, the stone-people. She is the mother of the fruits of the earth and of all things. She is the mother of our younger brothers, the French, and the strangers. She is the mother of our dance paraphernalia, of all our temples and she is the only mother we possess. She alone is the mother of the fire and the Sun and the Milky Way. She is the mother of the rain and the only mother we possess. And she has left us a token in all the temples,—a token in the form of songs and dances." [9]

She has no cult, and no prayers are really directed to her, but when the fields are sown and the priests chant their incantations the Kagaba say, "And then we think of the one and only mother of the growing things, of the mother of all things." One prayer was recorded. "Our mother of the growing fields, our mother of the streams, will have pity upon us. For to whom do we belong? Whose seeds are we? To our mother alone do we belong." [10]

Here we have pure pantheism and the recorder of the above data may perhaps be quite right when he insists that we can hardly expect an origin myth, for the All-Mother is obviously nature personified. I am not quite so convinced of this, but it is a fact that no creation myth has been recorded.

If there are traces, however faint they may be, of

[9] *Ibid.*, p. 169.
[10] *Ibid.*, p. 170.

a direct intervention of the All-Mother of the Kagaba in the ordinary affairs of man, there are absolutely none in the cases now to be cited, the Tirawa of the Pawnee of Oklahoma and the Earthmaker of the Winnebago of Wisconsin.

In the Pawnee pantheon Tirawa reigned supreme. To him the lesser gods, both of the heavens and of the earth, as well as the people themselves acknowledged authority. Tirawa rules from his position beyond the clouds and has both created and governs the universe by means of commands executed by lesser gods who are subject to him.[11]

The two temperaments which we see clashing incessantly in the interpretation of the supreme deity, that of the permanently devout man and the idealist, and that of the intermittently devout, the practical man, the realist, are transparently reflected among the Pawnee. The supremacy of Tirawa is never questioned by the latter, but something of his rôle as creator of all things is taken from him. The sun, moon, and stars are not mentioned as specifically formed by him. They are merely given their proper places and functions, i.e., Tirawa, somewhat like the culture-heroes, transforms things. The following is assuredly the account of the realist: "In the beginning was Tirawahut (the Universe-and-Everything-Inside); and chief in Tirawahut was Tirawa, the all-powerful,

---

[11] George A. Dorsey, *Traditions of the Skidi Pawnee* (see Introduction), and Alice C. Fletcher, "The Hako, a Pawnee Ceremony," 22d *Report of the Bureau of American Ethnology.*

and his spouse was Atira (Vault-of-the-sky). Around them sat the gods in council. Then Tirawa told them where they should stand. And at this time the heavens did not touch the earth. Tirawa spoke to the gods and said, 'Each of you gods I am to station in the heavens; and each of you shall receive certain powers from me, for I am about to create people who shall be like myself. They shall be under my care. I will give them your land to live upon, and with your assistance they shall be cared for. You, sun, shall stand in the east. You shall give light and warmth to all beings and to earth. You, moon, shall stand in the west to give light when darkness comes. You, evening star, shall stand in the west. You shall be known as Mother of all things; for through you all things shall be created.' "[12]

It is the same realist who in the following litany converts him merely into the most potent of gods:

> We heed as unto thee we call!
> Oh send to us thy potent aid!
> Help us, oh, holy place above!
>
> We heed as unto thee we call;
> Oh send to us thy potent aid!
> Help us, Hotoru, giver of breath! [18]

And it is unquestionably the idealist who speaks in the following. It is a final profession of faith.

---

[12] George A. Dorsey, *op. cit.*, pp. 3-4.
[18] Alice C. Fletcher, *op. cit.*, p. 285.

I know not if the voice of man can reach the sky;
I know not if the mighty one will hear as I pray;
I know not if the gifts I ask will all granted be;
I know not if the word of old we truly can hear;
I know not what will come to pass in our future days;
I hope that only good will come, my children, to you.

I now know that the voice of man can reach to the sky;
I now know that the mighty one has heard as I prayed;
I now know that the gifts I asked have all granted been;
I now know that the word of old we truly have heard;
I now know that Tirawa hearkens unto man's prayer;
I know that only good has come, my children, to you.[14]

There is no doubt whatsoever in the minds of the Pawnee that Tirawa reigns supreme and that the minor gods are his ministers only. In one of their prayers he is invoked in the following manner:

Father, unto thee we cry!
Father thou of gods and men;
Father thou of all we hear;
Father thou of all we see—
Father, unto thee we cry! [15]

His unapproachability and the realization that only through his ministers, the lesser gods, can man be brought into relation with him is forcibly brought out in such an invocation as this:

Father, thou above, father of the gods,
They who can come near and touch us,

---

[14] *Ibid.*, pp. 343 *ff.*
[15] *Ibid.*, p. 314.

Do thou bid them bring us help.
Help we need. Father, hear us! [16]

In the account of origins given by the Uitoto we saw the problem of the creation of the world out of nothing solved in a very ingenious manner. But no attempt was there made to create the creator. Yet this is precisely what the Winnebago essayed.

Their theory was not so different after all from that of the Uitoto. The creator is represented as being born and coming into consciousness. Water is formed from his tears. But this does not take place as the result of a conscious wish. It is only after he has recognized the water and inferred that it had originated from his tears that he realizes his powers and begins to create at first gropingly and then confidently and intelligently.

Earthmaker like the Tirawa of the Pawnee never holds direct communion with men. He acts only through his intermediaries, the deities and the culture-heroes he has created. At times, however, a daring realist will attempt to establish such a direct communion. I know of one instance where a man argued that if Earthmaker had created all the deities from whom we derive our powers, and if it is Earthmaker who bestowed them upon the deities, then he himself must possess even greater powers. Why not then supplicate Earthmaker directly; see him face to face, as one does the spirits? The man gives up everything —happiness, the goods of the world, lastly his own

---

[16] *Ibid.*

child, and finally he hears a voice from above saying, "My son, for your sake I shall come to earth." The man turns in the direction of the voice, perceives a ray of light extending from the heavens to his camp and a voice again speaking: "Only thus can you see me, my son. What you ask of me, to see me face to face, I cannot grant." [17] So not even the realist can alter him profoundly; he is a deity unapproachable and invisible.

In one of the cults, practically a feast to all the gods and a plea for victory in war, a further attempt has been made to convert him into a god of the general type:

"Hearken, Earthmaker, our father, I am about to offer you tobacco. My ancestor concentrated his thoughts upon you. The blessings you bestowed upon him, those I ask of you directly (i.e., and not through the customary intermediation of other spirits). Also that I may have no troubles in life." [18]

Or we get an even more definite attempt at transformation into a cult deity:

"Hearken, Father who dwells above, all things you have created. Yet if we were to offer you some tobacco you would thankfully accept it, you said. I am about to offer you a handful of tobacco and a buckskin for moccasins and a white-haired animal to be cooked so that you may have a holy feast. If you accept

---

[17] Paul Radin in 37th *Report of the Bureau of American Ethnology,* pp. 291-293.
[18] *Ibid.,* p. 447.

them, the first thing I ask of you will be the honor of killing an enemy in full sight of the people, of leading war paths." [19]

From the enumeration of these examples let us return to the general discussion.

If, then, as most ethnologists and unbiased students would now admit, the possibility of interpreting monotheism as part of a general intellectual and ethical progress must be abandoned and if social causations hardly touch the fundamental problem involved, only two alternatives remain open to us. We may either regard such a belief as innate in the theological sense or as the expression of a certain temperament. The first lies quite outside my province. The second will, I think, be found nearer the true solution— monotheism; its origin and development will seem to be bound up most intimately with the factor of man's temperament.

It is a matter of common experience that in any randomly selected group of individuals we may expect to find, on the whole, the same distribution of temperament and ability. Such a view, I know, has certain terrors because of national and class prejudices but I do not think it can be really seriously questioned. Primitive people are, we have seen, quite as logical as ourselves and have perhaps an even truer sense of reality. There is not the slightest indication of the existence of any fundamental difference in their emotional nature as compared with ours. I think we may

---

[19] *Ibid.*, p. 455.

confidently assume that the same distribution of ability and temperament holds for them that holds for us. Indeed, I think there is ample reason for believing, granted that chance mating has existed since man's first appearance on earth, that the distribution of ability and temperament never has been appreciably different. What has differed is the size of population with its corollary of a larger proportion of men of a certain type of ability and temperament. We must bear this in mind in estimating the culture of primitive peoples.

If we are right in assuming the same more or less fixed distribution of ability and temperament in every group of approximately the same size, it would follow that no type has ever been totally absent. I feel quite convinced that the idealist and the materialist, the dreamer and the realist, the introspective and the non-introspective man have always been with us. And the same would hold for the different grades of religious temperament, the devoutly religious, the intermittently, the indifferently religious man. If individuals with specific temperaments, for instance the religious-æsthetic, have always existed we should expect to find them expressing themselves in much the same way at all times. And this, it seems to me, is exactly what we do find. The pagan polytheistic religions are replete with instances of men—poets, philosophers, priests—who have given utterance to definitely monotheistic beliefs. It is the characteristic of such individuals, I contend, always to picture the world as a unified whole, always to postulate some first cause. No evolution from animism to monotheism was ever necessary in their case. What was required were individuals of a certain type. Alongside of them and vastly in the majority have always been found others with a temperament fundamentally distinct, to whom the world has never appeared as a unified whole and who have never evinced any marked curiosity as to its origin. Such, too, is the situation among primitive peoples. If anything, the opposition of the two types is much clearer. All the monotheists, it is my claim, have sprung from the ranks of the eminently religious individuals. Its precise formulation is due to those specifically religious individuals who happened to be thinkers at the same time. It is in the ritualistic version of the original myth, for example, that Earthmaker is depicted as a supreme deity who definitely creates the other deities and the culture-heroes; it is in the ritualistic version of the culture-hero cycle again that a nonmoral, buffoon-like hero, whose acts are only incidentally beneficial to mankind, is transformed into an ethical, intelligent, beneficent creator. No other explanation for the characteristics of the supreme deities, as I have attempted to sketch them, is indeed conceivable except upon the assumption that they reflect a definite type of temperament, examples of which we know actually exist in every primitive group. Such people are admittedly few in number, for the overwhelming mass belong to the indifferently religious group, are materialists, realists, to whom a god, be he supreme deity or not, is simply to be regarded as a source of power. If men of this type accept such a god, he is immediately equated with the more concrete deities who enter into direct relations with man, and as a result contamination ensues. It is thus that that particular type of creator arose, where a marked admixture of attributes belonging to the culture-hero and transformer was manifest.

On such an hypothesis a really satisfactory explanation of the existence and of the dominant traits of the monotheism among primitive peoples can be given. Monotheism would then have to be taken as fundamentally an intellectual-religious expression of a very special type of temperament and emotion. Hence the absence of cults, for instance, the unapproachability of the supreme being, his vagueness of outline, and his essential lack of function. Whatever dynamic force he possesses for the community is that with which the realists invested him. In so doing they frequently converted him into a cult deity, into a creator of gods; made him but one among many. This is merely monolatry if you wish, but this in no way detracts from the possibility that the faith of the religious man himself may have been different, may have been essentially explicit monotheism. Yet even if we should not care to press this claim, the existence of monolatry and implicit monotheism must constitute a definite challenge to the views still current as to the development of the concept of a supreme creator.

The view still held both by the ethnological theorist

and the student of comparative religion is frankly evolutionary. Only recently in a remarkably lucid address by the late Dr. C. Buchanan Gray, three stages in the development of Hebrew monotheism are assumed, the earliest extending perhaps even beyond the Exile, in which the Jews were divided into two groups, one, apparently the large majority, worshiping Jahveh and other deities at the same time, and the other worshiping only Jahveh but yet not denying the efficacy of other gods for the people. The second is represented by the belief of the prophets of the eighth century and after, where Jahveh is thought of as controlling the destinies of all nations but where, at the same time, it is not definitely asserted that no other gods exist. The last stage, that of Deutero-Isaiah, gives us the definite formulation that there is no god but one. Dr. Gray goes on to say, "The existence of this third type of belief in Israel cannot be definitely traced back beyond the sixth century. Implicit monotheism might, according to the judgment passed on the age and meaning of certain passages, be traced perhaps somewhat earlier than the eighth century; but wherever and so soon as we find the first type of belief, monotheism, whether implicit or explicit, is excluded."[20]

This is quite definitely in line with the orthodox evolutionary theory. The cardinal error is and always has been the assumption that every element in culture

---

[20] "Hebrew Monotheism," *Abstract of Proceedings for the Year 1922-1923* (Oxford Society of Historical Theology).

must have had an evolution and one generally comparable to that which exists in the animal world. But it is precisely in its application to culture, to thought, and to temperament that the evolutionary theory even in its heyday proved so unsatisfactory and even harmful. It requires no long preparatory stages for an individual with inborn artistic abilities to draw figures both correctly and with a remarkable feeling for line, and there is no reason whatsoever for supposing that certain concepts require a long period to evolve. What, concretely speaking, did Dr. Gray imagine had happened in Israel between the first and the third stages of monotheism? Apparently an increase in intelligence and in the capacity for abstract thought. This is but the old unconscious assumption that progress must make equal strides along the whole line. The general acceptance of explicit monotheism at one stage (if indeed there ever has been or could be such a general acceptance) and its apparent absence in the two earlier stages is taken to mean that it did not exist before. The existence of two varying attitudes toward God at one and the same time, as in the previously cited case of Hebrew monolatry, is regarded as somehow implying that explicit monotheism was absent. Dr. Gray himself partially realized the force of this criticism, for he says further on: "We may admit the possibility in the abstract that even before the eighth century there may have been individual Hebrew monotheists of whom no trace has survived; but the religion of the people as a whole—of the teachers, prophets, priests, as well as the mass of the people—was not monotheistic." [21]   To Dr. Gray the existence of such a monotheist was a bare possibility because at bottom he could not think of explicit or implicit monotheism except as the result of a gradual evolution and, I surmise, because he would have seen no way in which to explain it if it had actually been found.

Another theologian and historian of religion, the very stimulating Archbishop of Upsala, Dr. N. Söderblom, is also definitely evolutionistic in his interpretation. Instead of simply beginning with animism or pre-animism, however, he begins with three factors: animism, the belief in supernatural power, i.e., *mana,* and the belief in culture-hero creators (Urheber). He does not deny the existence of the all-father or creator concept but assumes it as something shadowy and vague among primitive peoples and in his opinion utterly distinct from real monotheism in any form. He, like so many people, can explain the marked resemblances of so many supreme creators to the culture-heroes in but one way, namely, that the latter have largely contributed toward the formation of the former. To explain the third, i.e., the mystical aspect, he has recourse to the *mana* concept. This in itself is exceedingly suggestive, especially if we take the belief in culture-heroes and the *mana* concept as being in the nature of psychological tendencies, but unfortunately Dr. Söderblom does not confine himself to this aspect of the question but predicates an evolutionary development

---

[21] *Ibid.,* pp. 8-13.

for both concepts.[22] For, like the most orthodox of evolutionists, he cannot bring himself to believe that the mentality of primitive people is not essentially different in kind from our own. He has been led astray, if I may say so, by the data he selected. He practically bases his analysis on the somewhat antiquated instances found in Lang, i.e., on the ridiculously inadequate and unsatisfactory material from Australia and the vague statements found in early accounts of the American Indians. But the real criticism of Dr. Söderblom's position is that just indicated, that to him explicit and implicit monotheism must represent the last phases of a long and gradual development.

Explicit monotheism, it is true, is rare among primitive peoples, but it is possibly not quite so uncommon as the literal reading of the facts might seem to indicate. Knowing the tremendous part symbolism plays in the interpretation of religious phenomena, particularly the godhead in our own civilizations, what right have we to assume that it played an inferior rôle in avowedly similar temperaments among primitive peoples, especially when it is universally admitted that symbolism permeates every aspect of primitive man's culture? What the facts really are it is admittedly difficult to ascertain, but from my own experience I am inclined to assume that a limited number of explicit monotheists are to be found in every primitive tribe that has at all developed the concept of a supreme

---

[22] *Das Werden des Götterglaubens.*

creator. And if this is true we can safely assume that they existed in Israel even at a time when the mass of the people were monolatrists.

The problem that confronts us is not, as has always been erroneously assumed, the origin of monotheism. That, I should say, antedates even Neanderthal man. The historical problem connected with monotheism, implicit and explicit, is, as I see it, not how monotheism arose but what made it the prevailing and exclusive official religion of a particular people. This we must assume to have been largely in the nature of an historical accident. The Jews and Mohammedans, the adherents of the purest form of monotheism known to-day, are certainly not innately gifted in this regard. It is true that the factors concerned in the complete credal triumph of monotheism in Judaism, Christianity, and Mohammedanism have never been satisfactorily explained, but they are emphatically of an individual, historical, and psychological nature. For myself, I am inclined to believe that the spread of monotheism is far more definitely a reflection of certain facts of a general sociological order than has hitherto been recognized. Certainly it has not been the triumph of the unifying principle over the disruptive, of abstract over concrete thought. Yet, on the other hand, there must be something subtly appealing in monotheism, for wherever it is found a definite influence is seen to be exercised over the thought of those who are stubborn polytheists and animists. Nowhere, indeed, has it ever been completely submerged once it has made its appearance, no matter how great the mass of foreign accretions piled upon it.

Most of us have been brought up in or influenced by the tenets of orthodox ethnology and this was largely an enthusiastic and quite uncritical attempt to apply the Darwinian theory of evolution to the facts of social experience. Many ethnologists, sociologists, and psychologists still persist in this endeavor. No progress will ever be achieved, however, until scholars rid themselves, once and for all, of the curious notion that everything possesses an evolutionary history; until they realize that certain ideas and certain concepts are as ultimate for man as a social being as specific physiological reactions are for him as a biological entity. Both doubtless have a history; but in the one case its roots lie in presocial man and in the other in the lower organisms. It must be explicitly recognized that in temperament and in capacity for logical and symbolical thought, there is no difference between civilized and primitive man. A difference exists—and one that profoundly colors primitive man's mental and possibly his emotional life; but that is to be explained by the nature of the knowledge the primitive man possessed, by the limited distribution of individuals of certain specific temperaments and abilities and all that this implied in cultural elaboration.

In no way, however, does this affect the question of the existence among primitive people of monotheism in all its different varieties. Such a belief, I cannot too often repeat, is dependent not upon the extent of knowledge nor upon the elaboration of a certain type of knowledge, but solely upon the existence of a special kind of temperament. When once this has been grasped, much of the amazement and incredulity one inevitably experiences at the clear-cut monotheism of so many primitive peoples will vanish, and we shall recognize it for what it is—the purposive functioning of an inherent type of thought and emotion—and this inherent type of thought and emotion has received expression among many primitive tribes, sometimes more, sometimes less elaborate, as the examples in this and other chapters amply demonstrate.

CHAPTER XIX

SKEPTICISM AND CRITIQUE

THE critical attitude assumed by some of the Ba-ila thinkers toward their supreme deity brings us to the whole subject of philosophical and scientific critique. Were there, for instance, any true skeptics among primitive people? Were they, or at least were some of them, capable of subjecting their beliefs to consistent criticism, capable of weighing their merits and demerits? I shall let the facts speak for me.

First let us turn to the out-and-out skeptics. Every ethnologist has encountered them. I will give one example in detail, one already mentioned.

Among the Winnebago it is narrated that there was once a man who doubted the powers of the most feared of Winnebago deities. The deity in question was named Disease-Giver. His was an open rebellion. "Why," he said, "do you always make offerings and feasts to Disease-Giver? What benefit has he ever been to you? If I were ever to see him I would kick him off the earth. The only thing he can give you is disease." Time passed, but in the fall of the year he saw a man coming toward him who proved to be the much slandered Disease-Giver. Disease-Giver disclosed himself and when he asked the man whether he still believed he could carry out his threat, the latter defiantly answered yes. Thereupon Disease-Giver pointed his deadly finger at him, straight at his heart. The man did not budge. And then we come to the complete depreciation of the god. The deity pleads with the man to die, at least for a short time, so that people might not say that he, Disease-Giver, had failed in his mission! [1] It is true that in the end the skeptic is punished but this in no way detracts from the skepticism, of course.

Skepticism and doubt, fear and bewilderment, mingle with acceptance and gratitude in the following discourses on the nature of the Ba-ila Leza. Something, indeed, of the atmosphere of the *Goetterdaemmerung* pervades their attitude.

Long ago the Ba-ila did not know Leza as regards his affairs—no, all that they knew about him was that he created us and also his unweariedness in doing things. As at present when the rainy season is annoying and he does not fall, why then they ask of Leza different things; they say now, "Leza annoys us by not falling"; then later when he falls heavily they say, "Leza falls too much." All the same, Leza, as he is the compassionate, that is to say, as he is the merciful, he does not get angry. He doesn't give up falling, he doesn't give up doing them all good—no, whether they mock him, whether they grumble at him, he does

---

[1] Paul Radin in 37th *Report of the Bureau of American Ethnology*, pp. 309-310.

good to all at all times. That is how they trust him always. But as for seeing always his affairs, no, the Ba-ila do not know. All they say is: Leza is the good natured one.

Today Leza has turned over and abandoned his old ways. Today he is not the same, he is altogether different, for he is not as he was in distant years before the white chiefs came. At that time he was truly the water giver and all things were still sufficient on earth as they had been established from the beginning. Then Leza was still young. Today Leza has grown old, he has become the ancient one of long ago. That is what we suppose, because the water which he rains down is supposed to be like tears from the eyes of men when they weep. So it is when one becomes aged. When he weeps tears he lets tears dribble down his chest—that is how we judge Leza to be. He is the-owner-of-his-things: all things are his. He cannot be charged with an offense, cannot be accused, cannot be questioned, cannot be claimed from: none of the things can be done to him which we do to our fellow-men on earth. He gives and rots. Vengeance is his own. There is no flood today—no great giver of floods. This is how he is judged of; today Leza is not as he is wanted to be. Long ago he was the one who could be urged to do well, but today he has left off being so.[2]

In the following example taken from a discourse on God of the Ewe of West Africa, we have a dispassionate presentation first of the good qualities of God and then of his inconsistency and rank injustice:

[2] E. W. Smith and A. M. Dale, *The Ila-Speaking Peoples of Northern Rhodesia*, II, pp. 200-201.

God made everything in the world. He alone has been great from the beginning of time. God made all men. When he is ready to send a person into the world he gives him some occupation by means of which he can earn his living. God is wise for he has created everything on the earth and accompanies men and animals everywhere. He made the high mountains and the woods that grow on them and he made the rivers. No person can understand his wisdom. He sent us Ewe here and he therefore consoles us and gives us food so that we may live for a certain span. He himself made the good and the bad people. He is compassionate but he does not always know how to act justly for he gave us death.

God acts unjustly for he made some people good and others bad. I and my companions work together in the fields; the crops of one prosper and those of others fail. This proves that God is unjust and treats men unequally. God treats us, our children and our wives who perish, unkindly. If men behaved like that we say nothing, but when God acts thus it hurts us. From this we are right in inferring that God is unjust.[3]

From ethico-philosophical critique of this kind it is but a step to definitely scientific or objective criticism, and I cannot do better than to begin by giving an instance of what is properly speaking the very highest type of scientific control. My example comes from the Maori.

In the early days of Christian influence the Maori

---

[3] Johann Spieth, *Die Ewe Staemme,* pp. 834-836.

were very much impressed by many aspects of European civilization. While not accepting them they yet believed them to be true. One thing, however, so the missionary who relates the following incident tells us, they did not believe and that was that a person could convey his thoughts to another person, separated many hundreds of miles, by writing. This a chief told the missionary he would believe only if all possibility of trickery and magic were definitely excluded. The chief thereupon proposed the following test. A white man was to write something on a piece of paper in his presence and the contents communicated to him alone. This was then to be taken by a Maori whose movements were under control, to a white man living many miles distant and who had had no communication with the sender of the message. If this white man could read the message correctly then he, the Maori, would accept this as proof. By one of those delightful ironies which fill the annals of our contact with primitive peoples, the missionary in question cites this incident to illustrate the ridiculous naïveté of savages and it was subsequently quoted in a paper entitled *Maori Beliefs and Superstitions.*[4]

But in critical caution and critical doubt the Maoris were excelled by many other peoples, particularly by the African Negroes. Take for example the following disquisition on Unkulunkulu, the supreme deity of the Amazulu of East Africa:

---

[4] Authority of Elsdon Best.

When black men say Unkulunkulu or Uthlana or the Creator they mean one and the same thing. But what they say has no point; it is altogether blunt. For there is not one among black men, not even the chiefs themselves, who can so interpret such accounts as those about Unkulunkulu as to bring about the truth, that others too may understand what the truth of the matter really is. But our knowledge does not urge us to search out the roots of it; we do not try to see them; if anyone thinks ever so little he soon gives it up and passes on to what he sees with his eyes and he does not understand the real state of what he sees. Such then is the real fact as regards what we know about Unkulunkulu, of which we speak. We say we know what we see with our eyes, but if there are any who see with their hearts they can at once make manifest our ignorance of that which we say we see with our eyes and understand too.

As to our primitive condition and what was done by Unkulunkulu we cannot connect them with the course of life on which we entered when he ceased to be. The path of Unkulunkulu through our wandering has not, as it were, come down to us; it goes yonder whither we know not.

But for my part I should say, if there be anyone who says he can understand the matters about Unkulunkulu, that he knows them just as we know him, to wit, that he gave us all things. But so far as we see, there is no connection between his gift and the things we now possess.

I say then that there is not one amongst us who can say that he knows all about Unkulunkulu. For we say, "Truly we know nothing but his name; but we no longer see his path which he made for us to walk in. *All that remains is mere thought about the things we like.* It is difficult to separate ourselves from these things and we make him a liar. For that evil which we like of our own accord, we adhere to with the utmost tenacity. If anyone says, "It is not proper for you to do that; if you do it you will disgrace yourself," yet we do it saying, "Since it was made by Unkulunkulu where is the evil of it?" [5]

The same Amazulu informant told Canon Callaway, our main authority on this tribe, the following:

The old men say, "Unkulunkulu came into being and gave being to man. He came out of the bed of reeds; he broke off from a bed of reeds." We children ask, "Where is the bed of reeds out of which Unkulunkulu came? Since you say there is a bed of reeds in what country is it? For men have now gone into every country. In which of them is the bed of reeds from which Unkulunkulu broke off?" They say in answer, "Neither do we know and there were other old men before us who said that neither did they know the bed of reeds from which broke off Unkulunkulu." They say they speak the truth in saying there is a bed of reeds. But we say there is no bed of reeds, for we do not know the land in which it is, of which they can say it is in such and such a country.[6]

But it is not merely the vague Unkulunkulu on whom the Amazulu exercise their very great critical

---

[5] Bishop Callaway, *The Religious System of the Amazulu*, pp. 22-24.
[6] *Ibid.*, pp. 31-32.

acumen and their half-ironical skepticism. Everything in their life is subjected to it, their ancestors, the nature of ecstasy, dreams, etc. In the following discourse on the *amatongo,* i.e., the ancestor-gods of the Amazulu, nothing escapes their boring inquiry—the ridiculousness of gods who are capricious without cause, and the fatuity of men who insist that their gods have been with them because they have, through some unforeseen chance, escaped destruction!

Men say they possessed *amatongo* as soon as they came into being. When they came into being men spoke already of there being *amatongo* and hence they too knew that they existed. It is not something which as soon as they were born they saw to be *amatongo.*

So all nations used to think when they were about to attack an army, that they should be assisted by the *itongo* (ancestors); and although they were killed by the army the friends of those who were killed said, "The *itongo* of our people has turned its back on us." They asked, "How is it that all our people have at length come to an end and not one man come back from the army?"

If there is one who has escaped he says, "As for me I escaped, I know not how. The *amatongo* had decreed that we should all die; one man would not assent. When we were destroyed by the enemy where was he, I wonder? I escaped I know not how; I no longer expected to be saved when I saw all our people destroyed."

At first the people say, "The *amatongo* of our people are good for nothing! Why has the whole village perished?

How is it that they never mentioned anything to us that we might understand why they were angry? Where had the *itongo* of so-and-so gone? Why was he not among the other *amatongo*? Those who weep for the dead say thus.

"And those who escaped say, 'We have been saved by the *amahlosi* of our people.'" [7]

Again what better recognition of the difference between our normal waking state and ecstasy can be demanded than this definition: "Ecstasy is a state in which a man becomes slightly insensible. He is awake but he still sees things which he would not see if he were not in a state of ecstasy."

As a final example I give the following Amazulu inquiry into the meaning of dreams:

Among black men the real meaning of dreams is not known. For some dreams have every appearance of reality but they are not true; others again point out something which is about to happen. For among black men it is supposed that if a man dream of a great assembly where they are dancing, if there is anyone ill, we have no confidence that he will get well, but immediately the man who dreamt of the dance is much alarmed.

But a dream which produces confidence among black men, when one is ill, is one in which they dream that someone is dead.

We do not understand how this happens. For as regards living and dying, it would appear proper that he who is

---

[7] *Ibid.*, p. 129.

about to die should die, if when he is ill people dream he is dead; and he who is about to live should live if people dream that he is well. But in truth I have seen both.[8]

We have now passed through the whole gamut of speculative philosophy and critical approach as vouched for among representative primitive people. In the face of this remarkable evidence which probably represents only a small portion of what is still to be obtained, it is manifestly unfair to contend that primitive people are deficient either in the power of abstract thought or in the power of arranging these thoughts in a systematic order, or, finally, of subjecting them and their whole environment to an objective critique.

[8] *Ibid.*, pp. 129-133.

CHAPTER XX

IN our introduction, we pointed out that certain of the assumptions current in anthropological literature to-day were arrived at more than fifty years ago, at a time when the older conception of the evolutionary process was making its triumphant procession through the intellectual world, and when our knowledge of primitive people was meager, one-sided, and largely erroneous. Within the last thirty years our material has increased to such a bulk that a new appraisal is not only urgent but obligatory. And this has been attempted from many sides. The foregoing chapters represent such an attempt made from a particular angle unusual in anthropology perhaps, but familiar enough to students of history and philosophy—the nature and the rôle of the intellectual in the community.

No qualified observer of the customs of primitive man has ever denied the existence of thinkers among them. He may have discounted their views and dismissed them as of no consequence, as having no perceptible influence on the attitude of the majority, but he has never denied their presence. Yet the preceding chapters will, I feel certain, convince even the most skeptical that to underestimate the contribution of these thinkers is a serious error, likely to distort our whole picture of the mentality of primitive man. Nor is this the only error arising from so superficial an attitude toward the culture of primitive peoples. A far larger question is involved. How are we ever to trace properly the development of thought and, more specifically, that of our fundamental philosophical notions if we begin with false premises? If it can be shown that the thinkers among primitive peoples envisage life in philosophical terms, that human experience and the world around them have become subjects for reflection, that these ponderings and searchings have become embodied in literature and ritual, then obviously our customary treatment of cultural history, not to mention that of philosophical speculation, must be completely revised.

Whether I have proved my contentions must be left for the reader to decide. There is not the slightest doubt in my own mind. It is not conceivable nor reasonable to suppose that material obtained in the original and translated by competent scholars is likely to be wrong, particularly when it is corroborated by statements contained in the ritual and the literature of primitive peoples. To those who would contend that the systematized philosophy found simply represents the influence of contact with Europeans and Oriental peoples during the last five hundred years, I would answer that this can, in many cases, be definitely disproved, and that even were it true, it would no more affect the real problem involved than the fact that Greek civilization influenced the rest of Western Europe. Indeed, it is from instances where we know European and Christian influence to have been definitely present that our best evidence for the existence of thinkers, and for the philosophical quality of their thoughts, can be derived. In no Christian creed of which I am aware—certainly in none with which American Indians ever came in contact—has God, for instance, become equated with the soul, or has the doctrine of a pantheistic soul been evolved, or has Man become synonymous with his Thought. Yet, as we have seen in the preceding pages, such was the philosophy elaborated by a Winnebago Indian after his conversion to a semi-Christian religion.

As we have stated the material must speak for itself. We must not, likewise, forget that our present data obviously represent only a fraction of what once existed, or of what could still be obtained if attention were specifically directed to the subject. Only when we have obtained this will we realize completely how erroneous has been the older contention so unfortunately revived by Professor Lévy-Bruhl's well known but completely misleading work *Les Fonctions Mentales dans les Sociétés Inférieures,* that the mentality of primitive man differs intrinsically from our own, and only then will we fully understand that what differentiates us from him is the written word and the technique of thinking elaborated on its basis.

In conclusion, lest I be misunderstood, let me again

emphasize the fact that it is not contended for one moment that what is contained in this book represents the viewpoint of the average man, or that of the overwhelming majority in any given primitive community. It is the thinker we have been describing and predominatingly the thinker.

APPENDIX

THE SOURCES OF THE POEMS QUOTED

All the poems quoted in this book represent accurate translations from the original. With the exception of the cases indicated below the originals are also available.

Page 103

I. *American Indian Life,* edited by E. C. Parsons and A. L. Kroeber, p. 19. Not available in original.

II. Frances Densmore, Bulletin 53, Bureau American Ethnology, p. 89

III. *Ibid.,* p. 114

IV. Johann Spieth, *Die Religion der Eweer,* p. 237

Page 104

V. John White, *The Ancient History of the Maori,* Vol. I, p. 35

I. H. A. Junod, *Les Chants et les Contes des Ba-Ronga,* p. 51. Translated from French.

II. Bureau of American Ethnology, 35th Report, p. 1292

Page 106

I. J. White, *op. cit.,* Vol. I, p. 7

Page 107

II. W. W. Gill, *Myths and Tales from the South Pacific,* pp. 281-282

III. J. Spieth, *op. cit.,* p. 237

Page 108

IV. W. W. Gill, *Darkness and Light in Polynesia,* p. 220

Page 110

I. Edward Tregear, *The Maori Race*, p. 73
II. J. C. Andersen, *Maori Life in Aotea*, pp. 61-62
All the references used from this book represent quotations that Andersen has taken from the older sources, where they are either given in the original Maori or in translations by scholars who knew Maori very well.

Page 112

III. E. Tregear, *op. cit.*, p. 75

Page 116

I. Edward Shortland, *Traditions and Superstitions of the New Zealanders*, pp. 178-181

Page 117

II. E. Shortland, *op. cit.*, pp. 170-171
III. *Ibid.*, p. 171

Page 118

IV. Henry Rink, *Tales and Traditions of the Eskimo*, p. 67
I. E. Shortland, *op. cit.*, pp. 178-179

Page 119

II. Nathaniel B. Emerson, Bulletin 38, Bureau of American Ethnology, p. 49
III. *Journal of the Polynesian Society*, Vol. II, pp. 35-37

Page 121

IV. J. Warneck, *Die Religion der Batak*, pp. 69-70
Translated from German. Not available in original.

Page 122

V. *Ioid.*, p. 69. Translated from German. Not available in original.

Page 123

VI. J. C. Andersen, *op. cit.*, p. 461

APPENDIX

Page 124

VII. E. Shortland, *op. cit.*, p. 184

Page 125

VIII. J. C. Andersen, *op. cit.*, p. 116

Page 126

IX. J. White, *op. cit.*, Vol. I, p. 178
X. *Ibid.*, pp. 33-34
XI. N. B. Emerson, *op. cit.*, pp. 133-134

Page 127

XII. *Ibid.*, p. 83

Page 128

XIII. J. R. Swanton, Bulletin 39, Bureau of American Ethnology, p. 415
XIV. *Ibid.*, p. 415
XV. F. Densmore, Bulletin 45, Bureau of American Ethnology, p. 89
XVI. E. Shortland, *op. cit.*, p. 178

Page 129

XVII. *Ibid.*, p. 180
XVIII. F. Densmore, *op. cit.*, pp. 151-152

Page 130

XIX. *Ibid.*, p. 154
XX. *Ibid.*, p. 184
XXI. E. Tregear, *op. cit.*, p. 75

Page 131

XXII. N. B. Emerson, *op. cit.*, p. 260
XXIII. W. W. Gill, *Myths and Songs of the South Pacific*, p. 104

Page 132

XXIV. *Ibid.*, p. 142
XXV. *Ibid.*, pp. 179-180

Page 133

XXVI. Smith and Dale, *The Ila-Speaking Peoples of Northern Rhodesia*, Vol. II, p. 276

Page 134

XXVII. Bureau of American Ethnology, 35th Report, p. 1306
XXVIII. *Journal of American Folklore*, Vol. XVI, p. 205
XXIX. Natalie Curtis, *The Indian Book*, p. 56

Page 135

I. H. Rink, *op. cit.*, pp. 67-68

Page 136

II. *Ibid.*, 68-69
III. *Journal of American Folklore*, Vol. I, pp. 210-211
IV. H. Junod, *op. cit.*, p. 64. Translated from French.

Page 137

V. F. Boas, *The Lkungen*, British Association for the Advancement of Science, 1890
VI. Richard Thurnwald, *Forschungen auf den Salomo Inseln*, p. 216. Translated from German.
VII. *Ibid.*, pp. 150-151

Page 138

I. E. Shortland, *op. cit.*, p. 62

Page 139

II. J. C. Andersen, *op. cit.*, p. 500
III. E. Tregear, *op. cit.*, p. 76

Page 140

I. *Journal of American Folklore*, Vol. XVI, pp. 205 *ff.* Not available in original.
II. N. Curtis, *op. cit.*, pp. 224 *ff.*
III. *Ibid.*, pp. 224 *ff.*

Page 141

IV. *Ibid.*, p. 431
V. Bulletin 45, Bureau of American Ethnology, p. 303
VI. Bureau of American Ethnology, 35th Report, p. 1315

Page 142

VII. *Ibid.*, p. 1315
VIII. N. Curtis, *op. cit.*, p. 104
IX. Bureau of American Ethnology, 35th Report, p. 1311

Page 143

X. J. R. Swanton, *American Ethnological Society,* Vol.
    III, p. 5
XI. *Ibid.,* p. 27
  I. N. Curtis, *op. cit.,* p. 50
 II. F. Densmore, *op. cit.,* p. 120

Page 144

III. *Ibid.,* p. 185
IV. *Ibid.,* p. 185
 V. J. Spieth, *op. cit.,* p. 287
VI. *Ibid.,* p. 287

Page 145

 VII. *Ibid.,* p. 287
V.II. N. Curtis, *op. cit.,* p. 50
 IX. H. Junod, *op. cit.,* p. 39. Translated from French.

Page 146

X. R. Thurnwald, *op. cit.,* p. 37

Page 147

 XI. *Ibid.,* pp. 221-224
XII. Bureau of American Ethnology, 35th Report, pp.
    1298 *ff.*

Page 149

XIII. *Ibid.,* pp. 1301 *ff.*

Page 212

I. N. B. Emerson, *op. cit.,* pp. 43-44

Page 214

 II. F. Russell, Bureau of American Ethnology, 23rd Re-
    port, p. 294
III. *Ibid.,* p. 299

Page 215

IV. *Ibid.,* p. 302
 V. *Ibid.,* p. 307
VI. *Ibid.,* p. 292

Page 216

VII. *Ibid.*, p. 317
VIII. *Ibid.*, p. 319

Page 217

IX. N. B. Emerson, *op. cit.*, pp. 43-44
X. *Ibid.*, pp. 45-46

Page 218

XI. Frank La Flesche, Bureau of American Ethnology, 39th Report, pp. 74-79

Page 220

XII. S. Percy Smith, "The Lore of the Whare Wanaga," *Memoirs of the Polynesian Society*, Vol. III, pp. 93-94

Page 221

XIII. F. Densmore, Bulletin 53, Bureau of American Ethnology, p. 254

Page 222

XIV. N. Curtis, *op. cit.*, p. 304
XV. N. B. Emerson, *op. cit.*, p. 89

Page 223

XVI. F. Russell, *op. cit.*, p. 322

Page 224

XVII. *Ibid.*, p. 284
XVIII. W. Skeat and C. Blagden, *The Pagan Tribes of the Malay Peninsula*, Vol. II, p. 129

Page 225

XIX. W. W. Gill, *Darkness and Light in Polynesia*, p. 129

APPENDIX B

AN AMERICAN INDIAN RELIGIOUS AND PHILOSOPHICAL FORMULATOR

It is only when a culture is breaking down, that is, only when crises, cultural and personal, are present that, generally speaking, an individual is prone to become sufficiently objective to examine the presuppositions, particularly the religious and philosophical presuppositions, on which his culture has been built. It is only at such times that real fundamental questions are likely to be asked by him and that disturbing doubts and fears arise. For that reason it is generally at such times that we catch a real glimpse into the nature of a personal religious experience and its philosophical implications and see it in all its multiform interconnecting aspects and varieties.

It is with the religious experience and philosophy of a particular Indian, a Winnebago named John Rave, and the new formulations which he arrived at in just such a period of personal crisis, that I shall deal here. Many of the different types of information necessary for a fruitful examination of such an experience are fortunately present here. Not all, unfortunately, nor ever in the detail I would have preferred. Let me stress what these are: authentic and adequate statements, *in the original,* from the individual whose experience is being described; adequate information about him and his experience from other members of his tribe, adequate personal acquaintance of the outside investigator with the man himself and with his culture. However, before we can profitably turn our attention to John Rave himself a few words about the state of the Winnebago culture of his time are necessary.

The Winnebago have been in contact with European civilization since the second quarter of the seventeenth century. Like every other American Indian culture they met the threats to their way of life which this contact presented in a number of different ways: either rejecting it in *toto*; compromising with it; or accepting it in *toto*. The vast majority in any tribe belonged, as always, to the second group. One of the consequences of this division of the tribe into factions disagreeing, often violently, upon so fundamental and vital an issue as to how the tribe was to survive as a distinct cultural entity, was, of course, a tremendous increase in personal frustrations. Cultural and personal demoralization in all its many aspects soon set in. This demoralization was markedly intensified when, from the middle of the eighteenth century on, white settlers spread in ever-increasing numbers throughout the area inhabited by the Winnebago. By the middle of the nineteenth century what remained of the tribe had been forced into a restricted area in Wisconsin. Then in the early sixties of the nineteenth century one-half of the tribe was forcibly removed to eastern Nebraska, that is, to surroundings completely different from those to which all their traditions had been interwoven.

Winnebago culture had, by that time, completely
lost its economic basis; its political structure, particularly its clan organization, was moribund. However,
the ideological structures, the religion, the rituals, the
mythology, the multiple customs and beliefs, which
had been reared upon them and in connection with
them, these all functioned fully and naturally. Men
still sought visionary experiences, and all the numerous ceremonies and rituals still flourished vigorously.
In fact it can be said that these ideological super-
structures functioned redundantly, that a hypertrophy
of religious rituals and visionary experiences existed.
Yet since, after all, for the Winnebago—for all other
Indians, indeed for all aboriginal peoples—religion
was in so large a degree a validation of reality, there
were some individuals who were bound to ask themselves what reality, what way of life, the visionary
experiences and the other practices of the old Winnebago religion to which they were so tenaciously ad-
hering, were supposed to validate. Obviously not the
drab, wretched and impoverished existence the Winnebago were being compelled by circumstances to lead
between, let us say, 1860 and 1890. Thus it became in-
creasingly difficult for essentially religious natures, for
individuals who were not content to be mere formal-
ists, to establish a satisfactory relationship between
themselves and their deities. Yet it goes without saying that these individuals were the ones who most
needed the contact with a deity which was normally

obtained in a visionary experience and all that this implied if they were to save themselves from inward psychical disintegration and attain some measure of inward security.

Now it was in the 60's of the nineteenth century that John Rave was born in Wisconsin. When I first met him, in 1910, he was so engrossed and wrapped up in the new religion, that is, the Peyote religion which he had brought back with him from Oklahoma and which he had completely reinterpreted and remodelled, that it was very difficult to extract from him any connected and coherent picture of his early life. He was too little of an exhibitionist, too inherently modest, to compose anything in the nature of an autobiography. However, certain facts about his early life emerged clearly. He had, for instance, not succeeded in obtaining a visionary experience in his childhood although he had sought it, and he had never become a member of the most important ritual society, the Medicine Rite. In short, he had failed to make a satisfactory adjustment to those aspects of Winnebago culture which demanded, ideally speaking, full acceptance of the religious conceptions of the old Winnebago way of life. Yet he apparently had had no difficulty in accepting other aspects of that way of life. His father had been one of the outstanding members of the community, the chief[1] of the Bear clan, the second in importance of all the Winnebago clans. Rave himself was unusually well-versed in everything that pertained to the old political and ceremonial structure of the tribe, more particularly to that of his own clan. The information he gave me and the texts[2] he dictated to me prove clearly that he must have accepted much of the older culture.

Why then, despite this, we must now ask, did he not obtain the proper visionary experience in his childhood? That he had been expected to do so we know from his own statements. He described the circumstances to me briefly. He and two other children were, as custom demanded, taken at dark to a comparatively isolated place, there to begin their fast and to wait for some deity to manifest himself to them. But he and those with him were thoroughly frightened, so he said, at being left alone and to forget their fears they played with each other and laughed all night. When dawn was about to break Rave suddenly realized that the elders in charge of their fasting would soon come to inquire about their success. He knew that they would have to indicate, in some fashion, that they had at least made some attempt to appeal to the deities. Now it was the custom when seeking visionary experiences for the faces of the suppliants to be blackened with charcoal and for the appeal to the deities to be made with outstretched hands and weeping. The streaks made by their tears on the children's charcoal-blackened faces was then the clearest evidence of the intensity of their appeals and prayers. But Rave and his youthful companions had not wept, so to protect themselves from being taken sharply to task and scolded, they took some saliva and ran it over their faces!

Assuredly this is not the complete story nor even a substantial part of it. But it brings out two facts that are very important for an understanding of Rave's psychology; his marked susceptibility to fears and his unwillingness to pretend that he had experienced something when he had not. Young fasters were given the most circumstantial details as to what they were to expect during their puberty fasts, so that it was really a simple matter to obtain a satisfactory "experience," and quite a number of Winnebago children brought back to their elders what they knew these elders wanted them to bring back. Ideally a faster and suppliant was expected to have an inward awareness of the presence of a deity and to put himself into a condition approximating to religious ecstasy. However, the elders of the tribe had no illusions about the rarity of religious ecstasy and were quite content if the young faster-suppliants followed the instructions and information given to them. Indeed an individual who insisted too strongly upon a true inward awareness of the presence of a deity as the *conditio sine qua non* often presented a considerable problem to them.

My own surmise would be that it was not simply recalcitrance on young Rave's part, no mere negativeness which brought his puberty-fasting to an end but, rather, his insistence upon an inward awareness of the presence of a deity which did not come to him. All his life, we shall see, he was to seek for just such an awareness and he was to attain it when he ate the peyote.

Of his life, apart from this brief description of his unsuccessful fasting, he told me only a few unimportant snatches. But some facts can be gleaned from the accounts he gave of his conversion to the peyote religion and from two accounts given by other members of the tribe, that of Oliver Lamere and that of John Baptiste.

Lamere had joined the peyote cult about 1908. He possessed some historical sense and knew a good deal about Rave, because he was married to Rave's niece. I shall quote only part of this account:

"John Rave belongs to the Bear clan. . . . He and his ancestors used to be in charge of the special lodge to which all malefactors were brought for punishment.

"Although he belonged to this highly respected family, Rave was a wicked man. He participated in all the Winnebago ceremonies, the Medicine Rite alone excepted. Up to 1901 he was a heavy drinker. In that year[3] he went to Oklahoma and while there ate the peyote. He had been married many times. . . .

"There was not much religion connected with it in the beginning and the only reason people drank it, i.e. the peyote infusion, was because of the peculiar effects it had upon them. Nevertheless these peyote people preached good things and gradually lost desire for intoxicating drinks or for participating in the old Winnebago ceremonies. Then Rave began to do away with the old Indian customs. About four years ago . . . the Bible was introduced by A. H."[4]

Baptiste's account adds some more details. It runs as follows:

"Among the Winnebago there is a man named Little Redbird (i.e. John Rave). When he reached middle age he began to travel around the world and to learn different languages. He used to travel inland (i.e. the United States) too.

"Once he joined a circus and crossed the ocean. He felt so ill while crossing that he wanted to die. Suddenly a wind came up and he got very frightened. He did not know what to do. Then he prayed to Earthmaker. . . .

"When he came back to his own people he told them that on the other side of the ocean the Thunderbirds did not thunder. All they did was to drizzle. There was no lightning either. As he crossed the ocean on his return it thundered and lightened.

"When he came back home he was very glad to see his relatives and he offered tobacco in thanksgiving.

"Shortly after his return he began to travel again and he visited a tribe of Indians who were eating peyote. Now it was his custom to try everything whenever he visited people. So he ate this medicine. He did not realize what he was doing when he took it but he ate it nevertheless. After he had partaken of it he suddenly began to think about the manner of life he was leading and he felt that it was wrong. He remembered all the evil things that he had done. Then he prayed to God. Suddenly it occurred to him, 'Perhaps I am the only one doing this.' But when he looked around and watched the others, he saw that they were all praying in this manner."[5]

"Not long after that he came home, taking with him some of the medicine (peyote). He knew it was holy. At home he offered tobacco to it and kept on eating it. Soon it cured him of a disease which he had. Then he tried to induce some other Winnebago to eat it but they refused. But, after a while, a few tried it and the peyote-eating began to spread. All the old customs which they had been accustomed to observe were abandoned. They gave up the Medicine Rite and all the ceremonies connected with the clans. For that reason, consequently, the conservative people hated the peyote-eaters, even the brothers and sisters of the peyote people hated them for they had abandoned matters that had always been considered holy."

To complete the picture let me now add the brief statement Rave himself makes, in retrospect, about these years. It relates exclusively to his psychological state.[6]

"It is now twenty-three years since I first ate peyote and I am still doing it. Before that time my heart was filled with murderous thoughts. I wanted

to kill my brother and my sister. It seemed to me
that my heart would not feel good until I killed one
of them. All my thoughts were fixed on the warpath.
This is all I thought of.

"Today I know that I was in that condition because some evil spirit possessed me. I was suffering
from a disease. I even desired to kill myself. I did
not care to live. This feeling, too, was caused by this
evil spirit living within me.

"Then I ate this medicine (peyote) and everything
changed. The brother and sister whom I wanted to
kill, to them I now became deeply attached. I wanted
them to live. This, the medicine had accomplished
for me."

From the above narratives two facts seem to emerge
clearly, first the nature of his early religion and his
attitude to the old Winnebago background and, secondly, the nature of the life he led before he ate the
peyote. It seems clear that until middle age, Rave, as
we have already pointed out, was a reasonably devout
believer in certain aspects of the old Winnebago way
of life, making offerings of tobacco to the spirits, etc.
In view of his later hatred of tobacco because of its
old associations, it is interesting to point out that
Baptiste represents Rave as offering tobacco to the
peyote in the early days of its worship. Apparently,
then, the old religious-ritualistic implications of
tobacco were not repudiated by Rave until some time
after his conversion.

All this makes it so much the more necessary to stress the facts of his inability to obtain the customary visionary experience in childhood.

With regard to the second fact, the marked deterioration of his character, about this there can be little question. The external side of that demoralization, his murder phantasies, his fears, his restlessness, his wandering, these have been vividly depicted by Lamere, Baptiste and by Rave himself. However the internal side of his behaviour is not so easily detected. What was it that was driving him to the psychical disintegration, to the murder phantasies he describes? And thus we are brought directly to the narrative concerning his conversion to the peyote religion which he dictated to me in 1911. I shall divide this narrative into three parts and then discuss each part. The first part deals with the visions he had immediately after eating peyote, the second with its sacred nature and curative powers, and the third consists of a series of exhortations extolling its virtues.

Rave's Narrative: Part I

I was in Oklahoma with the Peyote-eaters during 1893-1894.

In the *middle of the night*[7] we were to eat peyote. Since the other people present ate it *I did too*. Now it was just during the *middle of the night* that *I got frightened, for a living object seemed to have entered me*. Then I thought to myself, *"why did I do this?* I should never have done it, for now at the very beginning (of my visit) *I have injured myself*. I should not have done it! I am certain that it will injure me!" Surely the best thing I can do will be *to vomit it up*. "Yes, exactly," (so I thought to myself) "now you have really done something to yourself! *You have been going around trying everything* and now you have finally done something that has really harmed you.

"But what is it? It seems to be an object that is alive and moving around in my stomach.

"If only some of my own people were here! That would be better. Now no one will know what happened to me. *I have killed myself!"*

Just then the object within me *seemed about ready to come out*. Indeed it seemed just about out, so *I put my hand* (in my throat) to feel it but it slipped right back again.

"O my, I should never have done this (the eating of the peyote), never have started at all! Never again will I do it! Now I am most certainly going to die!"

And thus we continued until it became day. *Then we laughed*. Before, I had not been able to laugh.

On the following night preparations were again made to eat peyote. Then I thought to myself, "Last night *I almost injured myself*." Yet when those (gathered around) said "Let us do it again," then I answered "Good, I'll try it too!" So there we all ate seven peyote apiece.

Suddenly *I saw a large snake.* I was very much frightened. Then another snake (appeared) and *came crawling over me.* "O my! *Where are these coming from?"* Then I felt something behind me and I looked around me and *I saw a snake about to swallow me completely. It had legs and arms and a long tail and the end of its tail was like a spear.*

"O my, O my! Now I am surely going to die," I thought.

Then I looked around again and there in a different place, *I saw a man with horns and long claws and with a spear* in his hand. He jumped toward me so I threw myself on the ground. He missed me. Then I looked back at him and he appeared to be going back. Yet it seemed to me nevertheless that he was directing his spear at me. Again I threw myself on the ground and again he missed me. *Yet there seemed to be no possible escape for me.*

Then, suddenly[8] *the thought ran through me "Perhaps—yes,*[9] *it is this peyote that is doing this to me?"*

"Help me, O medicine, help me! It is you who are doing this! You are holy. It is not these fear-inspiring visions that are causing this!

"I should have known that you were doing this! Help me!"

Then *my suffering stopped.*

"As long as the earth shall last, so long will I make use of you."[10]

This (i.e. these sufferings and the release from them) had lasted a night and a day. For one whole night I had not slept at all.

Then we all breakfasted. When we were through it was I who said "Let us eat peyote again tonight."

That evening I ate eight peyote.

In the middle of the night *I saw God. To God, living above, our father, to him I prayed. "Have mercy upon me! Give me knowledge that I may not say or do evil things. Do thou, O Son of God, help me too.*

"This religion let me know! Help me, O grandfather, help me! Let me know this religion."

Thus I spoke and sat very quiet.

Soon *I beheld the morning star* and it was good to look upon. The light was good to look upon. Indeed, as the light appeared, it seemed to me that *nothing would be invisible to me. I seemed to see everything clearly.*

Then I thought of my home (in Nebraska). No sooner had I done so than, looking behind me, I saw the house in which I lived among the Winnebago, quite close to me. There, at the window, I saw my children playing.

Soon I saw a man making his way to the house carrying a jug of whiskey. He gave my people something to drink. Then he who had brought the whiskey got drunk and began annoying my family. Finally he ran away.

Then I saw my wife come out and stand outside the door of the house wearing a red blanket. She was thinking of going to the Flagpole[11] and was wondering which of the two roads she should take. *"If I take this road I am likely to meet some people* (who might annoy me) *but if I take the other road I am not likely to meet anyone."*

"Indeed, it is good. They are all well—my brother, my sister, my father, my mother." I felt very good indeed.

"O medicine, grandfather, most assuredly you are holy. All that is connected with you, that I would like to know and that I would like to understand!

"Help me! I give myself up to you completely!"

For three days and three nights I had not slept.

Throughout all the years that I had lived on earth, I now realized that I had never known anything holy. Now, for the first time, I knew something holy.

"O, would that some of the other Winnebago might also learn about it!"

Commentary on Part I

In trying to determine the meaning of the document we have before us we must, of course, bear in mind that it could not have been composed in one piece. Rave, in short, did not put into a coherent whole immediately the experiences he had on these first dreadful nights, but is speaking of them in retrospect and after many years had elapsed until the account of his conversion had taken on a definite pattern and had become something in the nature of a "creed" for all members of the peyote religion and ritual. We cannot be absolutely certain, consequently, that the succession of the visions themselves, for that matter, represents the order in which they actually took place. But the precise form and succession of the visions is not really of any great consequence here. The important fact is that he had hallucinatory visions and that he thought they had appeared in a specific order in time and in intensification.

In the long description given by S. B. of the visions he had after eating peyote, we find these same phenomena illustrated, namely a specific type of succession and intensification.[12]

But before discussing the visions as such, let us turn to the setting in which they appear. Rave is among strangers and is participating in a rite quite alien to Winnebago rites and beliefs, and it is the middle of the night. In addition, he is eating peyote for a variety of reasons; first, to be civil and, secondly, because, for reasons which will shortly be clear to us, he liked to experiment. Everything must have been strange and new to him here except the fact that the ceremony was taking place in the middle of the night. Yet the only Winnebago ceremony which can be said to have begun in the middle of the night was the puberty-fasting rite. Now for Rave, we know, this rite had multiple associations, none of them pleasant. And just as during his puberty-fasting, so here, once again, he is frightened.

At his puberty-fasting he was frightened at being alone, and, probably, also, at what those in charge of his fasting had told him. For a person of his temperament and make-up the mere expectation of establishing any type of contact with the spirit-deities must have held elements of terror.[13] However, whether what he was told was terrifying or not, he was there at least given a traditional pattern to expect.

Here at this, his first participation in the peyote religion he had no such traditional pattern. Thus he was delivered over to his innate fears and whatever patterns rose up from his unconscious memories.

His first sensation is that a living object has entered him. But what was this object? This is a question he puts to himself as soon as his initial fears have abated, only to repeat what he has already said, namely that this object is alive and is moving about his body. There can be little question but that he is describing here, fairly accurately, the physiological effects of the peyote as it manifested itself to him. That these physiological effects were different in different individuals we know. Yet there appears to be considerable agreement upon two points among those Winnebago who described these physiological effects; first, that something had "entered" them and, secondly, that this object inside them was strangling[14] them.

Rave, in his description, stresses not only the fact that the object inside him was choking him but that it was trying to come out. Rave is thus experiencing something entirely new here. It is, therefore, quite illuminating and significant to see how quickly he has analyzed and coordinated this new material. I think this must have been done immediately after he had this first experience, i.e. after the first night. I am strongly of the opinion that Part I must have constituted a unit by itself at first which was subsequently, and then only secondarily, and certainly much later, brought into connection with the visions obtained after the second eating of the peyote. All the stylistic considerations favor such an interpretation. In fact the first vision is tacitly abandoned when the peyote is suddenly recognized as the real instigator of the visions.

All this make Rave's retention and stressing of his first peyote-induced experience and the manner in which he coordinated and reinterpreted the events within it the more significant. The general physiological effects of the peyote are, we see, all unified and they are attributed to an object, not as yet identified, that has lodged itself in the body and is causing great physical suffering. Rave speaks of his attempt to vomit it up, then, of the object trying to come out of its own accord, of his attempt to aid it in emerging and of its finally slipping back. It never actually comes out. Nevertheless, in spite of this harrowing experience, as morning comes, everything seems to be forgotten. If he stresses the fact that he could laugh again, that is in order to make the contrast between the fears that the night engenders for him and the release which daylight brings all the more marked. This welcoming of the light of day is repeated, in intensified form, later on even after he had had his culminating vision of God. In that first vision he breaks out almost into a paean: "I beheld the morning star and it was good to look upon. The light was good to look upon."

Clearly this *object* which comes from nowhere, that fastens itself on him so tenaciously, and from which he tries so desperately to release himself, and this *darkness-night* that is dispelled by the light of day, these must have had a symbolical significance for him. As I see it, in that symbolism the object represents, basically, a concretization of his life-long struggle to maintain psychical equilibrium, to escape complete deterioration. In his demoralized state he offers the most desperate resistance to taking the bitter medicine which will cure him. Here, in this resistance, we find the real meaning of his repeated and frantic outcries that he has injured himself, that he has killed himself. It is the struggle of his evil self against the new life that is to bring him psychical unity and health; it is this drama that he is unconsciously portraying. That is why it was so easy for him and his followers, all of them completely demoralized and disoriented individuals, to clothe the physiological effects of the peyote so easily in the psychological-moralistic and Christian terms and to accept the peyote either as something in the nature of a divinity or as something through which alone divinity could manifest himself. The state of euphoria and release from tensions which the peyote frequently brought about was accordingly interpreted as willingness to give up one's evil ways, as a sign of true repentance. "If a person is truly repentant," so one of the peyote members said, "even if he is eating peyote for the first time, he will not suffer, but if he is bullheaded . . . he is likely to suffer a good deal."[15] Another one states that although he wished to give up his old ways, he could not get himself to do so and this unwillingness caused the peyote he was eating to strangle him.[16]

Only in this light can Rave's interpretation of his first peyote-induced experience be fully understood. That this interpretation came much later than his conscious organization of the sensations he felt, of this there can be little doubt. This implies that the emphasis upon his acute sufferings represents, in part, a later addition. And this brings up the further question of whether, originally, Rave actually postulated the presence of an object in him. If we could eliminate this object as part of the contents of his first experience, then the sensations he describes would be more in consonance with the frequent initial physiological effects of the peyote. The effects of the peyote upon Rave could then be arranged in the following order: first, the actual sensation he felt, with probably some vague hallucinatory images; secondly, the vision of snakes and of a figure that is evidently a merging of the old Winnebago Waterspirit and the Christian devil; and, thirdly, the vision of God.

But to return to the symbolism of darkness and light. This contrast is an old one in Winnebago religion and religious rituals. There, light had developed the secondary meaning of life, and darkness, by implication, that of death. For Rave, too, we have seen, darkness had always had the most sinister implications, in his childhood, when crossing the ocean and here in Oklahoma as he sat lonely among strangers, participating in an alien ceremony. The light of day had saved him in his childhood when he was fasting and it saves him after he has eaten his first peyote. It serves as the harbinger of the new life and of happiness after he has had his vision of God.

Let us now proceed to the effects of the peyote upon Rave during the second night. Why they should have been so different from those of the first night it is difficult to say.

That the first true vision he has is that of a snake is very significant. He had good reason to be thoroughly frightened, for to have a vision of a snake in the old puberty-fasts, in fact at any ritual-fast, meant death. It is therefore quite understandable that he

should exclaim in fear "Now I am going to die!"
However this snake is not like the ordinary one that
appeared to Winnebago in their visions. This snake is
not a divine being. It is a monster-snake and has
come to attack and devour Rave. As the latter describes it, it has the traits of two famous mythical
animals, first, of the enormous snakes whom the
Twins, in the well-known Winnebago myth, encounter
and overcome and, secondly, of the man-devouring sea
monster who swallows Hare as told in the Winnebago
Hare Cycle. One new element appears here, namely,
the legs, arms and the long tail with a spear at the
end of it. This, I feel, can only be a distorted description of a Winnebago waterspirit. Now to have
combined snake and waterspirit into one being, particularly where snake means so many things, indicates
the intensity with which Rave sensed that death was
all around him.

The image of the "snake" now disappears and its
place is taken by that of the devil who throws his
spears at him. What is important to remember here is
the contrast in the behaviour of the snake and the
devil toward Rave. While the snake threatens Rave
he is never represented as actually attacking him.
Rave does not run away in order to save himself. But
the devil attacks him and Rave has to dodge his
spear and to throw himself to the ground. The struggle
between the two, then, increases in intensity. Rave for
a time protects himself successfully but he realizes

that ultimately there is no escape for him. The phrase
he uses to describe his desperate situation is strangely
reminiscent of that used by the Twins[17] when they
are being pursued by *Rushewe* at the direction of
Earthmaker. Then, when he has resigned himself to
death, he is saved.

Now this situation, that of being saved when all
seems lost, is an old Winnebago religious-literary
cliché. The saviour in such myths is always some
spirit-deity. Here in Rave's narrative we also have a
"saviour" but he is of a very special type. Rave is
saved from destruction by his sudden recognition—a
recognition that comes in a flash—that his suffering is
being caused by the peyote. It is the recognition of
this fact that constitutes Rave's conversion, as the
prayer which immediately follows clearly indicates.

On the face of it, it is extremely difficult to believe
that his conversion could possibly have taken place
in this fashion. Something must have taken place
within him at that particular moment that he has
omitted. The most minute examination of the meaning and implications of the text, beginning with the
vision of the devil to the end of Part I, and all sup-
plementary material procurable are, consequently,
necessary in any attempt to try to understand what
it must have been which induced him to ponder about
the cause for his sufferings and to have this sudden
revelation just then.

Rave, of course, knew very well what a vision was

and he undoubtedly must have been told by some of the peyote people he was visiting that eating peyote produced visions. Actually, therefore, the revelation he receives is not at all in answer to his inward question "Who is doing this to me?" The revelation consists in his sudden illumination that the peyote is holy. This illumination has come after a long search. All his life had been an attempt to establish contact with the supernatural, with the holy, as he clearly says at the end of Part I. Now he has found it. The question we must accordingly now ask is, why did he find it just then? Such questions are not easy to answer. But let us try.

I shall begin with the vision of the snakes. That, of all the spirit-deities, just these should have appeared to him, makes us wonder whether they had not appeared to him before, appeared to him in his crucial puberty-fast. That, of course, would have brought his fast to an abrupt termination. Had he had such an ill-omened vision then, Rave, I feel quite certain, would never have spoken about it again. I am throwing this out simply as a suggestion. If true, it would help to explain not only the vision of the snake but the peculiarities they possessed and the fact that one of them took on the form of that other death-dealing Winnebago deity, the waterspirit. Rave's snake crawls over him and is ready to swallow him whole; one of the traits of the waterspirit was that he destroyed man by submerging him in water and devouring him.

However, we do not need any hypothesis of an earlier snake-vision to realize that death here is in active pursuit. After all, we have the progression: strangling object, man-swallowing "snake," spear-throwing devil. Further on in his narrative, Rave states that he wished to die, that he even contemplated suicide. Yet despite this, here he is terrified at the prospect of death. To understand this ambivalence we must turn to his anguished cry, "Help me, O medicine, help me!" Help him from what? one asks. Help him from a death that meant complete annihilation. Such a type of death all Winnebago dreaded. It is interesting to know that this is the accusation which the old conservative Winnebago hurled against the peyote-people. In one of the few statements that I was able to obtain from the old conservative Winnebago about the peyote-people, it was just this fact, namely annihilation after death, that was stressed.[18]

But Rave here is not thinking only of physical extermination. He is thinking of psychical extermination, thinking of that in fact primarily. The snake and waterspirit are, for him, the agents which have brought about the deterioration of his personality. They are the symbols of his psychical disunity. When, therefore, he is terrified by them, this terror is something quite distinct from that which a Winnebago would feel if a snake, or what the Winnebago termed an evil waterspirit, appeared to him in a vision-quest.

Undoubtedly the vision of the snake accentuated Rave's fears. But no more. That the devil should appear after the snake-waterspirit is clear. He was the great punisher, the great exterminator who is summoned when all other attempts to destroy a victim have failed.

We have the right to assume then from Rave's wording and his silence about any overt attack upon him by the snake-waterspirit that he has succeeded in warding them off. That much physical strength and unity he still possessed. From this success he has gained the courage to meet the new and far more dangerous threat represented by the devil. But courage is not enough; willingness to fight is not enough. To achieve the new psychical integration he is so desperately seeking, he must abandon his old way of life and all its implications. He must realize that his sufferings have a specific significance, that they do not simply represent extreme physical discomfort. These sufferings are not injuring him; on the contrary, they represent something positive. To put it in the language he subsequently developed, they are the evils within a man that are seeking to leave him. O. L., one of the most consistent members of the peyoterite, claimed that he threw up a bull-dog before he could become converted, the bull-dog being the concrete symbol for his greatest vice, his stubbornness.

Thus we have one more element to aid us in trying to understand why Rave is so concerned with finding out what is causing his sufferings. He wished to be clear about one thing in particular, namely, that his visions are not producing this suffering. To accept that would be tantamount to admitting that the old Winnebago visions were efficacious. But these latter had never functioned for him or, if they had, they had done so only in a life-destroying fashion.

Yet though this element in the old Winnebago religion had never meant anything to him, other elements in that culture had meant very much, at least formally. Probably before coming to Oklahoma and eating peyote, he would not have denied that other Winnebago had received power from the spirit-deities in their puberty vision quest. When, consequently, he arrives at the conclusion that, as he says, "it is not these fear-inspiring visions that are causing this (his sufferings)," he is then in fact, without his realizing it at the time, renouncing the whole old Winnebago religion in all its ramifications. It had failed him in his hour of need.

But here another question obtrudes itself. What made him feel that the peyote would help him? The only satisfactory answer would seem to be that, suddenly, for the first time in his life, he has had an ecstatic experience and been overwhelmed by all those sensations and affects that make up what we call holy. The ecstatic experience has made him one with himself, the inward knowledge of the holy has enlarged and reintegrated him. Both together have enabled him to substitute love and humility for hatred and arrogance. That this should have been ascribed to the peyote is an historical accident. In short, Rave does not know that the peyote is going to help him. All he knows is that the peyote was being worshipped when he happened to have his first experience of the holy.

It is very interesting to see how, at the very moment that he has renounced Winnebago culture, he falls back in his new prayer upon the old ritualistic terminology which he knew so well. Yet the prayer itself, apart from the last sentence, is a purely individual one, devised by Rave for his own needs. Take for instance the phrase "Have pity upon me." He has substituted for it the words "Help me." No spirit-deity had to be told he was holy. Nor should there ever have been any doubt in the suppliant's mind of who was bestowing "blessings" upon him. What this prayer then actually means is this: "Through you, O peyote, I have at last felt and recognized a holy thing, a knowledge which I should have obtained many years ago."

Perhaps a few words are in place here about the phrase that was to mean so much and to be so frequently employed by subsequent converts, namely: "Then my sufferings stopped." Rave's sufferings were, we know, of a double nature, the external ones caused by the effect of the peyote and the internal ones connected with his psychical disunity. However, there may also be an echo of the old fasting experiences in his stressing of suffering, for there, too, a person had to suffer and to be willing to suffer in order to gain the "blessings" of the spirits. Like Rave's sufferings they, likewise, stopped when the "blessings" had been obtained.

Stylistically—and this is important in the study of a document like the one before us—the phrase "my sufferings stopped" represents a full stop. It is clearly an oversight on Rave's part that the sentence beginning with "As long as . . ." follows it. We may then say that we have three stops connected with Part I; one after each experience, each having a different function and different implications. Let me enumerate them:

"Then we laughed. Before I had been unable to laugh." (End of first night.)

"Then my sufferings stopped." (End of second night.)

"I sat very quiet." (End of third night.)

We are now prepared to deal with the third vision, that of God.

Rave indicates the completeness of the change that has come over him when he says, preliminary to this vision, "It was I who said, let us eat peyote again." On the previous occasions it will be remembered, this eating of the peyote had to be suggested to him.

Formally and in content, the vision he has on the third night is a strange and subtle compound of old Winnebago and Christian beliefs. It is an old Winnebago belief that the spirit-deity appears during the middle of the night. It is not Winnebago, however, to say "I saw God." It should have been, "God saw me." The sentence that then follows is traditional old Winnebago phraseology—thus one addressed Earthmaker—except for one important and fundamental point, the word employed for "pray." In the old religion the word used meant "Here I stand in a pitiable condition." Here the word used means "I mention your name." The next sentence is, of course, Christian, but the phrase "to have mercy upon" is but a slight variation, i.e. in the original Winnebago, of the old "to have pity upon." The two sentences following that are purely Christian. The second paragraph with the exception of the word "help" is traditional Winnebago.

The word used for "quiet" in the next sentence is revealing. It signifies "to be at rest after turmoil," and it describes admirably the semi-euphoria which Rave had now attained. He was never to suffer again and he was always to remain, in fact, in a mild state of euphoria.

What follows now is truly amazing. Having, at last, attained his long-delayed experience and knowledge of the holy, all of this outside the Winnebago religion, he suddenly relapses into the latter again. It was, for instance, the custom for all ceremonies to stop as soon as the morning-star became visible, and a special person stood outside the ceremonial lodge to watch for it. Here we have the same thing except that Rave himself is watching for it. Not, let me add, to announce it to those about him, but in order to do something representing his own contribution, namely, to combine the appearance of the morning-star and the light that was now diffused over the sky with an old Winnebago belief specially connected, I believe, only with membership in the Medicine Rite, although generally known to the whole community. According to this belief, membership in the Medicine Rite gave the man the gift of foreseeing events many days ahead and, likewise, of seeing through space. This latter power could, however, be obtained in other ways as well.[19]

When Rave now says "Nothing *would be invisible,*" this is good old Winnebago doctrine. When, however, he adds "*I seemed to see everything clearly,*" this is also old Winnebago doctrine but here he is also talking about the inward change which has taken place within him.[20] But to what use does he put this newly-acquired gift? He thinks of his home and his relatives and he describes what he sees in two vividly-drawn pictures, each pointing a moral. The first picture stresses the evil of alcohol and how it leads to disunion and strife. His comment in the next sentence should really have read "So, that's what I have been doing," for before he ate the peyote he was a heavy drinker and frequently drunk. The second picture gives us the ideal of a virtuous married woman which, incidentally, his wife very definitely was not. The picture of the wife hesitating as to which road to take and the predicating of two roads, this represents the transference of an incident taken from the myth of The-Journey-of-the-Soul-to-Spiritland. That there are also secondary Christian implications involved here is very likely. Moreover I suspect that both of these pictures are very late interpolations and that what Rave saw was simply his home and his family.

In the next paragraph we have an expression of the love he feels for his blood relatives. That he mentions his brother and sister first is no accident, for it is against them, we have seen, that his murder phantasies had been directed.

A prayer to the peyote now follows which is essentially in the old Winnebago pattern. His reiteration of the phrase "O medicine, grandfather, assuredly you are holy" can be taken in two senses. Either it is simply an expression of his intense gratitude or it represents something in the nature of bewilderment in the presence of the new experience through which he has just passed.

I think it is worthwhile to compare, in this connection, the bewilderment which is so manifest in S. B.'s description of his conversion. He tells us that, after he had eaten a number of the peyote,[21] he was looking at the small peyote which the leader of the ceremony had placed in front of himself. ". . . I looked and there stood an eagle with outspread wings. . . . The eagle stood looking at me. I looked around thinking that perhaps there was something the matter with my sight . . . (But) it was really there . . . I then looked in a different direction and it disappeared. Only the small peyote remained. I looked around at the other people but they all had their heads bowed and were singing. *I was very much surprised.*" Other visions follow, traditional Winnebago ones, in fact, and which S. B. unquestionably must have recognized as such. Yet he says "I was much surprised indeed."

The final sentence of the prayer, "I give myself up completely," constitutes as complete a renunciation of the old Winnebago religion as did the sentence "It is not these fear-inspiring visions that are causing (these sufferings)." In the old Winnebago prayers the formula was "Here, humble and pitiable, I stand." One never surrendered one's person to the spirit-deity to do with as he wished. Yet I doubt very much whether Rave understood then or at any time of his life the full implications of this Christian doctrine. Later members of the peyote cult did, especially when the cult became overwhelmed by the Christian beliefs introduced by a partially Christianized Indian named Hensley.[22]

In the next to the last paragraph of this, the first part of Rave's narrative, he recapitulates what it is he has now acquired. Apparently this torn and disoriented soul had to reiterate, again and again, for his own benefit and for the benefit of others, "Come, look, behold, I have at last found and come into the presence of a holy thing." He cannot contain his joy and excitement. It spills over in all directions. It is, therefore, not at all strange that he should end the narrative of his conversion with a fervent prayer that the happiness which he has attained be brought to his fellow Winnebago as well.

And thus he launches out as a prophet and as the proclaimer of a new faith. How he proved his new faith and how it was disseminated we can best learn from the second and third part of his story.

Rave's Narrative: Part II

Many years ago I had been sick. It looked as if this illness was going to kill me. I tried all the Winnebago medicine-practitioners and then I tried all the white man's medicine. They were all of no avail. "*I am doomed,*" I said to myself, "I wonder whether I will be alive next year?" Such were the thoughts that came to me.

As soon as I ate the peyote I got over my sickness. After that I was not sick again.

My wife was suffering from the same disease. I told her that if she ate this medicine, it would unquestionably cure her. But she was afraid *although she had never seen it before.* She knew that I used it but, nevertheless, she was afraid. Her sickness however was getting worse so, one day, I said to her "You are sick. It is going to be difficult (to cure you) but try

this medicine anyhow. It will ease your (pains)."
Finally she ate some peyote. I told her to eat some,
then *to wash her face and comb her hair,* and then
she would get well. *I painted her face, took my gourd-
rattle and began singing.*[23] After a while I stopped.
"Indeed, you are right," she said, *"for now, I feel
well."* Now she is quite well. In fact from the time she
ate the peyote to the present day she has been well.
Today she is very happy.

A man named Black Waterspirit was having a
hemorrhage at about that time, and I wanted him to
eat the peyote. "Eat this medicine," I told him, "and
then you will soon be cured." Before this time con-
sumptives had never been cured. Now, for the first
time, one was cured. Black Waterspirit is living today
and he is very well.

Now again. There was a man named Walking-
Priest. *He was very fond of whiskey; he chewed and
he smoked tobacco; he gambled; he was very fond of
women.* He did everything that was bad. I gave him
some of the peyote. He ate it and, soon after, gave up
all the evil things he was doing. *Actually he was suffering from a very dangerous disease. He had even had
murder in his heart.* But today he is living a good life.
Such is his desire.

Whosoever has any evil thoughts, if he but eats this
peyote, he will get rid of them and abandon all his
evil ways. This medicine is a cure for everything evil.

Today the Winnebago say that *only God is holy.*
One of the Winnebago told me "Truly, the life I used

to lead was a very evil one. Never again will I lead such a life. This medicine is good and I will always use it."

John Harrison and Squeaking Wings were prominent members of the Medicine Rite. *They thought much of themselves as did all the members of the Medicine Rite.* These two knew everything connected with this Rite. *Both of them were gamblers and were rich* because they had won very much in gambling. Their parents had acquired great possessions by *giving medicine to the people.* They were rich and they believed they had *a right to be selfish with their possessions.*

Then they ate peyote and ever since that time they have been followers of this medicine. *These men were actually very ill* and now they have been cured of their illness.

If there existed any men who might be taken as examples for the effects of the peyote, it is these two. *Even if a man were blind* and only heard about (their conversion), he would realize that if any true medicine exists it is this one. It is a cure for all evil.

Before (eating the peyote) I thought I had knowledge but I really had none. It is only now that I have acquired it. In my former life *I was like one blind and deaf. My heart ached when I thought of what I had been doing.* Never again will I do it. This medicine alone is holy and has made me good and rid me of all evil.

The one whom they call God has given me this (knowledge). I know this positively.

Rave's Narrative: Part III

Let them all come here, men and women. Let them bring with them all they desire. Let them bring with them all their diseases. If they come here they will get well. This is all true; it is entirely true.

Bring whatever desires you possess along with you. Then come and eat and drink this medicine. This is life: this is the only life. Here you will learn something. about yourself, so come!

But even if you are not told anything about yourself, you will nevertheless learn something about yourself. Come with your disease, for this medicine will cure it! Whatever you have, come and eat this medicine and then you will obtain true knowledge, once and for all. *Learn about this medicine personally through actual experience.* If you just hear about it you are not likely to try it. If you desire true knowledge concerning it, try it yourself. *But you will learn of things that you had never known before. In no other way will you ever be happy.*

I know that all sorts of excuses will run through your head for not partaking of it. Yet if you wish to learn about something really good you had better try it.

Perhaps you will think to yourself that *it will be too difficult* for you and this will be your excuse for not trying it. *Now why should you behave like that?* If you partake of it, *even if you feel some uncertainty about its accomplishing* all the good that has been claimed for this medicine, I know you will nevertheless say to yourself, "Well, this life is good enough."

After you have eaten the peyote for the first time it will seem as if *a grave had been dug for you and that you are about to die. You will not want to take it again. "It is bad* (injurious)" you will say to yourself. You will believe that you are going to die and *will wonder what then will happen to you. The coffin will be set before you and there you will see your body.* If then you desire to make further inquiries as to where you are going, you will learn something you had not known before, namely, that there are *two roads,* that one leads to a hole in the ground, that *the other extends up above.* It is here that you will learn something you had not known before. Of the two roads *one is dark and the other is light.* You must choose one of these while you are *still alive,* and you must decide whether you wish to continue in your evil ways or whether you will abandon them.

These then are the two roads. *The peyote people see both.* They claim that *only if you weep and repent* will you be able to obtain true knowledge.

Do not, as I said before, listen to others talking about this medicine. Try it yourself. This is the only way to find out. *No other medicine can accomplish what this one has.* If, consequently, you make use of it you will live.

*After people have eaten peyote they throw aside all
the evil ceremonies they had been accustomed to perform before.* Only by eating the peyote will you learn
what is truly holy (not through the old ceremonies).
That is what I am trying to learn myself.[24]

Commentary on Parts II and III

The second part of the narrative is taken up primarily with accounts of the cures of disease which the
peyote effected. As far as Rave was concerned that
was enough. But the holiness of the peyote would be
immeasurably enhanced if it would do for others what
it had done for him. Like so many religious converts
and organizers, Rave was a practical man and an excellent psychologist. He wished to bring happiness
and new life to his demoralized fellow-Winnebago.
Although he knew from his own experience that any
psychical reintegration would have to come from
within, he realized that it was only common sense to
bring the new dispensation to his fellow-tribesmen in
a form that would not antagonize them and in a form
where the effects of the eating of the peyote would be
most immediate and most easily discernible. He consequently equated it, whether consciously or unconsciously it would be difficult to decide, with the
medicines of which there were very many among the
Winnebago.

It is therefore not surprising to see that in this part of his narrative the peyote is really only a medicine that effects cures. Only in the next to the last paragraph does he speak of its being holy.

But if the peyote was a medicine competing with the great medicines[25] of the conservative Winnebago, it would have to be accompanied by the same type of ritual observances. And so we see Rave having his wife wash and comb herself and then he himself painting her face and singing to the accompaniment of his gourd-rattle.

Nor can we discount the resemblances between the cures claimed for the peyote and those made for the *Stench-Earth medicine*. It probably is not an accident that the first person Rave mentions as having been cured by the peyote, i.e. apart from himself and his wife, was a consumptive. Compare Rave's description of *Black Waterspirit* with the beginning of the account of the *Stench-Earth medicine*. "There once was a man," so it begins, "who had consumption and who knew that he was going to die soon. . . . He decided to go out into the wilderness and die there. He went to the top of a hill and lay down. He noticed many birds of prey hovering around . . . (they) told him, however, that they had come to cure not to destroy him."[26]

However it is in the militant opposition of the peyote people to the *Stench-Earth medicine* and in the nature of their condemnation that we have the best indication of the essential resemblance between the

two. For example, in an aside by the Winnebago who described the *Stench-Earth medicine* and who was a devout peyote-man, we find the following: "The *Stench-Earth medicine* could undoubtedly cure the sick but it was also used to poison people. . . . These people cured the body but they killed the soul. It would have been much better had they saved their souls. They were really working for the devil. It is from him they got all the bad medicines. . . . The Indians were destroying their own souls. So Earth-maker decided to give them a new medicine (i.e. the peyote)."[27]

Rave himself makes no mention of any of the resemblances between the things he taught and the old Winnebago cultural heritage. He must certainly have known about them. But he was concerned with helping his fellow-Winnebago in their struggles against outward and inward demoralization, nothing else. At the beginning, he would unquestionably have had no objection to a retention of old Winnebago customs if that helped in the struggle and the power of the peyote was acknowledged. Later on he seems to have come to the conclusion that the whole Winnebago heritage was an obstacle in their rehabilitation and must therefore be abandoned. But that did not mean for him the adoption of Christianity or of the white man's ways, as it ultimately did for many of his followers.

But from these general remarks let us now turn to a more specific examination of parts II and III, to see what light they can throw upon Rave's psychology, upon the enlargement of the religious experience which he had attained and upon the development of his doctrine.

He begins, as in Part I, with the theme of doom and approaching death. He does not describe the specific physical illness of either himself or his wife because theirs was fundamentally a disease of the soul. Only in the case of *Black-Waterspirit* is a physical ailment mentioned by name and there he has probably been influenced by the description of the origin of the *Stench-Earth medicine*. The diseases which the peyote cured were not physical, even though some of them had physical manifestations. What they were he enumerates for the three converts specifically mentioned: whiskey-drinking, smoking, gambling, conceit, selfishness, avariciousness and, finally, evil thoughts and murder phantasies.

These can be divided into three groups. The first two are those introduced by the white man, like whiskey, and those resulting, he would have contended, from the drinking of whiskey, like the deterioration of one's personality. Here he would place violence, evil thoughts and murder phantasies. The third includes the use of tobacco, gambling, sexual debauchery, conceit, selfishness and avariciousness.

Against the evils flowing from the use of whiskey he, of course, was not the first one to preach. Its disruptive effects had always been recognized. But whereas the conservatives had always condemned it because it disrupted the old Winnebago culture, Rave condemned it because it disrupted a man's personality. As far as the "diseases" in the third group are concerned, with the exception of the use of tobacco, they were condemned specifically in the old Winnebago culture.[28] Rave was here therefore following strictly in the footsteps of all enlightened old conservative members of his tribe. In short, in none of these matters was he a radical or a reformer.

His condemnation of tobacco in all its uses is another matter, however. The conservatives would have gone along with him as far as its nonreligious use was concerned. But Rave, of course, did not stop there. Why, it is somewhat difficult to understand. It was not necessary. The Winnebago were not even in 1910 great smokers. That his rejection of all tobacco was of slow growth we know. His antagonism toward it can best be explained as part of his total rejection of Winnebago culture, particularly of Winnebago religion where tobacco played so fundamental a role.

It is not easy to follow Rave in the evolution and transformation of his ideas, especially in his relation to the old Winnebago culture and to the Christian ideas largely introduced, as previously indicated, by A. H., who quarrelled with Rave and subsequently seceded from Rave's group and formed one of his own. He, however, had few followers and soon disappeared from view. Nevertheless the strictly Christian elements he introduced into the Winnebago peyote[29] cult remained. Rave's attitude toward the innovations of A. H. had always been purely passive and external. As an example let us take Rave's statement in the paragraph preceding the account of John Harrison's conversion, "Today, the Winnebago say that only God is holy," or the one at the very end of Part II, "The one whom they call God has given me this knowledge." He makes no other references to God in Parts II and III and seems to be wavering as to whether he is here giving his own attitude or that of his followers. In Part I, it is true, he has a vision of God and he offers up a prayer to God, and to the Son of God. But this is, apparently, simply a verbal acceptance, particularly the second half of it. His vision of God may very well be little more than a remodelling of a famous fasting-experience that every Winnebago knew very well, called *How Wegishega Tried to See Earthmaker*.[30] At no time did Rave ever think of God, either the Christian God or the old Winnebago Earthmaker, as the source of his new life and dispensation or as responsible for his recognition of the holy. That came only from one source, the divine peyote.

It is very important, consequently, not to regard Rave's tolerance of Christian elements as an indication that they meant very much to him, and one must be very careful not to confuse the interpretations of Rave's statements made by his followers with the

statements that Rave himself actually made. Let me
give two examples. According to O. L., Rave baptized
individuals "by dipping his hand into . . . (the)
peyote and . . . saying 'I baptize thee in the name of
God, the Son, and the Holy Ghost, which is called
God's holiness.'" But this is a basically erroneous
translation of what Rave actually said. What he said
was simply "God, his holiness." To Rave, Holy Ghost
meant nothing. First of all he would not have thought
of a ghost as holy and, secondly, for him a deity could
not die and so could have no ghost. The next example
refers to O. L.'s statement that Rave began the peyote
ceremonies with a prayer called "Turning oneself over
to the care of the Trinity." This is simply a rendering
of Rave's phrase "I give myself up to you entirely,"
probably reinterpreted in this Christian sense by A. H.

The same tolerance that he exhibited toward the
introduction of Christian beliefs and dogmas as long
as they did not interfere with the one cardinal dogma
that man was made whole again by eating the peyote
and acknowledging its efficacy, that same toleration
he exhibited toward those who ate the peyote and
who attempted to throw over their evil ways. Since he
insisted that the peyote could only function completely
if an individual permitted it to do so, ample room was
left for those who wished to obtain the benefits of the
new religion and retain those of the old. The case of a
Winnebago named G. is very instructive here. G., a
member of the Thunderbird clan, believed that he

was living his second life on earth, that he was invulnerable, and that when he was tired of living among human beings he could return to the Thunderbirds. "For that reason," he states, "when I ate peyote I still held on to these beliefs for a long time, thinking that when I returned to the Thunderbirds *inasmuch as they dwell above it would be the same thing as going to everlasting life*,[31] as the peyote people said. Finally one night, at a peyote meeting, in thinking all these matters over I resolved to give them up. I could, nevertheless, not bring myself to do it. Then the peyote began to strangle me. At least I thought so."[32]

At times Rave, the organizer of a new cult, had to compromise with Rave, the devoutly religious man and the moralist, for the sake of spreading the new religion and gaining prestige for it. One can well imagine the joy with which he welcomed leaders of the Medicine Rite like Harrison and Squeaking Wings into the fold. But he had to pay the price. Harrison remained selfish and avaricious and continued the pursuit of women, married and unmarried, and Squeaking Wings remained the religious sceptic he had always been. Membership in the Medicine Rite, in the last quarter of the nineteenth century and after that, did not always imply any deep faith. It was frequently practically inherited.

It seems almost incredible that with Christian influences coming to him from all directions he should

have been so little touched by them. But it remains
an undisputable fact that this was so. Actually, as
might have been expected, he was more at home in
certain aspects of his old Winnebago cultural background than he realized. Thus the peyote-cult was
organized in the same fashion as were the old Winnebago societies based on blessings from the spirit
deities. Similarly, without the slightest hesitation he
introduced the feathered crooks which were the in-
signia of office in the Bear clan and the small earth-
mound used in the Buffalo ceremony, and he had no
objection to their being interpreted as the shepherds'
crooks or Mount Sinai. While his attitude toward
A. H.'s additions were, as I have indicated, passive,
he must have welcomed A. H.'s attempt to give the
peyote a proper Origin Myth. This myth is so important for the religious syncretism we are discussing
here that I shall quote most of it:

Once in the south an Indian belonging to the tribe
called Mescallero Apache was roaming . . . in Mexico
. . . and got lost. . . . He was about to die of thirst
but finally reached the foot of the hill. . . . It was
with the greatest difficulty he reached it. . . . There
he desired to die. . . . He fell over on his back and
lay thus with his body stretched toward the south,
his head pillowed on an object. He extended his right
arm to the east, and as he did this he felt something
cool touch his hands. "What is it . . . ?" he thought
to himself. . . . There was water in it and it also con-

tained food. . . . Then as he lay on the ground a holy
spirit entered him and taking the spirit of the Indian
carried it away to the regions above. There he saw a
man who spoke to him. "I have caused you to go
through this suffering, for had I not done it, you
would never have heard of the proper religion. It was
for that reason that I placed holiness in what you
have eaten. My Father gave it to me and I was permitted to place it on the earth. . . .

"At present this religion exists in the south but I
wish to have it extended to the north. . . . Long ago
I sent this gospel (knowledge) across the ocean but
you did not recognize it. Now I am going to teach you
to understand it." Then he led him to a lodge where
they were eating peyote. There he taught him . . .
all that belonged to this ceremony. . . . "Now go . . .
teach all that I have told you. I have placed my holiness in this that you eat."[33]

In this narrative we see how skillfully a Winnebago
could keep within the old form of an origin myth,
introduce Christian beliefs and phraseology, and yet
use the latter exclusively for purposes utterly alien
to Christianity, namely, to glorify and "deify" the
peyote. For Rave this was the only purpose that
Christianity could serve. "We would all join the Christian Church," he is reported as once telling a missionary, "if you would simply accept the peyote."[34]

The third part of Rave's narrative consists of exhortations. They are essentially miniature sermons.

There is no need for commenting upon them specifically. They largely explain themselves and, where they do not, they repeat ideas that we have already discussed at some length. A few words, however, are in order about their style and the insights they give us into John Rave, the man.

Rave was in no sense a literary artist nor, before his conversion, did he have any reputation as an orator. His style in the narratives he dictated to me was uneven, choppy and somewhat disconnected. Nor did he seem to possess any sense for plot elaboration, the narrative of his conversion always excepted. But in one thing he was always interested, namely the depiction of emotions and states of mind. There he was a master. I know of no other one of my numerous Winnebago informants who could remotely equal him. S. B. in his autobiography comes closest. This psychological interest is manifest everywhere and it is particularly evident, of course, in the narrative we have analyzed here.

All his stylistic inadequacies disappear, however, when he is talking about his own conversion and attempting to convert others. The narrative of his conversion is amazingly well-constructed and never loses its dramatic quality. All the sincerity, all the intensity and persuasiveness of the man—he converted half the tribe to his peyote faith in something like seventeen years—all this fairly leaps at us in these exhortations. What made him so convincing to so many of his fellow-Winnebago was the clarity with which he understood and analyzed what had happened to him and the skill and insight with which he conveyed to others, who were in as much need of psychical integration as himself, that the same miracle could and would happen to them.

When I first met him in 1910 it was hard to believe that this mild, gentle, outgoing, self-disciplined and manifestly well-integrated man had ever been a completely torn and disoriented individual. It would have been equally difficult to believe that he had founded a new religion.

[1] My informants were not all agreed on this point.

[2] Cf. "The Two Friends Who Became Reincarnated," in *The Culture of The Winnebago as Told by Themselves,* in *International Journal of American Linguistics,* pp. 12-41. Bloomington, Ind., 1949.

[3] Cf., however, the date given by Rave himself, p.

[4] An. Rep. Bur. Amer. Ethn., vol. 37, p. 394. Washington 1923.

[5] What Baptiste meant here is that, at first, Rave thought that he alone was being affected by the peyote but that afterward he saw that everyone was being affected in the same way. It was because the peyote had this influence not upon one person but upon everyone that it was so holy. This is one of the cardinal points in Rave's theology. We shall see him stressing it again and again in his conversion narrative. Although Rave does not mention this detail in his own narrative, it must have been something which he had actually said because it occurs in the conversion accounts of a number of Indians.

[6] An. Rep. Bur. Amer. Ethn. vol. 37, p. 394.

[7] I am italicizing those words and phrases which I am discussing specifically in the comments that follow the three sections into which I have divided Rave's narrative.

[8] The Winnebago word here really has the force of in the "twinkling-of-an-eye."

[9] The Winnebago here use an affix implying certain probability.

[10] "Make use of" here means *worship.*

[11] A place on the Winnebago reservation in Nebraska where celebration: like the Fourth of July took place and some exoteric Winnebago dances were given.

[12] Cf. *Autobiography*, etc., in *Univ. Calif. Publ. Am. Arch. Ethn.*, pp. 440-

[13] Among the Winnebago few of the fasting experiences contain any element of terror. S. B., however, who belonged to the Thunderbird clan, the clan specifically connected with war and warfare, states in his autobiography that he was told that he would be surrounded by spirits who could be heard whispering and whistling outside of his fasting place; that he would be thoroughly frightened and ill at ease; that he would be molested, on one night, by fearsome looking monsters and, on another night, by ghosts, etc. It may well be that Rave, who belonged to the clan entrusted with all the disciplinary functions in the tribe, may also have been told to expect some fear-provoking visions.

[14] Rave does not use the actual term "strangling" in his narrative but he frequently employed it when speaking about it and practically all members of the peyote-rite employed it and attributed it to Rave.

[15] An. Rep. Bur. Amer. Ethn., vol. 37, p. 395.

[16] Ibid., p. 301.

[17] Cf. P. Radin, *The Twin Myth of the American Indians*. Eranos-Jahrbuch XVII, Zuerich, 1949.

[18] "This medicine (peyote)," so runs his statement, "is one of the four spirits from below, and for that reason it is a bad thing. These spirits have always longed for human beings and now they are getting ahold of them.

Those who use this medicine claim that when they die they will only be going on a long journey. But that is not the truth, for when they eat peyote they destroy their souls (i.e. the immortal part of themselves) and death for them will mean extermination. If I spit upon the floor, the sputum will soon dry up and nothing will remain of it. So death will be for them." An. Rep. Bur. Amer. Ethn., vol. 37, p. 426.

[19] S. B. in his Autobiography does the same thing and, I think, quite independently. This is what he says, "all of us sitting there, we had altogether one spirit or soul . . . I instantly became . . . their spirit or soul. Whatever they thought of I immediately knew . . . Then I thought of a certain place, far away, and immediately I was there; I was my thought." Cf. Univ. Calif. Publ. Am. Arch. Ethn., pages 441-442.

[20] It should also be remembered that this *seeing of things clearly and vividly* is one of the effects of the peyote. Generally, however, this *clearness* is associated with color-visions. S. B. gives an excellent description of both in his Autobiography. Ibid., p. 440f..

[21] Autobiography, p. 440.

[22] Cf. An. Rep. Bur. Amer. Ethn., vol. 37, p. 397 ff.

[23] He has forgotten, probably, that he also offered up some tobacco.

[24] For the final section of Part III, cf. pp. —

[25] The two most important ones were called the *Stench-Earth medicine* and the *Black-Root medicine*. For a description of the former: Cf. *An. Rep. Bur. Amer. Ethn.,* vol. 37, pp. 259-270.

[26] Op. cit., pp. 259-260.

[27] Op. cit., pp. 264-265.

[28] Cf. the second part of S.B.'s Autobiography.

[29] The description given by O. L. of a peyote meeting as given in my Winnebago monograph, pp. 394-396, represents the cult when A. H. was still an active member of Rave's group.

[30] An. Rep. Bur. Amer. Ethn., vol. 37, pp. 290-293.

[31] The italics are mine.

[32] An. Rep. Bur. Amer. Ethn., vol. 37, p. 301.

[33] An. Rep. Bur. Amer. Ethn. Vol. 37, pp. 398-399.

[34] Even A. H., who was soaked in Christian ideas, had no doubts about that. "This is the true religion," he exclaims indignantly. "The peyote is fulfilling the work of God and the Son of God. When the Son of God came to the earth he was poor yet people spoke of him (despite this). He was abused. It is the same with the peyote. The plant itself is not much of a growth yet everyone is speaking about it. They are abusing it. They are trying to stop its use. When the Son of God came to earth the preachers. of that day were called Pharisees and Scribes. They doubted what the Son of God said and claimed that he was an ordinary man. So it is today with the Christian Church. They are . . . the doubters . . . they are calling it an intoxicant, but that is a lie." Op. cit. p. 400.

INDEX

A CATALOGUE OF SELECTED DOVER BOOKS
IN ALL FIELDS OF INTEREST

A CATALOGUE OF SELECTED DOVER BOOKS
IN ALL FIELDS OF INTEREST

AMERICA'S OLD MASTERS, James T. Flexner. Four men emerged unexpectedly from provincial 18th century America to leadership in European art: Benjamin West, J. S. Copley, C. R. Peale, Gilbert Stuart. Brilliant coverage of lives and contributions. Revised, 1967 edition. 69 plates. 365pp. of text.
21806-6 Paperbound $3.00

FIRST FLOWERS OF OUR WILDERNESS: AMERICAN PAINTING, THE COLONIAL PERIOD, James T. Flexner. Painters, and regional painting traditions from earliest Colonial times up to the emergence of Copley, West and Peale Sr., Foster, Gustavus Hesselius, Feke, John Smibert and many anonymous painters in the primitive manner. Engaging presentation, with 162 illustrations. xxii + 368pp.
22180-6 Paperbound $3.50

THE LIGHT OF DISTANT SKIES: AMERICAN PAINTING, 1760-1835, James T. Flexner. The great generation of early American painters goes to Europe to learn and to teach: West, Copley, Gilbert Stuart and others. Allston, Trumbull, Morse; also contemporary American painters—primitives, derivatives, academics—who remained in America. 102 illustrations. xiii + 306pp.
22179-2 Paperbound $3.00

A HISTORY OF THE RISE AND PROGRESS OF THE ARTS OF DESIGN IN THE UNITED STATES, William Dunlap. Much the richest mine of information on early American painters, sculptors, architects, engravers, miniaturists, etc. The only source of information for scores of artists, the major primary source for many others. Unabridged reprint of rare original 1834 edition, with new introduction by James T. Flexner, and 394 new illustrations. Edited by Rita Weiss. 6⅝ x 9⅝.
21695-0, 21696-9, 21697-7 Three volumes, Paperbound $13.50

EPOCHS OF CHINESE AND JAPANESE ART, Ernest F. Fenollosa. From primitive Chinese art to the 20th century, thorough history, explanation of every important art period and form, including Japanese woodcuts; main stress on China and Japan, but Tibet, Korea also included. Still unexcelled for its detailed, rich coverage of cultural background, aesthetic elements, diffusion studies, particularly of the historical period. 2nd, 1913 edition. 242 illustrations. lii + 439pp. of text.
20364-6, 20365-4 Two volumes, Paperbound $6.00

THE GENTLE ART OF MAKING ENEMIES, James A. M. Whistler. Greatest wit of his day deflates Oscar Wilde, Ruskin, Swinburne; strikes back at inane critics, exhibitions, art journalism; aesthetics of impressionist revolution in most striking form. Highly readable classic by great painter. Reproduction of edition designed by Whistler. Introduction by Alfred Werner. xxxvi + 334pp.
21875-9 Paperbound $2.50

THE PRINCIPLES OF PSYCHOLOGY, William James. The famous long course, complete and unabridged. Stream of thought, time perception, memory, experimental methods—these are only some of the concerns of a work that was years ahead of its time and still valid, interesting, useful. 94 figures. Total of xviii + 1391pp.
20381-6, 20382-4 Two volumes, Paperbound $6.00

THE STRANGE STORY OF THE QUANTUM, Banesh Hoffmann. Non-mathematical but thorough explanation of work of Planck, Einstein, Bohr, Pauli, de Broglie, Schrödinger, Heisenberg, Dirac, Feynman, etc. No technical background needed. "Of books attempting such an account, this is the best," Henry Margenau, Yale. 40-page "Postscript 1959." xii + 285pp.
20518-5 Paperbound $2.00

THE RISE OF THE NEW PHYSICS, A. d'Abro. Most thorough explanation in print of central core of mathematical physics, both classical and modern; from Newton to Dirac and Heisenberg. Both history and exposition; philosophy of science, causality, explanations of higher mathematics, analytical mechanics, electromagnetism, thermodynamics, phase rule, special and general relativity, matrices. No higher mathematics needed to follow exposition, though treatment is elementary to intermediate in level. Recommended to serious student who wishes verbal understanding. 97 illustrations. xvii + 982pp.
20003-5, 20004-3 Two volumes, Paperbound $5.50

GREAT IDEAS OF OPERATIONS RESEARCH, Jagjit Singh. Easily followed non-technical explanation of mathematical tools, aims, results: statistics, linear programming, game theory, queueing theory, Monte Carlo simulation, etc. Uses only elementary mathematics. Many case studies, several analyzed in detail. Clarity, breadth make this excellent for specialist in another field who wishes background. 41 figures. x + 228pp.
21886-4 Paperbound $2.25

GREAT IDEAS OF MODERN MATHEMATICS: THEIR NATURE AND USE, Jagjit Singh. Internationally famous expositor, winner of Unesco's Kalinga Award for science popularization explains verbally such topics as differential equations, matrices, groups, sets, transformations, mathematical logic and other important modern mathematics, as well as use in physics, astrophysics, and similar fields. Superb exposition for layman, scientist in other areas. viii + 312pp.
20587-8 Paperbound $2.25

GREAT IDEAS IN INFORMATION THEORY, LANGUAGE AND CYBERNETICS, Jagjit Singh. The analog and digital computers, how they work, how they are like and unlike the human brain, the men who developed them, their future applications, computer terminology. An essential book for today, even for readers with little math. Some mathematical demonstrations included for more advanced readers. 118 figures. Tables. ix + 338pp.
21694-2 Paperbound $2.25

CHANCE, LUCK AND STATISTICS, Horace C. Levinson. Non-mathematical presentation of fundamentals of probability theory and science of statistics and their applications. Games of chance, betting odds, misuse of statistics, normal and skew distributions, birth rates, stock speculation, insurance. Enlarged edition. Formerly "The Science of Chance." xiii + 357pp.
21007-3 Paperbound $2.00

ALPHABETS AND ORNAMENTS, Ernst Lehner. Well-known pictorial source for decorative alphabets, script examples, cartouches, frames, decorative title pages, calligraphic initials, borders, similar material. 14th to 19th century, mostly European. Useful in almost any graphic arts designing, varied styles. 750 illustrations. 256pp. 7 x 10. 21905-4 Paperbound $4.00

PAINTING: A CREATIVE APPROACH, Norman Colquhoun. For the beginner simple guide provides an instructive approach to painting: major stumbling blocks for beginner; overcoming them, technical points; paints and pigments; oil painting; watercolor and other media and color. New section on "plastic" paints. Glossary. Formerly *Paint Your Own Pictures*. 221pp. 22000-1 Paperbound $1.75

THE ENJOYMENT AND USE OF COLOR, Walter Sargent. Explanation of the relations between colors themselves and between colors in nature and art, including hundreds of little-known facts about color values, intensities, effects of high and low illumination, complementary colors. Many practical hints for painters, references to great masters. 7 color plates, 29 illustrations. x + 274pp.
20944-X Paperbound $2.50

THE NOTEBOOKS OF LEONARDO DA VINCI, compiled and edited by Jean Paul Richter. 1566 extracts from original manuscripts reveal the full range of Leonardo's versatile genius: all his writings on painting, sculpture, architecture, anatomy, astronomy, geography, topography, physiology, mining, music, etc., in both Italian and English, with 186 plates of manuscript pages and more than 500 additional drawings. Includes studies for the Last Supper, the lost Sforza monument, and other works. Total of xlvii + 866pp. 7⅞ x 10¾.
22572-0, 22573-9 Two volumes, Paperbound $10.00

MONTGOMERY WARD CATALOGUE OF 1895. Tea gowns, yards of flannel and pillow-case lace, stereoscopes, books of gospel hymns, the New Improved Singer Sewing Machine, side saddles, milk skimmers, straight-edged razors, high-button shoes, spittoons, and on and on . . . listing some 25,000 items, practically all illustrated. Essential to the shoppers of the 1890's, it is our truest record of the spirit of the period. Unaltered reprint of Issue No. 57, Spring and Summer 1895. Introduction by Boris Emmet. Innumerable illustrations. xiii + 624pp. 8½ x 11⅝.
22377-9 Paperbound $6.95

THE CRYSTAL PALACE EXHIBITION ILLUSTRATED CATALOGUE (LONDON, 1851). One of the wonders of the modern world—the Crystal Palace Exhibition in which all the nations of the civilized world exhibited their achievements in the arts and sciences—presented in an equally important illustrated catalogue. More than 1700 items pictured with accompanying text—ceramics, textiles, cast-iron work, carpets, pianos, sleds, razors, wall-papers, billiard tables, beehives, silverware and hundreds of other artifacts—represent the focal point of Victorian culture in the Western World. Probably the largest collection of Victorian decorative art ever assembled— indispensable for antiquarians and designers. Unabridged republication of the Art-Journal Catalogue of the Great Exhibition of 1851, with all terminal essays. New introduction by John Gloag, F.S.A. xxxiv + 426pp. 9 x 12.
22503-8 Paperbound $4.50

THE ARCHITECTURE OF COUNTRY HOUSES, Andrew J. Downing. Together with Vaux's *Villas and Cottages* this is the basic book for Hudson River Gothic architecture of the middle Victorian period. Full, sound discussions of general aspects of housing, architecture, style, decoration, furnishing, together with scores of detailed house plans, illustrations of specific buildings, accompanied by full text. Perhaps the most influential single American architectural book. 1850 edition. Introduction by J. Stewart Johnson. 321 figures, 34 architectural designs. xvi + 560pp.

22003-6 Paperbound $4.00

LOST EXAMPLES OF COLONIAL ARCHITECTURE, John Mead Howells. Full-page photographs of buildings that have disappeared or been so altered as to be denatured, including many designed by major early American architects. 245 plates. xvii + 248pp. 7⅞ x 10¾. 21143-6 Paperbound $3.00

DOMESTIC ARCHITECTURE OF THE AMERICAN COLONIES AND OF THE EARLY REPUBLIC, Fiske Kimball. Foremost architect and restorer of Williamsburg and Monticello covers nearly 200 homes between 1620-1825. Architectural details, construction, style features, special fixtures, floor plans, etc. Generally considered finest work in its area. 219 illustrations of houses, doorways, windows, capital mantels. xx + 314pp. 7⅞ x 10¾. 21743-4 Paperbound $3.50

EARLY AMERICAN ROOMS: 1650-1858, edited by Russell Hawes Kettell. Tour of 12 rooms, each representative of a different era in American history and each furnished, decorated, designed and occupied in the style of the era. 72 plans and elevations, 8-page color section, etc., show fabrics, wall papers, arrangements, etc. Full descriptive text. xvii + 200pp. of text. 8⅜ x 11¼.

21633-0 Paperbound $5.00

THE FITZWILLIAM VIRGINAL BOOK, edited by J. Fuller Maitland and W. B. Squire. Full modern printing of famous early 17th-century ms. volume of 300 works by Morley, Byrd, Bull, Gibbons, etc. For piano or other modern keyboard instrument; easy to read format. xxxvi + 938pp. 8⅜ x 11.

21068-5, 21069-3 Two volumes, Paperbound $8.00

HARPSICHORD MUSIC, Johann Sebastian Bach. Bach Gesellschaft edition. A rich selection of Bach's masterpieces for the harpsichord: the six English Suites, six French Suites, the six Partitas (Clavierübung part I), the Goldberg Variations (Clavierübung part IV), the fifteen Two-Part Inventions and the fifteen Three-Part Sinfonias. Clearly reproduced on large sheets with ample margins; eminently playable. vi + 312pp. 8⅛ x 11. 22360-4 Paperbound $5.00

THE MUSIC OF BACH: AN INTRODUCTION, Charles Sanford Terry. A fine, nontechnical introduction to Bach's music, both instrumental and vocal. Covers organ music, chamber music, passion music, other types. Analyzes themes, developments, innovations. x + 114pp. 21075-8 Paperbound $1.25

BEETHOVEN AND HIS NINE SYMPHONIES, Sir George Grove. Noted British musicologist provides best history, analysis, commentary on symphonies. Very thorough, rigorously accurate; necessary to both advanced student and amateur music lover. 436 musical passages. vii + 407 pp. 20334-4 Paperbound $2.25

CATALOGUE OF DOVER BOOKS

JOHANN SEBASTIAN BACH, Philipp Spitta. One of the great classics of musicology, this definitive analysis of Bach's music (and life) has never been surpassed. Lucid, nontechnical analyses of hundreds of pieces (30 pages devoted to St. Matthew Passion, 26 to B Minor Mass). Also includes major analysis of 18th-century music. 450 musical examples. 40-page musical supplement. Total of xx + 1799pp.
(EUK) 22278-0, 22279-9 Two volumes, Clothbound $15.00

MOZART AND HIS PIANO CONCERTOS, Cuthbert Girdlestone. The only full-length study of an important area of Mozart's creativity. Provides detailed analyses of all 23 concertos, traces inspirational sources. 417 musical examples. Second edition. 509pp.
(USO) 21271-8 Paperbound $3.50

THE PERFECT WAGNERITE: A COMMENTARY ON THE NIBLUNG'S RING, George Bernard Shaw. Brilliant and still relevant criticism in remarkable essays on Wagner's Ring cycle, Shaw's ideas on political and social ideology behind the plots, role of Leitmotifs, vocal requisites, etc. Prefaces. xxi + 136pp.
21707-8 Paperbound $1.50

DON GIOVANNI, W. A. Mozart. Complete libretto, modern English translation; biographies of composer and librettist; accounts of early performances and critical reaction. Lavishly illustrated. All the material you need to understand and appreciate this great work. Dover Opera Guide and Libretto Series; translated and introduced by Ellen Bleiler. 92 illustrations. 209pp.
21134-7 Paperbound $1.50

HIGH FIDELITY SYSTEMS: A LAYMAN'S GUIDE, Roy F. Allison. All the basic information you need for setting up your own audio system: high fidelity and stereo record players, tape records, F.M. Connections, adjusting tone arm, cartridge, checking needle alignment, positioning speakers, phasing speakers, adjusting hums, trouble-shooting, maintenance, and similar topics. Enlarged 1965 edition. More than 50 charts, diagrams, photos. iv + 91pp.
21514-8 Paperbound $1.25

REPRODUCTION OF SOUND, Edgar Villchur. Thorough coverage for laymen of high fidelity systems, reproducing systems in general, needles, amplifiers, preamps, loudspeakers, feedback, explaining physical background. "A rare talent for making technicalities vividly comprehensible," R. Darrell, *High Fidelity.* 69 figures. iv + 92pp.
21515-6 Paperbound $1.00

HEAR ME TALKIN' TO YA: THE STORY OF JAZZ AS TOLD BY THE MEN WHO MADE IT, Nat Shapiro and Nat Hentoff. Louis Armstrong, Fats Waller, Jo Jones, Clarence Williams, Billy Holiday, Duke Ellington, Jelly Roll Morton and dozens of other jazz greats tell how it was in Chicago's South Side, New Orleans, depression Harlem and the modern West Coast as jazz was born and grew. xvi + 429pp.
21726-4 Paperbound $2.50

FABLES OF AESOP, translated by Sir Roger L'Estrange. A reproduction of the very rare 1931 Paris edition; a selection of the most interesting fables, together with 50 imaginative drawings by Alexander Calder. v + 128pp. 6½x9¼.
21780-9 Paperbound $1.25

POEMS OF ANNE BRADSTREET, edited with an introduction by Robert Hutchinson. A new selection of poems by America's first poet and perhaps the first significant woman poet in the English language. 48 poems display her development in works of considerable variety—love poems, domestic poems, religious meditations, formal elegies, "quaternions," etc. Notes, bibliography. viii + 222pp.

22160-1 Paperbound $2.00

THREE GOTHIC NOVELS: THE CASTLE OF OTRANTO BY HORACE WALPOLE; VATHEK BY WILLIAM BECKFORD; THE VAMPYRE BY JOHN POLIDORI, WITH FRAGMENT OF A NOVEL BY LORD BYRON, edited by E. F. Bleiler. The first Gothic novel, by Walpole; the finest Oriental tale in English, by Beckford; powerful Romantic supernatural story in versions by Polidori and Byron. All extremely important in history of literature; all still exciting, packed with supernatural thrills, ghosts, haunted castles, magic, etc. xl + 291pp.

21232-7 Paperbound $2.00

THE BEST TALES OF HOFFMANN, E. T. A. Hoffmann. 10 of Hoffmann's most important stories, in modern re-editings of standard translations: Nutcracker and the King of Mice, Signor Formica, Automata, The Sandman, Rath Krespel, The Golden Flowerpot, Master Martin the Cooper, The Mines of Falun, The King's Betrothed, A New Year's Eve Adventure. 7 illustrations by Hoffmann. Edited by E. F. Bleiler. xxxix + 419pp. 21793-0 Paperbound $2.50

GHOST AND HORROR STORIES OF AMBROSE BIERCE, Ambrose Bierce. 23 strikingly modern stories of the horrors latent in the human mind: The Eyes of the Panther, The Damned Thing, An Occurrence at Owl Creek Bridge, An Inhabitant of Carcosa, etc., plus the dream-essay, Visions of the Night. Edited by E. F. Bleiler. xxii + 199pp. 20767-6 Paperbound $1.50

BEST GHOST STORIES OF J. S. LeFANU, J. Sheridan LeFanu. Finest stories by Victorian master often considered greatest supernatural writer of all. Carmilla, Green Tea, The Haunted Baronet, The Familiar, and 12 others. Most never before available in the U. S. A. Edited by E. F. Bleiler. 8 illustrations from Victorian publications. xvii + 467pp. 20415-4 Paperbound $2.50

THE TIME STREAM, THE GREATEST ADVENTURE, AND THE PURPLE SAPPHIRE—THREE SCIENCE FICTION NOVELS, John Taine (Eric Temple Bell). Great American mathematician was also foremost science fiction novelist of the 1920's. *The Time Stream,* one of all-time classics, uses concepts of circular time; *The Greatest Adventure,* incredibly ancient biological experiments from Antarctica threaten to escape; The *Purple Sapphire,* superscience, lost races in Central Tibet, survivors of the Great Race. 4 illustrations by Frank R. Paul. v + 532pp.

21180-0 Paperbound $3.00

SEVEN SCIENCE FICTION NOVELS, H. G. Wells. The standard collection of the great novels. Complete, unabridged. *First Men in the Moon, Island of Dr. Moreau, War of the Worlds, Food of the Gods, Invisible Man, Time Machine, In the Days of the Comet.* Not only science fiction fans, but every educated person owes it to himself to read these novels. 1015pp. 20264-X Clothbound $5.00

How to Know the Wild Flowers, Mrs. William Starr Dana. This is the classical book of American wildflowers (of the Eastern and Central United States), used by hundreds of thousands. Covers over 500 species, arranged in extremely easy to use color and season groups. Full descriptions, much plant lore. This Dover edition is the fullest ever compiled, with tables of nomenclature changes. 174 full-page plates by M. Satterlee. xii + 418pp. 20332-8 Paperbound $2.75

Our Plant Friends and Foes, William Atherton DuPuy. History, economic importance, essential botanical information and peculiarities of 25 common forms of plant life are provided in this book in an entertaining and charming style. Covers food plants (potatoes, apples, beans, wheat, almonds, bananas, etc.), flowers (lily, tulip, etc.), trees (pine, oak, elm, etc.), weeds, poisonous mushrooms and vines, gourds, citrus fruits, cotton, the cactus family, and much more. 108 illustrations. xiv + 290pp. 22272-1 Paperbound $2.50

How to Know the Ferns, Frances T. Parsons. Classic survey of Eastern and Central ferns, arranged according to clear, simple identification key. Excellent introduction to greatly neglected nature area. 57 illustrations and 42 plates. xvi + 215pp. 20740-4 Paperbound $1.75

Manual of the Trees of North America, Charles S. Sargent. America's foremost dendrologist provides the definitive coverage of North American trees and tree-like shrubs. 717 species fully described and illustrated: exact distribution, down to township; full botanical description; economic importance; description of subspecies and races; habitat, growth data; similar material. Necessary to every serious student of tree-life. Nomenclature revised to present. Over 100 locating keys. 783 illustrations. lii + 934pp. 20277-1, 20278-X Two volumes, Paperbound $6.00

Our Northern Shrubs, Harriet L. Keeler. Fine non-technical reference work identifying more than 225 important shrubs of Eastern and Central United States and Canada. Full text covering botanical description, habitat, plant lore, is paralleled with 205 full-page photographs of flowering or fruiting plants. Nomenclature revised by Edward G. Voss. One of few works concerned with shrubs. 205 plates, 35 drawings. xxviii + 521pp. 21989-5 Paperbound $3.75

The Mushroom Handbook, Louis C. C. Krieger. Still the best popular handbook: full descriptions of 259 species, cross references to another 200. Extremely thorough text enables you to identify, know all about any mushroom you are likely to meet in eastern and central U. S. A.: habitat, luminescence, poisonous qualities, use, folklore, etc. 32 color plates show over 50 mushrooms, also 126 other illustrations. Finding keys. vii + 560pp. 21861-9 Paperbound $3.95

Handbook of Birds of Eastern North America, Frank M. Chapman. Still much the best single-volume guide to the birds of Eastern and Central United States. Very full coverage of 675 species, with descriptions, life habits, distribution, similar data. All descriptions keyed to two-page color chart. With this single volume the average birdwatcher needs no other books. 1931 revised edition. 195 illustrations. xxxvi + 581pp. 21489-3 Paperbound $3.25

MATHEMATICAL PUZZLES FOR BEGINNERS AND ENTHUSIASTS, Geoffrey Mott-Smith. 189 puzzles from easy to difficult—involving arithmetic, logic, algebra, properties of digits, probability, etc.—for enjoyment and mental stimulus. Explanation of mathematical principles behind the puzzles. 135 illustrations. viii + 248pp.

20198-8 Paperbound $1.75

PAPER FOLDING FOR BEGINNERS, William D. Murray and Francis J. Rigney. Easiest book on the market, clearest instructions on making interesting, beautiful origami. Sail boats, cups, roosters, frogs that move legs, bonbon boxes, standing birds, etc. 40 projects; more than 275 diagrams and photographs. 94pp.

20713-7 Paperbound $1.00

TRICKS AND GAMES ON THE POOL TABLE, Fred Herrmann. 79 tricks and games— some solitaires, some for two or more players, some competitive games—to entertain you between formal games. Mystifying shots and throws, unusual caroms, tricks involving such props as cork, coins, a hat, etc. Formerly *Fun on the Pool Table*. 77 figures. 95pp.

21814-7 Paperbound $1.00

HAND SHADOWS TO BE THROWN UPON THE WALL: A SERIES OF NOVEL AND AMUSING FIGURES FORMED BY THE HAND, Henry Bursill. Delightful picturebook from great-grandfather's day shows how to make 18 different hand shadows: a bird that flies, duck that quacks, dog that wags his tail, camel, goose, deer, boy, turtle, etc. Only book of its sort. vi + 33pp. 6½ x 9¼.   21779-5 Paperbound $1.00

WHITTLING AND WOODCARVING, E. J. Tangerman. 18th printing of best book on market. "If you can cut a potato you can carve" toys and puzzles, chains, chessmen, caricatures, masks, frames, woodcut blocks, surface patterns, much more. Information on tools, woods, techniques. Also goes into serious wood sculpture from Middle Ages to present, East and West. 464 photos, figures. x + 293pp.

20965-2 Paperbound $2.00

HISTORY OF PHILOSOPHY, Julián Marias. Possibly the clearest, most easily followed, best planned, most useful one-volume history of philosophy on the market; neither skimpy nor overfull. Full details on system of every major philosopher and dozens of less important thinkers from pre-Socratics up to Existentialism and later. Strong on many European figures usually omitted. Has gone through dozens of editions in Europe. 1966 edition, translated by Stanley Appelbaum and Clarence Strowbridge. xviii + 505pp.   21739-6 Paperbound $3.00

YOGA: A SCIENTIFIC EVALUATION, Kovoor T. Behanan. Scientific but non-technical study of physiological results of yoga exercises; done under auspices of Yale U. Relations to Indian thought, to psychoanalysis, etc. 16 photos. xxiii + 270pp.

20505-3 Paperbound $2.50

Prices subject to change without notice.
Available at your book dealer or write for free catalogue to Dept. GI, Dover Publications, Inc., 180 Varick St., N. Y., N. Y. 10014. Dover publishes more than 150 books each year on science, elementary and advanced mathematics, biology, music, art, literary history, social sciences and other areas.